Aircraft
of
World War II

Focke-Wulf Fw 200C-3/U2 maritime reconnaissance bomber

KENNETH MUNSON

Aircraft
of
World War II

Doubleday & Company, Inc.
GARDEN CITY, NEW YORK

First published 1962
Second edition 1972

ISBN 0 385 07122 1

Library of Congress Catalog Card Number 72–84 207

© Ian Allan, Shepperton, Surrey, 1972

Published by Doubleday & Company, Inc.,
and printed in the United Kingdom by
Cox & Wyman Ltd, London, Fakenham and Reading

Contents

Jacket illustration shows a Messerschmitt Bf110
colliding with a North American P-51B Mustang of
the 354th Fighter Group from Boxted, Essex
during a 'dog fight' over Germany in February
1944 whilst engaged in a bomber escort mission
(*From a painting by George F. Heiron*).

Introduction

THE IDEA for this volume originated in 1960 with a small paperback which dealt with the German and Italian aircraft of World War II. Three other titles followed, and in 1962 these four small books were combined, with additional notes and some revision, in the first case-bound and fully indexed edition of *Aircraft of World War II*.

This second edition, first published in 1972, has an enlarged format, with bigger pages. Of the 310 photographs in the original edition, about 270 are new to this edition, which includes 8 extra pages of black and white illustrations and, for the first time, 8 pages of colour plates.

The author and publishers extend their grateful thanks to the following individuals and organisations for their kind assistance in helping to provide photographs for the first and second editions: Air-Britain; Miss Jean Alexander; Richard M. Bueschel; the Canadian Department of National Defence; J. B. Cynk; *Flight International*; James Gilbert; the Imperial War Museum, London; the Italian Air Attaché, London; the Italian Air Ministry; Neil A. Macdougall; the Ministère des Armées "Air"; V. Nemecek; H. J. Nowarra; Stephen Peltz; Eino Ritaranta; the Royal Canadian Air Force; the Royal Netherlands Air Force; the Royal Netherlands Navy; Hanfried Schliephake; Christopher F. Shores; John W. R. Taylor; the U.S. Air Force; and the U.S. Navy.

Background to the Belligerents

GERMANY

THE VERSAILLES TREATY of June 1919 required from Germany the surrender of all her considerable residue of World War I aircraft and aero-engines, and expressly forbade her either to manufacture new military types or to subsidise the construction of aircraft of any kind. A certain amount of private enterprise construction of civil types was allowed to continue, but the size of these and of the industry to produce them was similarly limited by the Treaty.

By continual agitation Germany secured, in the Paris Air Agreement of 1926, the withdrawal of all these limitations, and forthwith began to expand her civil aviation as a cloak for her para-military activities. The numerous small internal airlines were amalgamated to form the world's biggest commercial operator, Deutsche Luft Hansa, and the resurrected Luftsportverband, ostensibly a private flying organisation, was used to attract from wealthy industrialists and war profiteers the money necessary to finance the D.L.H. (and hence the Luftwaffe) by setting up new airfields and paying for the training of pilots.

The next step in the revival of German air power was the issue of specifications to leading manufacturers for civil airliners, fast " air taxis " and " sporting " single-seaters. The facility with which these types could be converted respectively to troop transports, bombers and fighters was later to be so painfully obvious as to need no further elaboration.

The ascension to power of Adolf Hitler and his National Socialist Party in 1933 gave the " disguised " German air force the opportunity it needed to come out into the open, and in March 1935 there followed official confirmation of the Luftwaffe's existence with the appointment of the former Air Minister, Hermann Goering, as its first Commander-in-Chief. At the end of 1935 the production of military aircraft had reached 300 a month, and it continued to increase at a steady rate thereafter.

The Spanish Civil War which broke out in July 1936 afforded a heaven-sent opportunity for the Luftwaffe to try out its newly-acquired air strength under authentic battle conditions. The revolution was barely a month old before Hitler sent Junkers Ju 52/3m and Heinkel He 51 aircraft to General Franco's assistance, and in November the famous Condor Legion of the Luftwaffe was formed expressly for participation in the Spanish conflict. By the time it returned to Germany early in 1939, the Condor Legion had accumulated a great deal of useful experience with such important types as the Bf 109, He 111, Do 17 and Ju 87.

In 1938 Hitler occupied Austria, expanding that country's aircraft industry to augment production in Germany itself, and by September 1939 the total aircraft production for the Luftwaffe had reached the astonishing rate of 1,100 machines a month. First-line strength was 4,840 aircraft, including 1,750 bombers and 1,200 fighters, with nearly as many more in reserve—giving Hitler's air force the strength and equipment he needed to fulfil his dominatory objectives. Without in any way belittling Allied aircraft, pilots or strategy, it can fairly be said that the Luftwaffe's ultimate failure to achieve those ends was to a considerable extent self-incurred, Hitler himself playing no small part in the process.

Germany's fortunes in the air reached their peak about the middle of 1940, but thereafter began to decline at a rate which increased steadily as the war progressed. Experience gathered in Spain, while valuable in many ways, led the Luftwaffe to base its World War 2 tactics on the evidence of its rather easy successes against the relatively inferior Spanish opposition. Misguidedly regarding air power as an auxiliary of the Army, Nazi policies had concentrated on short range, lightly armed day bombers which, while effective enough when used in conjunction with the ground forces, were far less successful when they were operated without such support. The reputations of several aircraft suffered as a result of this, the Ju 87 being a prize example. The blunder was extended by the continuation of daylight air attacks on the United Kingdom long after the Battle of Britain had clearly demonstrated the unwisdom of such a course; had the Luftwaffe changed over to night raids in the middle of 1940, when our night defences were practically non-existent, the course of the war might well have taken a very different turn. As it was, Germany went on to lose some 2,000 aircraft and 5,000 aircrew in daylight attacks before going over in any degree to night operations. The last, and perhaps the greatest, folly which marked down the Luftwaffe for ultimate defeat was Hitler's inexplicable decision to invade Russia in 1941.

By the middle of 1943 the first-line strength of the Luftwaffe was still in the region of 4,000 aircraft, but only by dint of cutting down the reserve to less than a quarter of its 1939 size. After the Battle of Britain lesson, the changing fortunes of the German air force were reflected in the changing roles of its aircraft. Fighters were adapted to defence, even brand new designs like the Fw 190, and began vastly to outnumber bombers in the total establishment. Escort fighters and dive bombers faded from the scene, their places being filled by interceptors and night bombers such as the Fw 190 already mentioned, the Ju 88C and the Do 217.

Following up their advantage, the Allies began in mid-1943 a full scale air attack against the industrial production centres of the Reich, an assault which was sustained until the Normanay invasion a year later and was probably one of the major turning points of the European war. Such was the devastating effect on German aircraft production that squadrons had to be recalled wholesale from other fronts, particularly Russia, to defend the homeland. After D-day, by dispersing factories and constructing new production centres underground, Germany managed to resuscitate its hard-hit aircraft industry, concentrating now almost exclusively on defensive fighter types such as the Fw 190D, Ta 152, He 219 and Do 335; Allied bombing attacks continued to take their toll, however, and it was largely because of their attentions that the three last-named fighters did not reach the Luftwaffe earlier or in larger quantities. Development of the promising new range of jet-propelled machines was similarly affected by the Anglo-American bombing offensive, and impaired still further by the obstinacy and stupidity of Hitler himself.

The Luftwaffe was finally and completely checked by lack of fuel. again thanks to Allied bombing, and in the closing weeks of the European war such fragments of the Luftwaffe as remained airworthy were mostly grounded, with empty tanks.

GREAT BRITAIN

AFTER THE ARMISTICE of 1918 the R.A.F. was the world's most powerful air force. It had 3,300 first-line aircraft (22,000 altogether) and over 290,000 men. Such a size was, however, uneconomical for a peacetime force, and in the following year drastic reductions in machines and manpower were made. Thereafter the R.A.F. began to grow again, slowly, though it was not until the middle 1930s that any large-scale expansion was attempted. Up to 1936 the standard fighter was still the two-gun biplane, and the bomber force was made up of obsolescent biplanes and ponderous monoplanes with poor speeds, short ranges and modest bomb loads. The advent to power of Adolf Hitler in 1933 and the subsequent official confirmation of the existence of the Luftwaffe stirred those in authority to recognise the potential danger from this quarter, and in 1934 plans began to be mooted for a realistic expansion of our land and naval air forces: the arms race was on. The first-line aircraft strength of the R.A.F. in 1933—two years before the Luftwaffe was " formed "—was 850 aircraft; a series of re-equipment plans aimed ultimately to increase this figure to 3,550, with nearly another 6,000 aircraft in reserve. The " shadow factory " movement was begun in 1936, with the resources of the British motor industry co-opted to supplement the production of the aircraft companies themselves. Not for another two years, however, was this production allowed to reach the limit of its capability; during this time it was still restricted by budgetary considerations. However, the types of aircraft which the enlarged industry was now engaged in building were at least a marked improvement upon previous equipment. The obsolescent bombers of the early 'thirties were already beginning to be replaced by a family of twin-engined monoplane types; in place of the two-gun biplane came the first eight-gun monoplane fighters; and the foundations were laid for the first really heavy bombers, the four-engined Stirlings, Halifaxes and Lancasters of the middle war years. The Fleet Air Arm, as had been its lot for almost the whole of its existence, lagged somewhat behind its land-based fellow service, and by the time the Second World War broke out could still put up no more modern a fighter than the Sea Gladiator. Specialised reconnaissance and torpedo bomber types, until as late in the war as 1943, were destined to be represented by such machines as the biplane Swordfish. However, the F.A.A. could draw some consolation from the seven new aircraft carriers which were ordered for it in 1938.

When Great Britain entered World War 2 on 3rd September, 1939, the R.A.F. could boast a fighter strength—although still low by comparison with the Luftwaffe—of over 1,000 machines, of which more than half were the new eight-gun types, the Hurricane and the Spitfire. Bomber Command was equipped with approximately equal numbers of Blenheims, Whitleys, Wellingtons and Hampdens, together with a few squadrons of single-engined Battles. Coastal Command was relatively poorly off, for apart from its Ansons, some American Hudsons and a small number of Sunderland flying boats, the reconnaissance squadrons were still equipped with ageing Stranraer and London flying boats and the torpedo bombing force was made up of antiquated Vickers Vildebeests. At the outset—in fact on 2nd September, the day before Britain declared war on Germany—the Advanced Air Striking Force was established in France with a force of ten Fairey Battle squadrons, two of Blenheims and two of Gladiators. The air component of the British Expeditionary Force sent to the Continent comprised a further four Blenheim squadrons together with four of Hurricanes and five of Lysanders. Coastal Command, meanwhile, was charged with patrolling the North Sea, with Blenheims, and with the de-gaussing of mines by specially fitted Wellingtons.

On the 17th December, 1939, the famous Empire Air Training Scheme was drawn up, to cope with the enormous task of training, quickly and thoroughly, the large number of aircrew who would soon be required to fly the rapidly-increasing numbers of aircraft now being built. Canada was by far the largest participator in the Scheme, but was ably joined by Australia, New Zealand and Southern Rhodesia. Eventually, though considerably later, the training of Allied pilots was to take place in the United States as well.

During these first few months of the war—the " Phoney War " as it has now become known—little positive happened on either side, apart from the campaign on the ground in Europe. The main German offensive, launched in the Spring of 1940, pushed us inexorably towards Dunkirk, and in the middle of June Italy joined the war on Germany's side. In those two months alone the R.A.F. lost nearly 1,000 aircraft, and those remaining at home to face the Luftwaffe were outnumbered by two to one.

On 18th June, Winston Churchill reported to the House of Commons: " What General Weygand called the Battle of France is over. I expect that the Battle of Britain is about to begin." Two months later he was proved right. Despite the fury of the fight and the heavy losses incurred, however, those two months were a valuable breathing space, in which we were able to get our second wind after Dunkirk and work out a redeployment of our forces for home defence. It is now a matter of history that during the ensuing seven weeks the skies above Southern England were thick with the vapour trails and gunsmoke of battling aeroplanes, from which the Luftwaffe emerged with 1,733 machines lost and the R.A.F. with 915 destroyed. With its back to the wall, outnumbered in both men and machines, the Royal Air Force had nevertheless proved to the world that the mighty German war machine was capable of being beaten. One of the men she had to thank for this, apart from the pilots themselves, was Air Chief Marshal Sir Hugh Dowding. Had it not been for his

9

stubborn resistance to all attempts to deplete our home fighter squadrons to prolong the conflict on the Continent, British resources to meet the aerial onslaught later that summer would have been even more slender. As early as 16th May, 1940, Dowding had told the Air Ministry that " if adequate fighter force is kept in this country, if the fleet remains in being, and if Home Forces are suitably organised to resist invasion, we should be able to carry on the war single-handed for some time, if not indefinitely. But, if the Home Defence Force is drained away in desperate attempts to remedy the situation in France, defeat in France will involve the final, complete and irremediable defeat of this country."

After the Battle of Britain, the German blitz on England by day and night increased, and many other theatres of war also began to make demands upon the British air forces: the fight spread to the Middle East, and the enemy invaded Greece. But the year was not completed without its compensations for the Allied cause: the Mediterranean island fortress of Malta began slowly to recover after its summer siege, and in November the Fleet Air Arm brought off a notable coup when it attacked and severely crippled the Italian Fleet at Taranto. In 1941, the tide was beginning to turn. No longer were we completely on the defensive, and the Battle of Britain began to give way to the Battle of Germany. Bomber Command started to hit back at night—daylight raids with our existing equipment having incurred severe losses during the early months of the war—against targets in France, Italy and Germany. Slowly the intensity of these attacks rose, and by the end of the year " Bomber " Harris's team were giving the enemy something to think about. This was not the only piece of food for Axis thought, for on the 7th December, 1941, Japan launched her murderous attack on the U.S. Fleet in Pearl Harbour and America, already sympathetic to the Allied cause, was precipitated into the war as a major participant. As the final result proved, the entry of the United States on the Allied side—despite the initial decimation of her vast naval strength—far outweighed the addition of Japan to the Axis powers, and Hitler himself in his more rational moments must have considered his new ally something of a mixed blessing.

As 1942 progressed, the United States Army Air Force, already striking back in the Pacific, also began to reinforce Allied air strength in the European theatre. Its Bostons and Venturas added to the Royal Air Force medium bomber strength against Germany, which itself was beginning to receive reinforcement in the shape of the de Havilland Mosquito. Although not to become regular practice for another year or so, the first of the famous thousand-bomber raids was launched, against Cologne, on the night of 30th/31st May, 1942. From September 1942 the pattern was established of daylight attacks by the U.S. air forces, followed up by night raids from the R.A.F., which was now beginning to receive the first of its four-engined heavy bombers. One of the most useful, although accidental, results of the independent development of aircraft design in Great Britain and the United States during the preceding years was that both countries had developed specialised designs for the particular strategic and tactical purposes which each country foresaw. Thus each possessed types which the other did not, and the subsequent interchange resulted in a more balanced array of individual types than could have been possible with any single air force. Another great advantage conferred by America's entry into the war was the increase in strength of transport aircraft. Up to the beginning of 1942 the enemy possessed nearly all the transport aircraft available for military purposes. This position was now changed; an agreement was reached whereby America would supply all the transports needed by the Allies, leaving Britain's smaller aircraft industry to concentrate on the production of fighters, bombers and trainers. At this time about one third of the total U.S. production of aircraft was given over to transport types

By 1943 the tide of war had definitely turned. The African campaign drew to its close, being followed by the invasion of Sicily and the Italian mainland, and the audacity of Allied air attacks against German targets was typified by the brilliant attack in May by 617 Bomber Squadron against the Ruhr dams. By this time the Fleet Air Arm was also giving a splendid account of itself, having acquired considerable new carrier strength and adequate quantities of long range patrol aircraft. It was fighting its own particular battle, the Battle of the Atlantic, in the form of convoy protection, anti-U-boat missions and harassing of enemy shipping in general. In March 1943, foreshadowing the forthcoming invasion of the European continent, R.A.F. Transport Command was formed as a replacement for the former Ferry Command; another hint of the coming Second Front was the formation of the Second Tactical Air Force in November. A new weapon was also introduced into the R.A.F. and F.A.A. armoury—the rocket projectile. Towards the end of 1943, and increasing through 1944, the war in both Europe and the Far East began to be carried back to the enemy.

D-day, as every schoolboy now knows, was 6th June, 1944. Fifteen Transport Command squadrons of Dakotas, Halifaxes, Stirlings and Albemarles, and British and American gliders, took part in the invasion of Normandy, covered by no less than 171 squadrons of Allied fighters and aided by diversions created elsewhere by Bomber Command and other squadrons. By now Bomber Command were carrying out day and night raids against Germany with complete impunity, and with the advance across Europe the ground attack aircraft, first used in any quantity in the Western Desert, now came really into its own. In the forefront of these attacks were machines like the Hawker Typhoon, which became famous for its train-busting and similar exploits both with cannon and with its under-wing barrage of rockets. Germany began a series of last-ditch efforts to stave off ultimate defeat, the first of which was the beginning of the V.1 flying bomb campaign against the United Kingdom. Large numbers of these got through the defences, but they were finally beaten by repeated bombing attacks on their launching sites and, in the air, by Fighter Command Tempests. The latter were joined in this task by Britain's first jet-propelled fighter, the Gloster Meteor, later to be transferred to Europe to counteract the German jet aircraft being pressed into service. Bigger and bigger bombs were being dropped on Germany, culminating in Barnes Wallis's fantastic 22,000 lb. " Grand Slam " which could be carried only by specially modified Lancasters. The end was in sight at last, and the war in Europe finally came to its inevitable conclusion on 8th May, 1945.

Meanwhile, from the end of 1944, South East Asia Command had undergone a steady and impressive expansion. It now held the offensive and, despite the frantic (though relatively successful) suicide attacks of the Japanese air forces, was placing its attacks nearer and nearer to the Japanese mainland. On conclusion of the European war, Britain remustered its aerial strength and formed a " Tiger Force " including some 20 bomber squadrons, to be sent to the Far East to hasten the end of the war there; but in August 1945, two small but potent pieces of hardware dropped from American B-29s on Hiroshima and Nagasaki rendered further preparation unnecessary. The war was over.

ITALY

THE ITALIAN AIR ARM which fought on the side of the Allies in World War 1 was quickly run down after 1918, and the existence of a full-scale air force was not re-established until Mussolini set up the Regia Aeronautica early in 1923. In the next ten years the first-line strength of this body was raised to some 1,200 aircraft, and the pattern of aeronautical activity in Italy during the early 1930s followed in many ways that of her future ally of World War 2: the setting up of various world air records, the invasion of smaller countries, the aid to General Franco's forces in the Spanish revolution. When she entered the Second World War on the 10th June, 1940, Italy could justifiably be regarded, numerically at least, as a major air power. She had almost a thousand bombers, nearly as many fighters and over 750 reconnaissance, transport and other types in her first-line armoury. With reserves included, her total strength was nearly 5,000 aircraft, although less than half of these could be considered a serious operational force; the weakest link was the fighter force,

11

which was composed largely of obsolescent biplanes and under-powered monoplanes.

For a few months in 1940/41, Italian bombers flying from Belgian bases supported the Luftwaffe in day and night raids on the United Kingdom, but they were soon withdrawn to resume home-based operations in the Mediterranean theatre and to back up Rommel's forces in North Africa.

In 1942 and 1943, Italian fighter quality began to benefit considerably from the acquisition of Daimler-Benz liquid-cooled engines from Germany—the Macchi C.202 Folgore and Fiat G.55 Centauro in particular being extremely good machines—and the Piaggio P.108B long range heavy bomber entered service. The Italian aircraft industry, however, could not keep pace with the requirements (and losses) of the Regia Aeronautica, and several German types, notably the Bf 109 and 110, the Do 217, and the Ju 87, were supplied as reinforcements.

On the 8th September 1943, Marshal Badoglio surrendered to the Allies, and Regia Aeronautica squadrons in the southern half of the country were formed into the Italian Co-Belligerent Air Force, fighting with a mixture of Italian, British and American aircraft on the side of the Allies. The northern part of the country, still under German control, was re-named the Repubblica Sociale Italiana, and Italian air force units in this territory continued in support of the Luftwaffe as the Aviazione della RSI until the occupation of Italy was completed.

JAPAN

SERVICE AVIATION IN JAPAN began in 1909, and by 1911 separate Army and Navy air arms were beginning to take shape. For the first few years, Army aviation progressed somewhat more rapidly than that of the Navy, but by the outbreak of World War I both units were still quite small, and their participation in the war was extremely limited. Nevertheless they picked up a considerable amount of experience which they were able to put to good use in the years after the war.

By 1917, the three major industrial concerns in the country—Mitsubishi, Nakajima and Kawasaki—had begun to take a close interest in aviation. The Mitsubishi enterprise, founded in 1884, had a network of trading posts throughout the Far East; the " Hudson's Bay Company" of the Pacific, they were merchant bankers, industrialists and shipbuilders. The Nakajima company was founded in 1914, and most of its early aircraft manufacturing experience consisted of building, under licence, the products of European and American designers, notably those of Fokker and Douglas. Kawasaki was also an important shipbuilding firm, one of whose earliest aeronautical " stars " was the German Dr. Richard Vogt, later to become more widely known for his work on the aircraft side of Blohm und Voss at Hamburg.

These three companies, guided by the advice of a French Air Mission sent to Japan at the behest of the Army in 1919, and a British one similarly requested by the Navy two years later, formed the backbone of Japan's young aircraft industry for the next ten to fifteen years. To begin with, they were mainly occupied in the purchase and licence construction of foreign designs, but Mitsubishi did turn out one or two home-designed basic warplane types which were in service by 1922-23, and at the end of 1922 the Navy began to build its first aircraft carrier, the *Hosho*.

By the end of the first post-war decade both Japanese air arms were fairly well established, though they were still small in size by world standards; and from September 1931 until February 1932 their men and equipment had the opportunity of testing themselves under battle conditions, during the Japanese invasion of Manchuria. By now the J.N.A.F. had edged ahead of the Army in development, but the aircraft designed by the companies at home had so far been disappointing, and continued reliance had to be placed on variants of foreign types, by now mostly British or German. More promising indigenous designs were, however, on the way, and the first of these began to emerge in the early 1930s. By the middle 1930s such machines as the Mitsubishi A5M fighter and G3M bomber, comparable with any of the foreign types so far employed, were entering service; and behind these was coming yet another generation of new and advanced aircraft, among them the famous A6M Zero fighter, which were to be encountered by the Allies upon the outbreak of World War 2. Meanwhile, in 1937 the campaign against China had re-opened, and in 1938/39 there were clashes with Russia over the borders of Manchuria and Mongolia.

By 1941, Japan was possessed of Army and Naval air forces which were equipped with fairly modern machines and staffed by a large percentage of battle-experienced aircrew; and a further generation of replacement aircraft was well under way, backed by considerably larger production orders than the aircraft industry had ever before known. The undoubted quality of the Japanese air forces was one of the war's major surprises. Due in part to wishful thinking, but largely to an amazing ignorance by the Western nations of the true state of aeronautical affairs in the country, it was widely believed that Japanese air power did not need to be taken too seriously. These beliefs were rudely shattered by the Imperial Japanese Fleet's attack on the U.S. Navy base at Pearl Harbour. On 7th December 1941, a task force comprising the aircraft carriers *Soryu*, *Hiryu*, *Zuikaku*, *Shokaku*, *Kaga* and *Akagi*, with seventeen other warships, sailed across the Pacific towards Hawaii. The six carriers unleashed a combined force of 353 aircraft—Aichi D3A1 dive bombers, Nakajima B5N2 torpedo bombers, and Mitsubishi A6M2s for escort and ground attack—against the American ships and shore installations, and so complete was the element of surprise that the raid was successfully completed for the loss of only 29 Japanese aircraft.

Following up the advantage gained by this decimation of U.S. naval strength, Formosa-based units launched attacks upon U.S. strongpoints in the Philippines within hours of the Pearl Harbour raid, and set the pattern for a series of similar assaults on island and mainland bases in the south-west Pacific. Inside six months, Japan was master of the area, but this was not achieved without fairly heavy losses of aircraft, losses with which the existing production machine was barely keeping pace. The Japanese air forces were thus unable to capitalise fully their territorial gains by building up a comparable arial strength over the much vaster area now under their domination. Nor did they escape effective retaliation: an isolated but significant event, the famous Doolittle B-25 raid on Tokyo in April 1942, struck a sharp blow at Japanese pride and complacency, and the Midway battle, in the summer of the same year, cost the Japanese Navy four aircraft carriers and over three hundred aircraft.

After these and other setbacks, the initiative in the Pacific passed gradually from the Japanese forces to those of the Allies as 1942 drew to its close, and the island bases were gradually won back as the Allied offensive steadily mounted through 1943. As a result of some reorganisation, following the reversals of the previous year, naval interest was now inclined more towards aircraft capable of operation from naval shore bases rather than from carriers at sea. The replacement aircraft which had been under study before the war were now beginning to make their appearance: the H8K flying-boat, the D4Y and B6N torpedo bombers, the Mitsubishi G4M long-range bomber, and improved models of the A6M Zero. The Army too was bringing into service such new types as the Ki.45 and Ki.84 fighters, and the Ki.49 and Ki.67 bombers.

During the second half of 1944, the Japanese war machine suffered its biggest reversals of the war to date. The Navy lost more carriers and several hundred aircraft in the Marianas campaign and, after the Philippines battles, was so greatly diminished that what remained of its sea and air power no longer constituted a serious threat. Similar punishment was meanwhile being meted out to J.A.A.F. formations on the mainland, in India, Burma and China.

Faced with this depletion of her strength, Japan resorted to a more extreme measure—the suicide attack—to try to halt the Allied advance. Although in keeping with Japanese religious beliefs and figeting traditions, this venture was, if viewed dispassionately, even more illogically and wasteful of resources than a normal air fighting campaign would have been.

Yet for some time it was successful in achieving its desired object, thus giving the home industry a breathing space in which to endeavour to replace in some measure the heavy losses already incurred.

The first suicide attack was made in the Philippines, on 25th October 1944, by a force of bombed-up Zero fighters, which succeeded in sinking one American carrier and damaging four others. Encouraged by this success, further suicide raids were made in the Philippines during the next three months, and a considerable variety of other aircraft types was adapted for similar missions—indeed, by the time that the war ended there was scarcely a single type which had not been used in this role. Quite apart from this adaptation of existing aircraft for Kamikaze missions, there also appeared at the end of 1944 a machine designed specifically for this role: the Yokosuka MXY-7 Ohka piloted flying bomb, carrying about a ton of high explosive in its nose, which was air-launched from a modified G4M " mother " aeroplane. These and "conventional " suicide aircraft were again used in substantial quantities at Okinawa and Iwo Jima in the early months of 1945, but even the weight of these attacks was insufficient to deter the massive U.S. invasion fleet.

With the capture of the Marianas, America's long range Superfortress bombers at last had advanced bases from which they could mount sustained and heavy bombing attacks against Japanese industrial and military targets at home, and the remaining Japanese air strength was driven back upon defence of the homeland. In a final effort to stave off defeat, existing aircraft types were modified to undertake high altitude or night interceptions, and production orders were hastily given to new and half-developed types in an attempt to provide adequate defence strength. However, the obliteration of Hiroshima and Nagasaki by atomic bombs demonstrated the futility of further resistance, and on 15th August 1945 Emperor Hirohito indicated to the Allies that Japan had, at last, admitted defeat.

RUSSIA

THE BEGINNINGS of military aviation in Russia were much the same as those in other countries; 1910 saw the establishment of army and navy air schools, and two years later the first purchases were made of foreign types—British, French and American—upon which the Imperial Russian Flying Corps was founded. During Russia's participation in World War I, these foreign aircraft fought alongside designs of purely Russian origin, outstanding among which was Igor Sikorsky's four-motor bomber, the *Ilya Mourometz*, the first of its kind in the world. Following the Socialist Revolution of 1917, air affairs became somewhat disorganised for a time, but the basis for the future Red Air Force was formulated during 1918—although the " Workers' and Peasants' Red Air Fleet ", as it was known, could initially command only a rather motley collection of aircraft.

By the middle 1920s, things were beginning to settle down more, and the Red Air Force had begun to re-stock with newer Russian and foreign designs in about equal proportions. The names of other Russian pioneer designers—Tupolev and Polikarpov amongst them—were beginning to make themselves known, and the performance of their new aeroplanes was convincingly demonstrated by record-breaking flights of one type or another. Throughout the remainder of the 1920s and the 1930s, a succession of five-year plans, the Russian aircraft industry, formed of a series of design bureaux, continued to grow in stature, and the Red Air Force seized the opportunity of the Spanish Civil War to obtain actual battle experience for its aircraft and aircrew. Further experience was gained from the clashes with Japanese formations in the Siberian border disputes of 1938/39.

From these campaigns it was realised that Soviet design thought was still lagging behind that of the other major aeronautical powers, and as a result several foreign designs were studied in an effort to make up lost ground. By the time of the German invasion of Russia in June 1941, a number of promising new designs were under way, most of them fighters and—since the Red Air Force had always been viewed primarily as a supporting body to the Army—ground attack types.

The front-line aircraft in service at that time, although numerically greater than those ranged against them by the Luftwaffe, were inferior technically, and this, coupled with the element of surprise in the German attack, led to their initial defeat by the enemy. Before the Russo-German war was a year old, however, the more modern replacements—the Yak-1, LaGG-3, MiG-1 and MiG-3 fighters, and the famous Il-2 Shturmovik close support aircraft—were getting through to the Red Air Force squadrons, and Lend-Lease supplies of American fighters and bombers, as well as similar types from Great Britain, began to reach the U.S.S.R. These included Airacobra, Kingcobra, Warhawk, Thunderbolt, Spitfire and Hurricane fighters, Havoc, Mitchell and Mosquito bombers, Douglas C-47 transports and Catalina maritime patrol aircraft. Between 1942 and 1944 the United States alone delivered to Russia almost 15,000 aircraft, of which approximately two-thirds were fighters; added to this total, the Russian aircraft industry itself turned out between thirty and forty thousand machines during the war period. By VE day, the front-line strength of the Red Air Force was in the region of 17,500 aircraft. Russian air superiority was finally obtained by a combination of superior Russian tactics, and dwindling Luftwaffe resources, due both to losses in Russia and to the reduction of remaining German squadrons to reinforce Luftwaffe units on other fronts.

U.S.A.

WHEN THE " war to end wars " came to its end in November 1918 the United States of America, like every other armed nation, immediately began to make wholesale cuts in the size and strength of its military forces. As in other countries too, there continued against this background the inevitable tug-of-war between the Army and the Navy for outright control of the newly-born air arm; at the same time, leading personalities—notable among them the outspoken William H. (" Billy ") Mitchell—campaigned vigorously for the establishment of an air force as a separate and independent body, but to no avail. Not until 18th September, 1947, did the United States Air Force drop the " Army " from its title and become fully autonomous, although it had enjoyed a certain amount of self-direction for some seven years previously. As the events of World War 2 were to prove, however, the joint efforts of the two air arms worked well together towards final victory, for although Army aircraft administered the *coup de grace* to Japan, they did so from bases won for them at great expense by the naval forces.

In 1920, the Army Reorganisation Act set up an Air Service under the jurisdiction of the U.S. Army, and in June of the following year a Bureau of Aeronautics was established to advise the Navy on air affairs. Throughout the 1920s political, policy and economic fluctuations hampered the full implementation of various re-equipment programmes for both services, but although some wartime equipment remained at the end of the decade the Army Air Corps did by then have a substantial measure of new material in service. The Navy fared slightly better during this period. Conversion of the collier *Jupiter* as its first carrier, the *Langley*, was completed in 1922, eight battleships were adapted for the carriage of small " spotter " aircraft, and by the end of the decade two more new carriers had been delivered, the *Saratoga* and the *Lexington*, which at that time were the largest of their kind in the world.

By the middle of the 1930s, a number of advanced designs had appeared for both services: one of the most significant, later to play such an important part in the coming conflict, was the concept of the long range strategic heavy bomber, as typified by the Boeing B-17 and the Douglas XB-19. The Navy had two more carriers launched in 1936, and in January 1938 a 20 per cent increase in its expansion programme was authorised. Within a few more months this was to be increased still

15

further. Thanks to these Army and Navy air force expansions, and to substantial orders from Great Britain and Europe, the American aircraft industry's order books at this time were in an extremely healthy state although, at the time of the outbreak of war in Europe, American home forces were still relatively poorly equipped. However, with the rapid drive across the Continent by Germany the go-ahead was given for a much quicker build-up of home strength, coupled with an enormous training scheme to produce the pilots to fly the increasing numbers of aircraft envisaged. The famous Lend-Lease Act, passed in March 1941, involved the outpouring of many thousands more aircraft in support of the Allied cause, to which America had always been openly sympathetic. The U.S. Army Air Corps was again re-organised and raised in importance on 20th June, 1940, and became known as the United States Army Air Force. By December 1941 the U.S.A.A.F. could boast a growing force of modern aircraft types, and the Navy possessed six aircraft carriers and over 5,000 aircraft of various descriptions, with a further eleven carriers on order.

On the morning of 7th December, 1941, a force of Japanese Navy bombers attacked the U.S. naval base at Pearl Harbour in the Hawaiian Islands, striking a crippling blow at America's Pacific sea power. Eight battleships were either destroyed or damaged, together with over a hundred aircraft, more than two thirds of the total in the area at the time. With opposition thus immensely reduced—and within six months of Pearl Harbour the carriers *Langley* and *Lexington* had also been sunk—the Japanese forces quickly overran the island bases in the south-west Pacific in preparation for their assaults on the mainland. Even so, they did not have things all their own way. They incurred an expensive set-back in mid-1942 in their vain attempt to secure the island of Midway, losing four aircraft carriers and over 250 aircraft in the process; and earlier that year, in April, the Japanese homeland was on the receiving end of the famous Army/Navy raid by sixteen B-25 Mitchell land bombers which, lead by Lt. Col. J. H. Doolittle, successfully took off from the carrier *Hornet*, flew 700 miles to bomb Tokyo and then continued their journey to land at pre-arranged bases in China.

Meanwhile, units of the U.S.A.A.F. were beginning to arrive in the European Theatre of Operations. forming the Eighth Air Force for attacks against German-held targets on the Continent. Part of the Eighth was later detached, in the autumn of 1942, to the Middle East to form the Twelfth Air Force in the North African campaign. The Naval Air Transport Service was formed during 1942 in support of Pacific operations, and eventually established a network of 40,000 miles. Production lines at home were by now turning out substantial quantities of excellent fighters and heavy and medium bombers, and by the end of the year the total number of aircraft in U.S. service had increased threefold from Pearl Harbour, though the defence of the United States itself was, until then, somewhat neglected. To relieve this situation the Navy accepted, through necessity rather than choice, some assistance from the A.A.F. in the provision of long range aircraft for maritime patrol, assistance which continued until late in 1943.

It was during 1943 that the tide began to turn for America. Daylight bombing attacks by A.A.F. Fortresses and Liberators against European targets were maintained. Losses continued to be heavy, but the increased armament of the bombers and an improved breed of escort fighters—the Lightning, the Thunderbolt and, particularly, the superb P-51 Mustang— also increased the attrition rate among enemy interceptors. The Navy began in 1943 to build up a strong anti-submarine force, and by the middle of the year its total strength was nearly thirty carriers and upwards of 16,500 aircraft. The "island-hopping" campaign for the recovery of the Pacific air bases was going well, and the Atlantic sea forces were also extremely active against submarines on the convoy routes.

One of the biggest assets to the Allied cause conferred by America's entry into the war was the huge force of transport aircraft which thus became available. Perhaps the most notable achievement of these aircraft—leaving aside such other valuable contributions as their tremendous support in operations like the D-day landings—was the long but invaluable airlift "over the Hump" between India and China after the fall of Burma. Between the end of 1942 and the middle of 1945, Skytrains, Commandos, Skymasters and other aircraft transported thousands upon thousands of tons of vital food, equipment, medical and other supplies via this route.

At the same time as the Normandy landings were taking place in Europe, one of the biggest battles of the Pacific war was also under way: the Battle of the Philippine Sea. This was the attempt to recapture the Marianas Islands of Saipan, Tinian and Guam, which were urgently wanted as bases for the new B-29 Superfortress bombers designed to attack the Japanese mainland. The A.A.F. introduced the B-29 in the spring of 1944, and the first bombing attack on Japan by this type was made on 15th June; in November Tokyo was attacked by a force of over a hundred B-29s, and attacks were steadily maintained. Meanwhile, however, the Navy was in for a surprise. At the Battle of Leyte Gulf, undertaken as a supporting move in the Marianas battle, they made severe inroads upon the fast-dwindling warship strength of the Japanese Navy, but the price was a heavy one, for it was at this stage that the Japanese *Kamikaze* (Divine Wind) suicide attacks began. Futile though these attacks may seem, in retrospect, as an attempt to alter the course of the war, they were remarkably successful while they lasted, and by VJ day they had accounted for nearly a quarter of all U.S. warships sunk during the whole of the war. Their efficacy was considerably diminished in the later stages, after a rapid increase in U.S.N. carrier-borne fighter strength.

After " mopping-up " around the south-west Pacific islands, the U.S. Navy turned its attention to the invasion of Iwo Jima and Okinawa as a prelude to strikes against the Japanese mainland. Those attacks already being made by the A.A.F's B-29s were, however, having the desired effect. Between VE and VJ days the saturation bombing of Japanese cities and installations with conventional high explosive and incendiary bombs was so great that the final outcome was never in doubt. In August 1945, however, it was dramatically advanced by the devastation of Hiroshima and Nagasaki with atomic bombs. Pearl Harbour had been avenged.

Nomenclature of Service Aircraft

GERMANY

THE German system of aircraft nomenclature, although essentially and typically methodical, can give rise to a certain amount of confusion if the system is not clearly understood.

The basic designation consisted of a letter-number combination, utilising a contraction of the name of the designing firm followed by a type number—*e.g.*, Ju 88 = Junkers Flugzeug und Motorenwerke A.G., Type 88. Occasional deviations from this practice were made. Towards the end of the war, an abbreviation of the name of the designer himself was sometimes used; thus, Kurt Tank's development of the Fw 190D, coupled with a new type number, was known as the Ta 152. The aircraft bearing type numbers 108, 109 and 110 were prefixed by the contraction *Bf*, from Bayerische Flugzeugwerke, the title of the Messerschmitt company at the time when they were designed. The contraction *Ha* used on some early Blohm und Voss types indicates that they originated at the Hamburg works of that Company.

This basic title was followed by a suffix letter indicating the sub-type (*e.g.*, Ju 88A), and eventually by a figure indicating the series (*e.g.*, Ju 88A-6). With one exception the sub-type letters were allotted consecutively, although the aircraft concerned may not necessarily have entered service in that order. For instance, the Ju 88A-5 was in service before the Ju 88A-4, which was a much-improved version.

The suffix letter V was reserved for prototype aircraft: thus, the He 177V3 was the third prototype of the Heinkel He 177. Note that in this instance no hyphen is used between the final letter and figure.

Type numbers were allotted from a central body in the R.L.M. (*Reichsluftministerium*, the German Air Ministry), and the same number was seldom duplicated in two different types of aeroplane. Persistent reports of the existence of an "Fw 198" fighter, for example, should never have arisen, since this type number had already been allocated to the Arado Ar 198. However, there were one or two instances of aircraft and *engine* type numbers coinciding, as in the case of the Me 323 and the Bramo 323.

One other frequent ingredient of German aircraft designations was the contraction "Trop." (as in Fw 190A-4/Trop.), indicating that the aircraft had been adapted for tropical service.

JAPAN

THE naming and numbering of Japanese service aircraft during the five years of war was inordinately complex, and was one of the prime reasons behind the Allied code naming system whereby fighters and floatplanes were allocated boys' Christian names, and most other types (except trainers) girls' names, transport aircraft having female names beginning with T. Until mid-1943 the Japanese used a clumsy system based on the Japanese calendar, which was 660 years ahead of the western one. For the sake of simplification such designations have been omitted from this book; the later system is outlined below.

Japanese Army Air Force types, whilst still in the experimental stage, were given a serial number prefixed with the contraction Ki (from *Hikoki*, meaning aeroplane). The numbers were allotted chronologically regardless of manufacturer or function. Major modifications during production were indicated by a model number (e.g., Ki.43-II). Names, in addition to designation numbers, were allotted to Army aircraft comparatively rarely.

The J.N.A.F. system was more complicated, though not altogether dissimilar to that used by the U.S. Navy. The basic designation was a letter-number-letter-number combination, the first letter signifying function and the second the manufacturer. These were allocated as follows:—

Functional Letters

A	Carrier-borne fighter	K	Trainer
B	Carrier-borne attack	L	Transport
C	Carrier-borne reconnaissance	M	Special aircraft
D	Carrier-borne bomber	N	Fighter floatplane
E	Reconnaissance floatplane	P	Land-based bomber
F	Observation floatplane	Q	Anti-submarine
G	Heavy and medium bomber	R	Land-based reconnaissance
H	Flying boat	S	Night fighter
J	Land-based fighter		

Manufacturers' Letters

A	Aichi	N	Nakajima
D	Showa	P	Nippon
G	Tokyo Gasu Denki	S	Sasebo
H	Hiro	W	Kyushu
K	Kawanishi		(formerly Watanabe)
M	Mitsubishi	Y	Yokosuka

The two numbers indicated, respectively, the order of the aeroplane designs entering service, regardless of manufacturer, and the individual aircraft model number.

Thus the designation A6M2 indicated that the Zero was a carrier-borne fighter (A), the sixth to go into Japanese Navy service (6), was built by Mitsubishi (M), and was the second version of the design (2) to be produced. Where a design was later adapted to fulfil a different function, the letter of the new function was added after the basic designation (e.g. A6M2-N).

Names, as well as numbers, were given to the major operational Navy aircraft. Fighters were named after meteorological phenomena; attack aircraft after mountains, bombers after stars and constellations, patrol aircraft after seas, transports after skies and training aircraft after trees or plants.

RUSSIA

UP to 1940, the Red Air Force employed a designation code consisting of letters denoting the function of the aircraft concerned, followed by an Air Force series number. The chief functional prefixes were:—

ARK	Arctic service	I	Fighter
BB	Short range bomber	KOR	Shipborne
DB	Long range bomber	PS	Transport
SB	Medium bomber	U	Trainer
TB	Heavy bomber	UT	Trainer

A simplified system was introduced in 1941, whereby a new designation was allotted, consisting of a contraction of the designer's surname followed by a design bureau series number. The designers' names were abbreviated as follows:—

ANT	A.N. Tupolev	Pe	V. Petlyakov
Il	S.V. Ilyushin	Po	N. Polikarpov
La	S.A. Lavochkin	Su	P. Sukhoi
LaGG	Lavochkin, Gorbunov and Gudkov	Tu	A. N. Tupolev
MiG	A.I. Mikoyan and M.I. Gurevich	Yak	A.S. Yakovlev

The continued existence of both systems, for a while, side by side, inevitably led to some confusion at the time. As an example, the heavy bomber which began life as the TB-7 later became known as the ANT-42, after Andrei Tupolev, by one of whose design bureaux it was created. It finally received the designation Pe-8, in recognition of its actual designer, Vladimir Petlyakov.

U.S.A.

THE United States army and naval air force authorities each employed —and until 1962 still employed—separate codes to designate their respective aircraft. Although the two schemes have some points in common, there are certain significant differences between them; because of this, and of further detail differences between the codes used during the war and those prevailing today, the following explanation may be helpful.

The designations of both army and naval aircraft opened with a letter or letters denoting their function, as follows:—

U.S.A.A.F.

A	Light Bombing	O	Observation
AT	Advanced Training	OA	Observation Amphibian
B	Medium or Heavy Bombing	P	Fighting
BT	Basic Training	PT	Primary Training
C	Transport	R	Rotary Wing
CG	Transport Glider	TG	Training Glider
F	Reconnaissance	UC	Utility Transport
L	Liaison		

U.S. Navy and Marine Corps

B	Bombing	N	Training
F	Fighting	O	Observation
G	Transport (single engined)	P	Patrol
H	Rotary Wing	R	Transport (multi-engined)
J	General Utility	S	Scouting
L	Glider	T	Torpedo

These functional letters were followed, in the case of U.S.A.A.F. aircraft, by a hyphen and a number indicating the model. The numbers ran consecutively, regardless of manufacturer, throughout each class: thus, the B-24 and B-25 were consecutive designs for the U.S.A.A.F., although from different manufacturers.

Combat aircraft modified for other duties were sometimes given entirely fresh designations, as in the case of the C-87, which was the transport version of the B-24. Others simply added the letter of their new function ahead of the original designation—for example, the TP-39 was the trainer version of the P-39 Airacobra.

The use of two or more prefix letters (e.g., PB=Patrol Bomber) was also practised for dual-function naval aircraft, the first letter always denoting the primary function. Following the prefix letter or letters came a number-letter combination denoting the design sequence and the name of the manufacturer, then a hyphen and a final number indicating successive modifications. Thus, the designation PB4Y-2 revealed that the aircraft was a patrol bomber (PB), the fourth of its kind (4) to be designed by Consolidated (Y), and was the second major variation (-2) of that design.

The following letters identified the principal aircraft manufacturers in the U.S. Navy system:—

A	Brewster; Allied Aviation	O	Lockheed
B	Beech; Boeing; Budd	P	Piper; P-V Engineering;
C	Curtiss-Wright; Cessna;		Spartan
	Culver	Q	Bristol
D	Douglas; McDonnell	R	Ryan; Interstate; Aeronca;
E	Bellanca; Gould; Piper; Edo		American Aviation
F	Grumman; Fairchild Canada	S	Sikorsky; Stearman; Schweizer
G	Goodyear	T	Northrop; Taylorcraft; Timm
H	Howard; Hall-Aluminium	U	Chance Vought
J	North American	V	Vultee; Canadian Vickers;
K	Fairchild; Fleetwings		Vega
L	Bell; Columbia; Langley	W	Waco; Canadian Car &
M	Martin; Eastern		Foundry
N	Naval Aircraft Factory	Y	Consolidated-Vultee

The prefix X, on both army and naval aircraft, indicated that the machine was an experimental prototype; the prefix Y signified that it was one of a pre-production batch for service testing.

D3AI

Aichi D3A

Country of origin: **JAPAN**　　　*Designers:* **Aichi Tokei Denki K.K.**
Purpose: **Dive bomber.**　　　*In operational use:* **1941/45.**

The Aichi D3A (code name *Val*) somehow seemed to typify Japan's entry into World War 2. Apart from the fact that this type of aeroplane predominated in the force which attacked Pearl Harbour, it was that most unpleasant of warplanes, a dive bomber; not, admittedly, so angularly awe-inspiring as the Ju 87, but no less lethal for that. The *Val* did in fact, owe much to German design thought, and it was conceived by the Aichi company in 1936 after a prolonged study of the Heinkel He 66, 70 and 74. As the D3A1, powered by a 1,075 h.p. Kinsei 44 engine, the type entered production during 1937, and from then until 1942 a total of 478 D3A1s were completed. In 1942 it was replaced on the assembly lines by the more powerful D3A2, of which 816 had been built when production terminated in 1944. The *Val*, which had the distinction of being Japan's first all-metal low-wing mono-plane dive bomber, was extremely effective during the early years of the war in the hands of a skilled pilot; as the latter became more rare, however, and more modern replacement machines became available, its success began to wane. Although it was not an unduly light aeroplane, and was strongly stressed to withstand steep diving, the D3A was highly manoeuvrable and capable of engaging opposing fighters after delivering its bombs.

BRIEF TECHNICAL DETAILS (D3A2):
Engine: One 1,300 h.p. Mitsubishi Kinsei 54 radial.
Span: 47 ft. 1¼ in.
Length: 33 ft. 6¾ in.
Height: 10 ft. 11¼ in.
Weight Empty: 5,772 lb.
　　　Loaded: 8,378 lb.
No. in crew: Two.
Max. Speed: 266 m.p.h. at 18,536 ft.
Service Ceiling: 35,695 ft.
Max. Range: 970 miles.
Armament: Two 7.7 mm. machine guns; Up to 816 lb. of bombs.

Airspeed Oxford

Country of origin : GREAT BRITAIN
Purpose: **Advanced trainer and ambulance.**
Makers **Airspeed (1934) Ltd.**

Specification: **T.23/36.**
In operational use: **1939/45.**

Known to hundreds of R.A.F. aircrew as the "Ox-box", the Oxford first appeared in 1937 as a military development of the 1934 Envoy feeder-liner, and was the first twin-engined monoplane trainer in the Royal Air Force. The first Oxfords joined the Central Flying School in November 1937, and by the time of the outbreak of World War 2 nearly 400 were in service. Production was subsequently stepped up, Airspeed building nearly four and a half thousand Oxfords, and with sub-contracts placed with de Havilland, Percival and Standard Motors the total number of Oxfords completed came to 8,751. Although used most widely in its intended role as aircrew trainer, the Oxford gave valuable service on communications and anti-aircraft co-operation duties, and was also used in some numbers as an ambulance, particularly in the Middle East. As a trainer, it served in Canada, Australia, New Zealand and Southern Rhodesia as well as in the United Kingdom. Outwardly there was little difference in appearance between the various mark numbers, the principal variations being in power-plant and internal equipment. The Oxford I was a bombing and gunnery trainer, and featured a dorsal Armstrong-Whitworth turret—the only Oxford to do so. The Mk. II was similarly powered, and was equipped as a navigation and radio trainer. This was likewise the function of the Mk. III, powered by two 425 h.p. Cheetah XV, which was also the usual ambulance version. The designation Mk. IV applied to a single Oxford used as test-bed for de Havilland Gipsy Queen motors; while the Mk. V, a standard trainer model, was powered by 450 h.p. Pratt & Whitney Wasp Juniors and was chiefly used in Rhodesia and Canada. During the war period a number of Oxfords were also in service with the Fleet Air Arm as naval crew trainers.

BRIEF TECHNICAL DETAILS (Mk. I):
Engines: Two 355 h.p. Armstrong-Siddeley Cheetah IX or X radials.
Span: 53 ft. 4 in.
Length: 34 ft. 6 in.
Height: 11 ft. 1 in.
Weight Empty: 5,380 lb.
Loaded: 7,600 lb.
No. in crew: Three.
Max. Speed: 182 m.p.h. at 8,300 ft.
Service Ceiling: 19,200 ft.
Range: 550 miles.

23

Ar 196A-2/H. J. Nowarra

Arado Ar 196

Country of origin: **GERMANY**
Purpose: **Reconnaissance and anti-submarine.**

Makers: **Arado Flugzeugwerke G.m.b.H.**
In operational use: **1939/45.**

Probably the most successful seaplane produced and employed by the German Naval air forces during the period of the European War, the Arado Ar 196 was for many years the standard catapult seaplane of the German Navy, 435 aircraft of the type being completed. Its wide range of seagoing duties included those of general reconnaissance, light bombing and submarine hunting—two aircraft of this type being instrumental in the capture of the British submarine "Seal". As many as four of these twin-float aircraft (the Ar 196V3 was fitted with a single float only, but a return to the twin arrangement was made with production aircraft) could be carried at one time aboard the larger German battleships, and the first examples of the Ar 196 to be observed during the war were those, in December 1939, on the short-lived pocket battleship "Graf Spee". Arado Ar 196s were, during their service, encountered over every major sea area in the European theatre of operations, and were often employed on coastal patrol in addition to their seagoing missions.

BRIEF TECHNICAL DETAILS (Ar 196A-3):
Engine One 900 h.p. BMW 132K radial.
Span: 40 ft. 10½ in.
Length: 36 ft. 1 in.
Height: 14 ft. 6 in.
Weight Empty: 6,580 lb.
       Loaded: 8,200 lb.
No. in crew: Two.
Max. Speed: 193 m.p.h. at 13,120 ft.
Service Ceiling: 23,000 ft.
Normal Range: 670 miles.
Armament: Two 20 mm. MG FF cannon and two 7.9 mm. MG 17 machine guns. One 110 lb. bomb beneath each wing.

Whitley Mk. V/*Flight International*

Armstrong Whitworth Whitley

Country of origin: **GREAT BRITAIN**
Purpose: **Bomber.**
Makers: **Sir W. G. Armstrong Whitworth Aircraft Ltd.**

Specification: **B.3/34.**
In operational use: **1939/44.**

Although it was overshadowed by more modern bombing types as the war progressed, the Whitley, one of the mainstays of Bomber Command in September 1939, nevertheless had a distinguished operational record. It was the first British bomber to fly over Berlin, and the first to drop bombs on both Germany and Italy. From the outset of the war it was used as a night bomber and leaflet dropper; later it served with Coastal Command on reconnaissance and anti-submarine work, and it also saw service as a glider tug and paratroop trainer. The Whitley prototype (K 4586) made its maiden flight in March 1936, followed by a second prototype and the first production Mk. Is (795 h.p. Tiger IX), which entered service in March 1937. The 34 Mk. Is were followed by 46 Mk. II (920 h.p. Tiger VIII) and 80 Mk. III, similar except for a ventral " dustbin " turret. After the 40 Mks. IV (1,030 h.p. Merlin IV) and IVA (1,075 h.p. Merlin X) of 1938 came the major production version, the Mk. V, in 1939. Deliveries of the Mk. V continued until June 1943, during which time 1,476 were completed. At the end of the first month of the war a squadron of bombers was transferred to Coastal Command, and in March 1941 a number of Whitley Vs joined the anti-submarine force of that Command. Some of these were later converted for reconnaissance as the G.R. VIII (there was no Mk. VI), and a further 146 aircraft, built from the outset as Mk. VIIs, were the first Coastal Command aircraft to carry the long range A.S.V. Mk. II radar. In the summer of 1940 a number of Whitley Mk. IIs were supplied to No. 1 Parachute Training School as paratroop trainers and Horsa glider tugs, though they were never used operationally in the latter role. Twelve Mk. Vs were converted in 1942 for civil use by British Airways as freighters.

BRIEF TECHNICAL DETAILS (Mk. V):
Engines: Two 1,075 h.p. Rolls-Royce Merlin X inlines.
Span: 84 ft. 0 in.
Length: 72 ft. 6 in.
Height: 15 ft. 0 in.
Weight Empty: 19,350 lb.
Loaded: 28,200 lb.
No. in crew: Five.
Max. Speed: 228 m.p.h. at 17,750 ft.
Service Ceiling: 17,600 ft.
Normal Range: 1,500 miles.
Armament: Five .303 machine guns; up to 7,000 lb. of bombs.

Lancaster Mk. I

Avro Lancaster

Country of origin: **GREAT BRITAIN** *Makers:* **A. V. Roe & Co. Ltd.**
Purpose: **Heavy bomber.** *In operational use:* **1942/45.**

Apart from the many famous actions in which it participated with distinction, the Lancaster will be remembered as the aeroplane which, more than any other, carried the war back to the German homeland. It grew out of the downfall of the twin-engined Manchester (see page 172), and the prototype Lancaster I (BT 308, which first flew on 9th January, 1941) was originally the Manchester III —triple tail unit and all—modified to take four 1,130 h.p. Rolls-Royce Merlin X engines. The first production Mk. I flew just over nine months later, powered by Merlin XX and incorporating dorsal and ventral gun turrets. Production, begun at Avro, was also delegated to Vickers-Armstrongs, Metropolitan-Vickers, Armstrong Whitworth and Austin Motors. Deliveries to the R.A.F. began just after Christmas 1941; the first squadron (No. 44) was equipped with the type at the beginning of 1942, and it made its first raid in March of that year. Total U.K. production of Mk. I Lancasters eventually topped the 3,500 mark, and during 1942 construction was further sub-contracted to Victory Aircraft Ltd. of Malton, Ontario, who delivered in August 1943 the first of over 400 Canadian-built Lancasters. Designated B. Mk. X, these were generally identical with the British Mk. I apart from the employment of Packard-built Merlin 28, 38 or 224 powerplants. Meanwhile there had appeared in Britain a radial-engined version, the Lancaster II. Built by Armstrong Whitworth, it was powered by 1,725 h.p. Bristol Hercules VI or XVI as a safeguard against possible supply difficulties with the Merlin. In the event there proved to be no shortage of Merlins, and only 300 Lancaster IIs were completed. Production continued with the Mk. III, the second major version (about 3,000 built), which was almost identical to the Lancaster I, the primary difference being the adoption of Packard-Merlins to provide the power. The Mks. IV and V eventually became proto-types for the Lincoln bomber, and only a handful of Mk. VI (special conversions of a few Mks. I and III) were completed. The final production Lancaster was the Mk. VII, of which 180 were built by Austin Motors. These had a Martin

26

Lancaster Mk. II/*Canadian Department of National Defence*

Lancaster Mk. I modified to carry "dams" bomb

Mk. I with "Tallboy" bomb

dorsal turret, re-located further forward, instead of the Nash and Thompson turret of earlier Lancasters. Variants of the Lancaster 1 were the Mk. I (F.E.), intended to bomb the Japanese mainland with the " Tiger Force ", but too late for operational service, and the Mk. I (Special), which was the designation of those Lancasters specially modified to take the 22,000 lb. " Grand Slam " bomb.

Lancasters figured in many notable adventures during World War 2, but undoubtedly two of their most famous exploits were the dams raid of 1943 and the sinking of the battleship *Tirpitz* in the following year. The breaching of the Moehne, Eder and Sorpe dams was carried out on the night of 17th May, 1943, using Barnes Wallis' specially-developed " bouncing bomb ". Eight of the force of 19 Lancasters were lost that night, and amidst several decorations awarded, the C.O. of No. 617 Squadron, Wing Commander Guy Gibson, received the Victoria Cross. Throughout the war, eleven V.Cs. were awarded to Lancaster crew members.

The *Tirpitz* was finally sunk in Tromso Fjord, Norway, on 12th November 1944, by a force of 31 Lancasters each carrying a 12,000 lb. " Tallboy " bomb (another Barnes Wallis development), though she had been severely crippled in another Lancaster raid two months earlier.

The grand total of Lancaster production reached 7,374 aircraft, of which many continued to serve the R.A.F., on air/sea rescue and maritime reconnaissance duties, long after the end of the war.

BRIEF TECHNICAL DETAILS (Mk. I):
Engines: Four 1,460 h.p. Rolls-Royce Merlin 20 or 22, or 1,640 h.p. Merlin 24 inlines.
Span: 102 ft. 0 in.
Length: 69 ft. 6 in.
Height: 20 ft. 0 in.
Weight Empty: 36,900 lb.
Loaded: 68,000 lb. (70,000 lb. with " Grand Slam ").
No. in crew: Seven.
Max. Speed: 287 m.p.h. at 11,500 ft.
Service Ceiling: 24,500 ft.
Max. Range: 1,660 miles.
Armament: Ten .303 Browning machine guns; up to 14,000 lb. of bombs normally.

Lancaster transport/B.O.A.C.

Avro Anson

Country of origin: **GREAT BRITAIN**
Purpose: **Reconnaissance and trainer.**
Makers: **A. V. Roe & Co. Ltd.**

Specification: **18/35 (first production).**
In operational use: **1939/45.**

Few aeroplanes can so thoroughly have lived up to their nicknames as " Faithful Annie ".   Clearly there can be little wrong with an aeroplane that remains in production or service for more than twenty years, and this was well borne out by the thousands of Ansons which served throughout World War 2 and for many years afterwards.   A military development of Imperial Airways' six-seater Avro 652, and incorporating much of the company's earlier experience in building the rugged Fokker F.VII, the Anson design was evolved in 1934 to meet a requirement for a twin-engined shore-based reconnaissance aircraft. Avro's design was accepted that September, and the first prototype (K 4771) flew on 24th March 1935.   Four months later 174 Anson Mk. I were ordered, the first of these entering service in March 1936.   From then until the outbreak of war Ansons continued to be delivered at a steady rate, although by the latter date they had just begun to be replaced by Hudsons from the U.S.A.   Nevertheless the Anson continued to give a good account of itself with Coastal Command —numbering even the Messerschmitt Bf 109 among its victims—and remained on reconnaissance duties until 1942.   By this time it had also come into its own as a training aircraft: in 1939 an order had been placed for 1,500 Anson trainers, and in December of that year the type was chosen as a major part of the equipment for the huge Commonwealth Air Training Plan.   As a result of this, several new versions appeared as the war progressed, many of them converted or entirely constructed in Canada.   The Anson II was Canadian-built with two Jacobs engines: the Mk. III a British conversion to Jacobs; the Mk. IV a British conversion to Wright Whirlwinds.   To conserve strategic materials the Canadian-built Mks. V and VI (450 h.p. Wasp Junior) made extensive use of plywood construction.   In Britain, Mk. Is converted as light transports or ambulances included 103 Mk. X, 90 Mk. XI and 246 Mk. XII, the latter employing 425 h.p. Cheetah XV motors.   Total Anson production in Britain (which ceased in May 1952) was 8,138 of which 6,704 were built as Mk. I. Canadian factories completed 2,882 Ansons.

BRIEF TECHNICAL DETAILS (Mk. I):
Engines: Two 350 h.p. Armstrong Siddeley Cheetah IX radials.
Span: 56 ft. 6 in.
Length: 42 ft. 3 in.
Height: 13 ft. 1 in.
Weight Empty: 5,375 lb.
Loaded: 8,000 lb.
No. in crew: Six.
Max. Speed: 188 m.p.h. at 7,000 ft.
Service Ceiling: 19,000 ft.
Normal Range: 790 miles.
Armament: Two .303 machine guns; up to 360 lb. of bombs.

29

P-39F/U.S.A.F.

Bell P-39 Airacobra

Country of origin: **U.S.A.**
Purpose: **Fighter and fighter-bomber.**

Makers: **Bell Aircraft Corporation.**
In operational use: **1941/45.**

The P-39 Airacobra departed from orthodox fighter design in that its Allison inline engine was installed below and behind the pilot's seat, driving the propeller by means of an extension shaft coupled to a gearbox in the nose of the aircraft. It was also one of the first production fighters in the world to feature a tricycle undercarriage. The XP-39 prototype first flew in 1939 and was followed by the usual evaluation batch of 13 YP-39s, although no U.S. orders were immediately forthcoming. The initial contracts, placed by the French Government, were taken over by the British Purchasing Commission in 1940, the first Airacobras reaching the R.A.F. in July 1941 and becoming operational three months later. After limited use on ground attack duties, however, the type was withdrawn and the undelivered aircraft were taken over by the U.S.A.A.F. for training duties. The first version produced expressly for U.S. use was the P-39C, originally designated P-45 and generally similar to the R.A.F.'s Airacobra I and IA. Production of the P-39C amounted to 80 aircraft: 60 of these were subsequently converted to P-39D, followed by a further 863 of the D model with self-sealing fuel tanks. Apart from a trio of XP-39Es completed with laminar-flow wings as test aircraft for the P-63 Kingcobra, Airacobra production continued with moderate-sized batches of the P-39F (229), P-39J (25, engine change), P-39K (210, uprated engine and extra ammunition), P-39L (250), and P-39M (240). There was no P-39H, and 1,800 aircraft originally to have been designated P-39G were eventually divided among the K, L, M and N models. By far the greatest production of the Airacobra was centred on the P-39N and Q, of which 2,095 and 4,905 respectively were built, bringing total production of the type to 9,558 machines by July 1944. Some 5,000 Airacobras, mostly of the N and Q type, were supplied to Russia under Lend-Lease. Both the N and the Q were similarly powered; the latter was slightly faster and featured a .50-inch gun armament in place of the .30s of earlier models.

BRIEF TECHNICAL DETAILS
(P-39Q):
Engine: One 1,200 h.p. Allison V-1710-85 inline.
Span: 34 ft. 0 in.
Length: 30 ft. 2 in.
Height: 12 ft. 5 in,
Weight Empty: 5,645 lb.
    Loaded: 8,300 lb. (max.)
No. in Crew: One.
Max. Speed: 385 m.p.h. at 11,000 ft.
Service Ceiling: 35,000 ft.
Normal Range: 675 miles.
Armament: One 37 mm. cannon and four .50 machine guns; one 500 lb. bomb optional.

Blohm und Voss Bv 138

Country of origin: **GERMANY**
Purpose: **Reconnaissance.**

Makers: **Blohm und Voss.**
In operational use: **1940/45.**

One of the most distinctive products of a company that produced several unorthodox aeroplanes, the Bv 138 soon earned itself, for obvious reasons, the nickname of " The Flying Shoe ".   A pre-war design by Dr. Richard Vogt, the prototype (D-ARAK) flew in 1937, but considerable modification was carried out before the aircraft entered military service.   It was, incidentally, the only Blohm und Voss design to achieve quantity production status during the Second World War.   The first production version was the Bv 138A-1, which was powered by Jumo 205C engines.   Production then continued, in 1940, with the higher-powered Bv 138B-1 with Jumo 205Ds, modified tail structure and revised armament and followed with the Bv 138C-1 which was essentially similar. The Bv 138 was in general use throughout the war, operating in the later stages over the North Sea from bases in occupied Norway and over the Baltic Sea from airfields in Germany.   Its variety of duties included long range reconnaissance, convoy patrol and U-boat co-operation.   Production of all variants totalled 276 aircraft.

> **BRIEF TECHNICAL DETAILS**
> **(Bv 138C-1):**
> *Engines:* Three 880 h.p. Junkers Jumo 205D inlines.
> *Span:* 88 ft. 4¼ in.
> *Length:* 65 ft. 1½ in.
> *Weight Empty:* 17,820 lb.
> *Loaded:* 34,100 lb.
> *No. in crew:* Five.
> *Max. Speed* 170 m.p.h. at 8,200 ft.
> *Service Ceiling:* 18,700 ft.
> *Max. Range:* 2,670 miles.
> *Armament:* Two 20 mm. MG 151 cannon, one 13mm MG 131 and one 7.9mm. MG15 machine gun. Up to six 110 lb. bombs, four depth charges or two sea-mines.

Boeing B-17 Flying Fortress

Country of origin: **U.S.A.**
Purpose: **Bomber.**
Makers: **Boeing Aircraft Company.**

Other U.S. designations: **F-9, C-108, PB-1.**
In operational use: **1941/45.**

The B-17 Fortress was in service from start to finish of America's participation in World War 2. It was designed in response to a U.S.A.A.C. competition in 1934, the prototype (four 750 h.p. P. & W. Hornets) flying on 28th July, 1935. Thirteen Y1B-17 and one Y1B-17A (four 930 h.p. Wright Cyclones) were ordered for evaluation; after their test period these became the B-17 and B-17A respectively. The first production batch of 39 B-17B, featuring a modified nose, enlarged rudder and various internal modifications, were all delivered by the end of March 1940; meanwhile a further order had been placed for 38 B-17C (four 1,200 h.p. Cyclones) with armament and other minor changes. Twenty of these were supplied to the R.A.F. as the Fortress I in 1941, but after several losses the remainder were diverted to Coastal Command or the Middle East. By the time the Pacific war commenced the B-17D, 42 of which had been ordered during 1940, was in service. This was generally similar to the C, and the Cs in service were subsequently modified to D standard. The new tail design, hallmark of

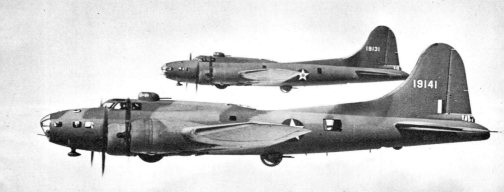

B-17F

later Fortresses, was introduced with the B-17E, with improved defensive armament which included, for the first time, a tail turret. The R.A.F. received 45 B-17Es in 1942 as the Fortress IIA; one E was converted as the 38-passenger XC-108 transport for General MacArthur, another as the XC-108A freighter, and one, as the XB-38, was fitted with Allison engines, a project later abandoned, In April 1942 the B-17F, with further refinements, entered production; Coastal Command received 19 as the Fortress II. As the F-9, -9A and -9B, 61 of this model were converted for reconnaissance. The last production Fortress was the B-17G, 8,680 being completed by Boeing, Douglas and Vega. A standard feature (later added to some B-17Fs) was a "chin" turret mounting twin .50 guns. This model was the R.A.F's Fortress III, 85 being delivered. Ten B-17Gs were converted to F-9Cs, the U.S. Navy and Coast Guard employed 24 PB-1W and 16 PB-1G for aerial patrol duties, and about 130, with a lifeboat under the belly, became B-17H or TB-17H air/sea rescue aircraft Total B-17 production exceeded 12,700 machines.

BRIEF TECHNICAL DETAILS (B-17G):
Engines: Four 1,200 h.p. Wright GR-1820-97 Cyclone radials.
Span: 103 ft. 9½ in.
Length: 74 ft. 4 in.
Height: 19 ft. 1 in
Weight Empty: 32,720 lb.
Loaded: 55,000 lb.
No. in crew: Ten.
Max. Speed: 300 m p.h. at 30,000 ft.
Service ceiling: 35,000 ft.
Max. Range: 1,850 miles.
Armament: Thirteen .50 machine guns; up to 17,600 lb. of bombs over short ranges.

B-17G

487775

Boeing B-29 Superfortress

Country of origin: **U.S.A.**
Purpose: **Long range heavy bomber.**
Makers: **Boeing Aircraft Company.**

Other U.S. designations: **F-13.**
In operational use: **1943/45.**

Evolved as a " super bomber " to bomb the Axis powers into submission, the Superfortress was the outcome of a prolonged series of design studies begun in the late 1930s.   The heaviest combat aircraft of World War 2, and the first in quantity production to employ pressurisation, authority was given in 1940 for three XB-29s, and a large number of B-29s were ordered " off the drawing board " to follow the 14 YB-29s.   By the time the first XB-29 (four 2,200 h.p. Duplex Cyclones) made its maiden flight on 21st September, 1942, total orders stood at 1,664 machines and production had been sub-contracted to a number of factories. By mid-1943, when the first unit was formed, it had been decided to use the bomber against Japan only, and during the early summer of 1944 the type began bombing operations in the Far East, making its first raid on Tokyo in June.   From March 1945 raids were made by night as well as by day, primarily with incendiaries, which were most effective against the lightly-constructed Japanese buildings.   The Superfortresses built thus far comprised over 3,600 B-29s and B-29As, all of which had an extensive (and largely remote-controlled) gun armament; the negligible opposition which was encountered, however, led to this being reduced to the bare minimum, with a consequent improvement in performance and bomb load, and the completion of a further 311 B-29B Superfortresses with tail guns only.   On 6th August 1945 the history-making B-29 " Enola Gay ", under the captaincy of Col. Paul Tibbetts, dropped the first atomic bomb on Hiroshima, heralding the end of World War 2.   With the arrival of VJ-day further B-29 orders were curtailed, production finally ceasing in May 1946 after 3,970 machines had been completed.   Wartime conversion of a number of B-29 and B-29A aircraft produced the F-13A photo-reconnaissance model;   various other modifications, both during and after the war, included the XB-39 (a converted YB-29 with Allison inline engines), the XB-44 (testbeds for the later B-50 Superfortress), and the SB-29 (search and rescue), TB-29 (trainer), WB-29 (weather reconnaissance) and KB-29 (tanker).

BRIEF TECHNICAL DETAILS (B-29):
Engines: Four 2,200 h.p. Wright R-3350-23 Cyclone radials.
Span: 141 ft. 3 in.
Length: 99 ft. 0 in.
Height: 27 ft. 9 in.
Weight Empty: 74,500 lb.
 Loaded: 120,000 lb.
No in crew: Ten to fourteen
Max. Speed: 357 m.p.h. at 30,000 ft.
Service Ceiling: 33,600 ft.
Normal Range: 3,250 miles.
Armament: Twelve .50 machine guns and one 20 mm. cannon; 12,000 lb. of bombs normally

Bristol Beaufighter

Country of origin: **GREAT BRITAIN**
Purpose: **Night fighter and anti-shipping strike**
Makers: **Bristol Aeroplane Co. Ltd.**

Specification: **F.17/39.**
In operational use: **1940/45.**

Based on the Beaufort (page 36), the first of four Beaufighter prototypes (R 2052) flew on 17th July, 1939, a fortnight after 300 Mk. IF had been ordered. The first reached Fighter Command in September 1940, being fitted two months later with A.I. radar for night fighting. With its high speed, 1,500-mile range and a firepower from its four cannon and six machine guns of 9,600 rounds a minute, the Beaufighter was a most welcome arrival. The Mk. IC joined Coastal Command in the Spring of 1941 and was followed into production by the dihedral-tailplane Mk. IIF—powered by 1,280 h.p. Merlin XX, since the Stirling programme had first call on Hercules production. No Mks. III or IV and only two Mk. V were built, the next major version being the Hercules-powered Mk. VI which came into service in 1942. More than 1,000 Mk. VI were built, including the first rocket-firing version (" Flakbeau ") and the first to carry a torpedo (" Torbeau "). In January 1943 the Mk. VI arrived in the Far East, where it quickly acquired the title " Whispering Death " from the Japanese. It also served with U.S.A.A.F. night fighter units. The Mks. VII, VIII and IX did not materialise, and the Mk. XIC (163 built) was an interim version of the VIC without torpedo gear. The last major version (2,231 built) was the Mk. X, probably the finest torpedo and strike aircraft of its day, counting many U-boats among its victims. This version introduced the " thimble " radar nose and compensating dorsal fin, which were afterwards added to certain earlier models. R.A.A.F. Beaufighters included the Fairey-built IC and the Australian-built Mk. 21. The latter (to which the R.N.Z.A.F. Mk. XX was also similar) resembled the Mk. X except for the 0.5-in. gun armament. Beaufighter production at home and abroad totalled 5,962; the type · performed the last operational sortie of the European war and remained in R.A.F. service, latterly as a target tug, until 1959.

BRIEF TECHNICAL DETAILS (Mk. X):
Engines: Two 1,770 h.p. Bristol Hercules XVII radials.
Span: 57 ft. 10 in.
Length: 41 ft. 8 in.
Height: 15 ft. 10 in.
Weight Empty: 15,592 lb.
Loaded: 25,400 lb.
No. in crew: Two.
Max. Speed: 320 m.p.h. at 10,000 ft.
Service Ceiling: 19,000 ft.
Max. Range: 1,470 miles.
Armament: Four 20 mm. Hispano cannon, six .303 Browning and one .303 Vickers machine guns. One 1,650 lb. or 2,127 lb. torpedo, 8 R.P. or two 250 lb. or 500 lb. bombs.

Bristol Beaufort

Country of origin: **GREAT BRITAIN**
Purpose: **Torpedo bomber and reconnaissance.**
Makers: **Bristol Aeroplane Co. Ltd.**

Specifications: **M.15/35 and G.24/35.**
In operational use: **1939/44.**

Based on experience gained with the Blenheim (opposite), the Bristol 152 Beaufort was the Royal Air Force's standard torpedo bomber for four years of the war, and saw action in practically every theatre of operations. Altogether 1,120 Beauforts were built, of which 955 were Mk. Is. Evolved to meet two Air Ministry Specifications, one for a torpedo carrier and the other for a reconnaissance bomber, design work on the Beaufort began in 1937 and the first prototype (L 4441) flew on 15th October 1938. The first production aircraft (Mk. I), incorporating various modifications, entered service with Coastal Command in December 1939, following an initial contract placed in August 1936 for 78 machines. These early aircraft were powered by 1,010 h.p. Taurus II engines. The Beaufort I was followed into production by the Mk. II, of which 166 were built with a powerplant of two Pratt & Whitney Twin Wasp radial motors. Later examples of the Mk. II were built as training aircraft, having the dorsal twin-gun turret removed. Beauforts took part in several memorable adventures during World War 2, including the attempt in February 1942 to prevent the escape of the German ships *Scharnhorst*, *Gneisenau* and *Prinz Eugen* up the English Channel. They were eventually superseded in the torpedo bomber role in 1943 by the " Torbeau " Beaufighter.

BRIEF TECHNICAL DETAILS (Mk. I):
Engines: Two 1,130 h.p. Bristol Taurus VI radials.
Span: 57 ft. 10 in.
Length: 44 ft. 7 in.
Height: 12 ft. 5 in.
Weight Empty: 13,107 lb.
Loaded: 21,228 lb.
No. in crew: Four.
Max. Speed: 265 m.p.h. at 6,000 ft.
Service Ceiling: 16,500 ft.
Normal Range: 1,035 miles.
Armament: Four .303 machine guns; up to 2,000 lb. of bombs or mines, or one semi-external 1,605 lb. torpedo.

Blenheim Mk. IV

Bristol Blenheim

Country of origin: **GREAT BRITAIN**
Purpose: **Medium bomber.**
Makers: **Bristol Aeroplane Co. Ltd.**

Specification: **B.28/35.**
In operational use: **1939/44.**

When it first appeared, the Blenheim was fast—some 40 m.p.h. better than the fighters then in service—but it did not enjoy the successful career which at one time seemed certain. Nevertheless it performed some useful service during the first half of the war, when there was little else available. Designed as a development of the Type 142 " Britain First ", the Blenheim was ordered " off the drawing board ", the first two production aircraft serving as prototypes; the first of these (K 7033) flew on 25th June, 1936. The initial order was for 150 Mk. I (840 h.p. Mercury VIII), the final figure for this version reaching 1,552, and first deliveries reached the R.A.F. in January 1937. During this time the Blenheim I was widely exported or licence-built in several foreign

Blenheim Mk. IF

countries. By the outbreak of World War 2 the short-nosed Blenheim I, though it continued in service for some time afterwards in the Western Desert, had been succeeded at home by the Mk. IV. Meanwhile, some 200 Mk. Is had been modified as Mk. IF night fighters; these, with a four-gun pack fitted under the bomb bay, made the first large-scale use of the new A.I. radar. The Blenheim IV began to supersede the Mk. I in production during 1938, and six squadrons carried this model on the outbreak of war. A much-improved aeroplane, the Blenheim IV continued with Bomber Command until replaced by Bostons and Mosquitos in 1942, though in the Middle and Far East it served for at least a year more. Production of the Mk. IV totalled 1,930 aircraft, of which the first 68 were converted Mk. Is. An extensive redesign to Spec. B.6/40 produced the Mercury 30-powered Blenheim V (at first known briefly as the Bisley), which first flew in 1941 and was followed by 940 production aircraft. Although this model had many refinements, its performance was not spectacular and it was not over-popular with its crews; nevertheless it remained in service in the Far East until late 1943, after which a number were converted to dual control for training purposes. The Canadian-built Type 149 Bolingbroke was originally based on the Blenheim I.

BRIEF TECHNICAL DETAILS (Mk. IV):
Engines: Two 905 h.p. Bristol Mercury XV radials.
Span: 56 ft. 4 in.
Length: 42 ft. 7 in.
Height: 9 ft. 10 in.
Weight Empty: 9,790 lb.
Loaded: 13,500 lb.
No. in crew: Three.
Max. Speed: 266 m.p.h. at 11,800 ft.
Service Ceiling: 27,260 ft.
Max. Range: 1,460 miles.
Armament: Five .303 Browning machine guns; 1,000 lb. of bombs.

Bolingbroke floatplane

38

Z.506B Serie XIV/Italian Air Ministry

Cant Z.506B Airone (Heron)

Country of origin: **ITALY**
Purpose: **Torpedo-bomber and reconnaissance.**

Makers: **Cantieri Ruiniti dell'Adriatico.**
In operational use: **1940/45.**

The original Cant Z.506 was a commercial transport seaplane of pre-war vintage, from which appeared, in later years, the Z.506B, Z.506C and Z.506S military developments. Of these the most numerous in wartime activities was the Z.506B, which first appeared in 1937 as a bomber and reconnaissance aircraft. When Italy entered the Second World War two groups of the Regia Aeronautica were equipped with the type, which served throughout the years of Italy's participation, primarily on sea patrol, reconnaissance and anti-shipping duties. The Z.506B became obsolescent as a front-line aircraft towards the end of hostilities and was very vulnerable to attack unless heavily escorted, large numbers being destroyed in the Mediterranean and North African theatres where the type was chiefly employed. When Italy surrendered, a small number of Z.506Bs were left on the Allied side, where they fought on with the Co-Belligerent Air Force. After the war a few of these aircraft survived until 1959 with the reconstituted Italian Air Force, on air-sea rescue duties.

BRIEF TECHNICAL DETAILS:

Engines: Three 750 h.p. Alfa Romeo 126 RC 34 radials.
Span: 86 ft. 11 in.
Length: 63 ft. 1½ in.
Height: 22 ft. 2½ in.
Weight Empty: 19,290 lb.
  Loaded: 28,008 lb.
No. in crew: Five.
Max. Speed: 217 m.p.h. at 13,120 ft.
Service Ceiling: 25,750 ft.
Max. Range: 1,430 miles.
Armament: One 12.7 mm. and three 7.7 mm. Breda-SAFAT machine guns; up to 2,645 lb. of bombs or torpedos.

39

Italian Air Ministry

Cant Z.1007 *bis* Alcione *(Kingfisher)*

Country of origin: **ITALY**   Makers: **Cantieri Ruiniti dell'Adriatico.**
Purpose: **Medium bomber.**   In operational use: **1940/45.**

Official interest in the trimotor Z.1007 bomber began when it was realised that Zappata's alternative design, the twin-engined Z.1011, would be very much underpowered. Designed about 1935, the first prototype of the Z.1007 flew towards the end of 1937 and was followed by further machines during the ensuing two years, production commencing in 1939. The prototype aircraft had been powered by 840 h.p. Isotta-Fraschini Asso engines, but the considerably better performance conferred by the 1,000 h.p. Piaggio P.IX led to the latter engine being specified for production aircraft, which were designated Z.1007*bis*. The additional power available from the use of the Piaggio engines enabled the Z.1007*bis* to be made a slightly larger machine than the prototypes, with a greater all-up weight and improved armament. Even so, the armament of the Alcione remained inadequate for defensive purposes and was one of the aircraft's serious shortcomings. An unusual feature of the Alcione was the production of both single- and twin-finned versions during the bomber's service life.

The type was employed by several Regia Aeronautica squadrons on bombing and anti-shipping missions in the Mediterranean area, and was second only in importance to the S.M.79 Sparviero (see page 148). Improved versions included the higher-powered Z.1007*ter* and Z.1015, but neither of these achieved quantity production. The most important development, which came belatedly into service in 1943, was the twin-engined Z.1018 (1,320 h.p. Piaggio P. XII RC 35), featuring an improved all-round performance, bomb load and defensive armament.

BRIEF TECHNICAL DETAILS:
Engines: Three 1,000 h.p. Piaggio P.XI RC 40 radials.
Span: 81 ft. 4 in.
Length: 60 ft. 1¾ in.
Height: 17 ft. 0 in.
Weight Empty: 19,338 lb.
        Loaded: 28,622 lb.
No. in crew: Five.
Max. Speed: 288 m.p.h. at 17,220 ft.
Service Ceiling: 26,500 ft.
Max. Range: 1,370 miles.
Armament: Two 12.7 mm. and two 7.7 mm. Breda-SAFAT machine guns; 2.600 lb. of bombs (4,410 lb. max.) or two 1,000 lb. torpedos.

40

Chance Vought F4U Corsair

Country of origin: **U.S.A.**
Purpose: **Carrier-based fighter.**
Makers: **Chance Vought Aircraft Division,
United Aircraft Corporation.**

Other U.S. designations: **FG, F3A.**
In operational use: **1943/45.**

Bearing the same name as Vought's earlier O2U-1 of 1926, the Corsair was, at the time of its appearance, the most-powerful naval fighter ever built; later it was to become the last piston-engined fighter to be built in the U.S.A. Although it was only fully operational during the second half of World War 2, it was an extremely potent addition to the striking force of Allied navies, and by VJ day Corsairs had accounted for well over two thousand enemy aircraft, apart from their attacks on submarines and surface vessels; they well justified the name "Whistling Death" bestowed upon them by the Japanese. The XF4U-1, powered by the new Double Wasp engine developing 1,800 h.p., made its first flight on 29th May, 1940, less than two years after it had been ordered by the U.S. Navy, and in the summer of 1941 a production contract was awarded. The first production F4U-1 (2,000 h.p. Double Wasp) had flown by the end of June 1942, and in February 1943 the type flew its first operational mission with the U.S. Marine Corps, being assigned initially to shore stations. Two other companies were called upon to augment the Corsair programme, Brewster building 735 (designated F3A-1) before their contract was cancelled in July 1944, and Goodyear completing some 4,000 as the FG-1 and -2. Total Corsair production by all three companies reached 12,681 aircraft. Variants included the F4U-1C cannon-armed fighter, F4U-1D fighter-bomber, F4U-2 night fighter, F4U-3 high-altitude research version, and F4U-4 fighter; post-war developments were the F4U-5 fighter-bomber, F4U-5N all-weather fighter, F4U-5P photo-reconnaissance aircraft, F4U-6 (later AU-1) attack aircraft and the F4U-7, also supplied to the French Navy. Just over 2,000 Corsairs were supplied to the R.N.Z.A.F. and Royal Navy from mid-1943, nineteen F.A.A. squadrons being equipped eventually with the type. Known as the Corsair I, II, III and IV, these corresponded respectively to the F4U-1, F4U-1A, F3A-1 and FG-1.

> **BRIEF TECHNICAL DETAILS
> (F4U-4):**
> *Engine:* One 2,450 h.p. Pratt & Whitney
> R-2800-18W Double Wasp radial.
> *Span:* 40 ft. 11 in.
> *Length:* 33 ft. 8 in.
> *Height:* 14 ft. 9 in.
> *Weight Empty:* 9,230 lb.
> *Loaded:* 12,399 lb.
> *No. in crew:* One
> *Max. Speed:* 446 m.p.h. at 26,000 ft.
> *Service Ceiling:* 41,000 ft.
> *Max. Range:* 1,562 miles.
> *Armament:* Six .50 Browning machine
> guns; two 1,000 lb. bombs or eight
> R.Ps. optional.

B-24D

Consolidated B-24 Liberator

Country of origin: **U.S.A.**
Purpose: **Long range bomber, transport and reconnaissance.**

Makers: **Consolidated-Vultee Aircraft Corporation.**
Other U.S. designations: **C-87, F-7, PB4Y-1**
In operational use: **1941/45.**

" Go anywhere, do anything " might well have been the Liberator's watchword, for this versatile machine showed considerable adaptability, being employed as a bomber, passenger and cargo transport, tanker, maritime patrol, reconnaissance and anti-submarine aircraft during a distinguished career with the U.S. forces and those of Great Britain and the Commonwealth. It was built in far greater numbers than its running mate, the B-17 Fortress—or indeed, any other U.S. aircraft—and is credited with dropping nearly 635,000 tons of bombs in the European, African and Pacific zones and with the destruction of 4,189 enemy aircraft. The design, produced to a U.S.A.A.C. requirement in 1939, was particularly noteworthy for the very high aspect ratio Davis wing and capacious fuselage. By the time the XB-24 (four 1,200 h.p. Twin Wasp) flew on 29th December, 1939, orders had been placed by the U.S.A.A.C. (for seven YB-24 and 36 B-24A for evaluation), France (120) and Great Britain (164). After France fell, the French orders were diverted to Britain, and the first half dozen Liberators (designated LB-30A) were handed over to B.O.A.C. for transatlantic ferry flights; twenty more found their way to Coastal Command as the Liberator I, modified for patrol duties. The first U.S. deliveries were nine B-24As in June 1941, and these too were put into use as transport aircraft. Coastal Command's Liberator II (which had no U.S. counterpart) incorporated a lengthened nose, additional armament and a crew of ten; a few of the 139 delivered were employed as LB-30 transports, one of them becoming Winston Churchill's personal transport " Commando ". The majority, however, went into action in the bombing role, the first Liberators to do so. Following the flight in America of the XB-24B, an improved model with self-sealing fuel tanks and turbo-supercharged engines, came a batch of nine B-24C and the first major production version (and first U.S. bomber version), the B-24D. Among the 2,738 examples of this model were to be found various permutations of gunnery

PB4Y-I/U.S. Navy

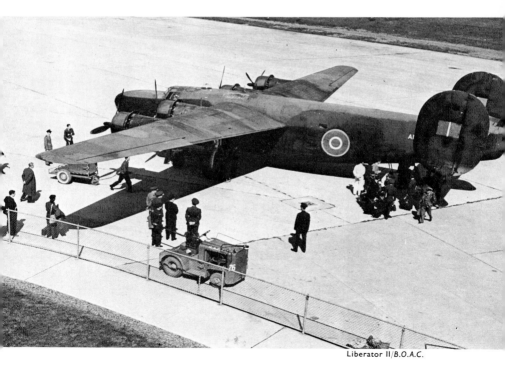

Liberator II/B.O.A.C.

43

and bomb load, and some of the later series also underwent a change of power-plant. To the R.A.F. went 260 B-24Ds (with minor modifications) as the Liberator III and IIIA, and a further 122 later fitted with ventral and " chin " radar housings and a Leigh light as Coastal Command's Mk. V. In the summer of 1943 the U.S. Navy took over those U.S.A.A.F. B-24Ds already used for anti-submarine duties, plus a further quantity of the same version, as the PB4Y-1. Several B-24Ds joined with the Fortresses over Europe at this time, and others served in the Mediterranean and Middle East, but it was in the Pacific that the Liberator's unrivalled range made it particularly useful, and this undoubtedly accounts for its success as a bomber. The C-87 Liberator Express transport appeared in the middle war years, 276 being built for the U.S.A.A.F., 24 for the R.A.F. and a number as RY-2s for the U.S. Navy; the C-87A and the Navy's RY-1 were specially fitted for V.I.P. use. Other factories now joined the production team, and the combined efforts of Consolidated, Douglas and Ford produced 791 B-24E, generally similar to the B-24D. North American contributed 430 of the longer, turret-nosed B-24G, and the 3,100 B-24Hs also featured a power turret in this position. A substantial number of B-24H were distributed among Bomber and Coastal Commands and F.E.A.F. as the Liberator IV. Again very similar to the G model was the B-24J, 6,678 of which were built; some 1,200 of this model were supplied to the R.C.A.F. and further quantities to other Commonwealth air forces. Over 90 B-24H and J Liberators were converted as photo-reconnaissance aircraft with F-7 series designations. The B-24L and M were generally similar to earlier variants apart from tail gunnery changes, 1,667 and 2,583 respectively being completed. The XB-24K, modified from a D in 1943, led to the single-finned B-24N, but only eight of these were completed before B-24 production ceased in May 1945. Of more than 18,000 Liberators built, the U.S. Navy received 977 as the PB4Y-1 and -1P for anti-submarine and reconnaissance purposes; the PB4Y-2 which was developed from these is described on page 186.

BRIEF TECHNICAL DETAILS (B-24J):

Engines: Four 1,200 h.p. Pratt & Whitney R-1830-65 Twin Wasp radials.
Span: 110 ft. 0 in.
Length: 67 ft 2 in.
Height: 18 ft. 0 in.
Weight Empty: 38,000 lb.
   Loaded: 56,000 lb.
No. in crew: Twelve.
Max. Speed: 300 m.p.h. at 30,000 ft.
Service Ceiling: 28,000 ft.
Normal Range: 2,100 miles.
Armament: Ten .50 machine guns; 5,000 lb. of bombs normally (12,800 lb. max. for short ranges).

B-24H/U.S.A.F.

44

PBY-6A

Consolidated PBY Catalina

Country of origin: **U.S.A.**
Purpose: **Maritime patrol and reconnaissance.**
Makers: **Consolidated-Vultee Aircraft Corporation.**

Other U.S. designations: **PB2B-I, PBN-I, PBV-I, OA-I0.**
In operational use: **1941/45.**

One of the most famous and familiar aircraft of its time, the " Cat " had a distinguished service record in many theatres of war with the U.S. and Allied air forces. Having few equals for toughness and dependability, not to mention adaptability, the Catalina was noteworthy for its excellent range. Several civil Model 28s became famous pre-war for exploration missions, and the XP3Y-1, after its flight tests, set a distance record of 3,443 miles. First flight of the XP3Y-1 took place in 1935, and 60 were ordered by the Navy under the designation PBY-1. By the time the first of these flew, on 5th October, 1936, further contracts had been placed for 50 PBY-2 and 66 PBY-3. The PBY-4 first appeared in 1938, a longer and heavier model with 1,200 h.p. Twin Wasp motors and the first to introduce the prominent blisters at the waist which characterised all subsequent Catalinas. The PBY-5 was similar to the -4, but the PBY-5A (OA-10 in the U.S.A.A.F.), adopted in 1940, was an amphibious version produced for operation in northern waters, and was fitted with a tricycle undercarriage. The final models, the PBY-6 and -6A, had improved armament and a still greater range. Following evaluation of a civil Model 28 which it bought in 1939, the British Government placed orders for successive PBY versions for the R.A.F., which eventually received over 650 Catalinas. The PBY-5 was built in Canada as the Canadian-Vickers PBV-1 and the Boeing (Canada) PB2B-1, and was known as the Canso in R.C.A.F. service. A further version, the PBN-1, was undertaken by the Naval Aircraft Factory to examine various modifications without disrupting established production lines; subsequently introduced on the PBY-6A, these included a re-designed nose, strengthened wings and a taller fin and rudder in addition to improved firepower and fuel capacity. Widely used in the Pacific, Atlantic and off the coasts of Europe and North and South America, the Catalina saw service as a bomber, torpedo-carrier, convoy escort, anti-submarine and air/sea rescue aircraft, mail and freight transport, and even as a glider tug. The bulk of the production aircraft went to the U.S. Navy, who received 1,196 of the various flying-boat models and 944 amphibians.

BRIEF TECHNICAL DETAILS (PBY-5A):
Engines: Two 1,200 h.p. Pratt & Whitney R-1830-92 Twin Wasp radials.
Span: 104 ft. 0 in.
Length: 63 ft. 10 in
Height: 20 ft. 2 in.
Weight Empty: 20,910 lb.
　　　Loaded: 33,975 lb.
No. in crew: Eight.
Max. Speed: 179 m.p.h. at 7,000 ft.
Service Ceiling 14,700 ft.
Max. Range: 3,100 miles.
Armament: Five .50 machine guns.

45

Curtiss C-46 Commando

Country of origin: **U.S.A.**
Purpose: **Transport.**
Makers: **Curtiss-Wright Corporation.**

Other U.S. designations: **R5C-1.**
In operational use: **1943/45.**

Like most American military transports of World War 2, the Commando was originally designed and built as a civil airliner.   The basic 1936 design, known as the CW-20, was completed as a 36-passenger aircraft and flew for the first time on 26th March, 1940.   After some military modification it was given the U.S. Army designation C-55, later being re-converted to civil standard and flown to Great Britain, where it operated for a time between the U.K. and Eire.   Meanwhile, with further modification, the type was ordered into quantity production for the U.S.A.A.F.   A preliminary batch of 25 C-46 passenger transports was followed by 1,491 C-46A cargo aircraft with a single large loading door, and by 1,410 C-46D with double doors and a modified nose. The single-door C-46E (17 built) and the double-door C-46F (234 built) were more or less similar except for a change in powerplant, and 160 Commandos were completed as R5C-1s for the U.S. Marine Corps.   The XC-46B, XC-46C, C-46G, C-46H, XC-46K and XC-46L were various projects, differing in minor detail only, which did not achieve production status.   With the Marines, the Commando played a prominent part in the Pacific island campaigns, taking in supplies and bringing out wounded.   With Air Transport Command, Air Service Command and Troop Carrier Command of the U.S.A.A.F. it was widely used in the Far East as a trooper, ambulance and freighter, typical loads including light artillery pieces, small vehicles, fuel and ammunition supplies or spare aircraft engines.   The type was also employed on occasion as a glider tug.   First European appearance of the Commando was not made until March 1945, when it dropped paratroops to take part in the Rhine crossing.

BRIEF TECHNICAL DETAILS:
Engines: Two 2,000 h.p. Pratt & Whitney R-2800-51 Double Wasp radials.
Span: 108 ft. 1 in.
Length: 76 ft. 4 in.
Height: 21 ft. 9 in.
Weight Empty: 29,483 lb.
      Loaded: 45,000 lb.
No. in crew: Five (plus 36-40 passengers or equivalent freight).
Max. Speed: 265 m.p.h. at 13,000 ft.
Service Ceiling: 24,500 ft.
Normal Range: 1,600 miles.
Armament: None.

Curtiss P-40 Warhawk

Country of origin: **U.S.A.**
Purpose: **Fighter and fighter-bomber.**

Makers: **Curtiss-Wright Corporation.**
In operational use: **1941/45.**

 The first mass-produced U.S. single-seat fighter, the Curtiss P-40, together with the Bell P-39, constituted more than half the U.S.A.A.F. fighter strength for the first half of the war, in addition to being supplied in considerable numbers to the R.A.F. and other Allied air forces. It was not a brilliant aircraft, and was inferior technically and in performance to many of its contemporaries, yet it acquired a justifiable reputation for ruggedness and dependability and was the subject of extensive development as the war progressed. The XP-40, derived from the P-36A (Model 75) Hawk and powered by a 1,160 h.p. Allison V-1710-19, flew in the autumn of 1938 and the P-40 was put into production the following year. (There were no YP-40s, three P-40s being used as test aircraft). The P-40 was produced in moderate numbers for the U.S.A.A.F., for the R.A.F. (as the Tomahawk I, IA and IB) and for France—these last being ultimately taken over by the R.A.F. Only a small number of P-40B (there was no P-40A) went to the U.S.A.A.F., the bulk of the production going either to the R.A.F. (Tomahawk IIA and IIB) or to Russia, and the P-40C and D (Kittyhawk I) were likewise built in comparatively small numbers. The P-40, P-40B and P-40C (1,040 h.p. Allison V-1710-33) were basically similar except for armament and internal variations. The P-40D introduced the 1,150 h.p. V-1710-39 in a slightly shorter fuselage, and carried an armament of four .50 wing guns, with provision for a drop-tank or single 500 lb. bomb beneath the fuselage and six 20 lb. bombs underwing. The first large-scale production model was the P-40E (Kittyhawk IA), of which 2,320 were built; this version, similar to the D but with two additional .50 wing guns, was a marked improvement over the P-40B which it replaced, and a small number were later converted as tandem two-seat trainers. The first version to be named Warhawk by the U.S.A.A.F. was the P-40F (Kittyhawk II). This model, of which 1,311 were completed, marked a change in powerplant to the 1,300 h.p. Packard-Merlin 28 engine and, on later examples, a lengthened fuselage; armament was similar to the P-40E. There was only ône P-40H, and the P-40J supercharged high altitude project was abandoned,

47

the next major production version being the P-40K (Kittyhawk III). This had the 1,325 h.p. V-1710-73 engine and, on later examples, the long fuselage of the P-40F. A number of P-40K were "winterised" for service for the U.S.A.A.F. and R.C.A.F. in Alaska and the Aleutian Islands. Following the K, the P-40L (Kittyhawk II) was a lighter-weight F development with the Packard Merlin 28 and the longer fuselage; 700 of these were completed. From the batch of 600 P-40M (Kittyhawk III and IV), similar to the K model apart from a 1,200 h.p. V-1710-81 engine, one squadron was supplied to the South African Air Force. The final—and most numerous—production version of the Warhawk was the P-40N (R.A.F. Kittyhawk IV), a development of the lightweight P-40L. Altogether more than 5,200 P-40Ns were completed, utilising various Allison powerplants and permutations of armament. This version was supplied to several Allied air forces, including the R.N.Z.A.F., and saw most of its service in the Pacific theatre. The designation P-40R covered the conversion of some 300 P-40F and L Warhawks from Packard-Merlin powerplants to Allisons. Total production of the P-40 series reached over 14,000 aircraft, including a number of experimental projects which never attained production status. Among these were the XP-40Q (a modified K with 1,425 h.p. V-1710-121, cut-down rear fuselage and blister canopy), the XP-46 (two only completed), the XP-60 (five prototypes for a P-40 replacement, with various inline or radial powerplants) and the XP-62 (a radial-engined fighter-bomber development of the XP-60).

BRIEF TECHNICAL DETAILS (P-40N):
Engine: One 1,200 h.p. Allison V-1710-99 inline.
Span: 37 ft. 4 in.
Length: 33 ft. 4 in.
Height: 12 ft. 4 in.
Weight Empty: 6,200 lb.
   Loaded: 8,350 lb.
No. in crew: One.
Max. Speed: 350 m.p.h. at 16,400 ft.
Service Ceiling: 31,000 ft.
Normal Range: 750 miles.
Armament: Six .50 Browning machine guns; up to three 500 lb. bombs.

Tomahawk of the American Volunteer Group, Chinese Air Force/I.W.M.

Kittyhawk IIIs/I.W.M.

P-40N

TP-40N/U.S.A.F.

Curtiss SB2C Helldiver

Country of origin: **U.S.A.**
Purpose: **Carrier-based dive bomber.**
Makers: **Curtiss-Wright Corporation.**

Other U.S. designations: **SBF, SBW, A-25.**
In operational use: **1943/45.**

The Helldiver's operational career began on 11th November, 1943, in the attack on the Japanese-held island of Rabaul. Yet this SB2C-1 was a vastly different machine from the XSB2C-1 which had first flown in November 1940. Designed to a 1939 U.S. Navy specification, the Helldiver was ready to enter production when, a few days before Pearl Harbour, the prototype was destroyed in a crash. The delays occasioned by the investigation into this, and by revision of the official concept of the dive bomber following actual combat experience, set back the flight of the first production Helldiver until June 1942. By this time, 889 major and thousands of minor modifications had been made to the original design, the chief results of which were increased armament and armour protection for the pilot and a completely new rear fuselage and tail assembly. A substantial quantity of the SB2C-1 (978) were completed, as well as a batch of 900 for ground attack missions with the U.S.A.A.F. as the A-25A. The floatplane XSB2C-2 did not achieve production status, but development continued with the SB2C-3, featuring an uprated Cyclone. The SB2C-4 had underwing bomb or rocket attachments and perforated landing flaps. During the latter half of the war, production of the Helldiver was augmented by sub-contracts to Fairchild (Canada) and the Canadian Car and Foundry Co., who built 300 and 894 examples of the type as the SBF and SBW respectively. Twenty-six C.C. & F.-built SBW-1B Helldivers were supplied under Lend-Lease to the Fleet Air Arm, but were not used operationally by this service; the type did however serve in moderate numbers with the R.A.A.F. Despite its rather slow start, the Helldiver played an important part in the Pacific island campaigns, and was a welcome reinforcement for the older Dauntless which had borne the main burden of dive-bombing in the early years of America's participation in the war.

BRIEF TECHNICAL DETAILS (SB2C-3):
Engine: One 1,900 h.p. Wright R-2600-20 Cyclone radial.
Span: 49 ft. 9 in.
Length: 36 ft. 8 in.
Height: 13 ft. 2 in.
Weight Empty: 10,400 lb.
Loaded: 14,042 lb.
No. in crew: Two.
Max. Speed: 294 m.p.h. at 16,700 ft.
Service Ceiling: 29,300 ft.
Max. Range: 1,925 miles.
Armament: Two 20 mm. cannon and one .50 machine gun; up to 1,000 lb. of bombs or one torpedo internally.

50

Mosquito prototype taking off for first flight, 25 November 1940

de Havilland Mosquito

Country of origin: **GREAT BRITAIN**
Purpose: **Bomber, fighter, ground attack and reconnaissance.**

Makers: **The de Havilland Aircraft Co. Ltd.**
Specification: **B.1/40 (first production).**
In operational use: **1941/45.**

Adapted with conspicuous success to such widely varied roles as high and low level day and night bomber, long range day and night fighter, fighter-bomber, minelayer, pathfinder, rocket-armed ground attack, shipping strike, high and low altitude photographic reconnaissance, trainer and transport, the supremely versatile D.H.98 Mosquito was one of the outstanding aeroplanes of World War 2. It was conceived in 1938 as an unarmed day bomber, but official interest did not crystallise until December 1939, and in the following March 50 aircraft were ordered. In the post-Dunkirk period, although the Mosquito was temporarily dropped from the M.A.P. programme, the prototype (W 4050) was completed, and flew in November 1940. The fifty aircraft ordered eventually materialised as ten P.R. Mk. I, thirty N.F. Mk. II and ten B. Mk. IV, these being delivered to the R.A.F. between July 1941 and March 1942. The designation T.III was reserved for a trainer version which appeared later, and the B. Mk. V did not go into production. By this time assembly lines had been set up at the Percival, Airspeed and Standard Motors factories, and production of the Mosquito continued with over 1,000 F.B. VI, numerically the most important version, which began to enter service in May 1943. In addition to performing as a day and night intruder the F.B. VI became, with the addition of eight 60-lb. R.Ps. to its armament, a shipping strike aircraft with Coastal Command. This model was followed by a batch of 27 F.B. XVIII, carrying eight rockets and two 500 lb. bombs and with a single 57 mm. (6-pdr.) gun in a separate fairing under the nose. The first high-altitude bomber version was the B.IX (1,290 h.p. Merlin 72), of which 54 were completed, and this was succeeded by 387 examples of the B.XVI (Merlin 72/3 or 76/7), fitted with a pressurised cabin. The successor to the B.XVI, the B.35, did not reach R.A.F. squadrons until after VJ-day. Photo-reconnaissance equivalents were also built, designated P.R.IX, XVI and 34, with cameras and additional fuel in the bomb bay. A crop of night fighter versions followed the original N.F. Mk. II, including 97 aircraft converted from Mk. II to Mk. XII standard with the new centimetric A.I. radar in a " bull " nose. A higher loaded weight and longer range characterised the N.F. XIII, of which 270 were built; a further 100 Mk. IIs were converted to Mk. XVII with U.S.-built radar; the N.F. XIX (220 built), also using this radar, was otherwise similar to the Mk. XIII; and there were five N.F. XVs, which were B.IVs converted to Merlin 77 engines. The last night fighter was the N.F. 30, similar to the Mk. XIX, also with improved Merlins. Canadian production of the Mosquito ran to just over 1,000 machines, powered by Packard-built Merlins and including the Mk. XX and 25 bombers, Mk. 26 fighter-bomber and Mk. 22 and 27 trainers. Forty Canadian-built reconnaissance Mosquitos were supplied to the U.S.A.A.F., who employed them under the designation F-8. Production of the Mosquito in Australia, also with Packard-Merlin powerplants, reached a total of 178 machines; chief among these were the F.B.40, P.R.40, and T.43. In 1943 about half a dozen Mks. III and IV were " demilitarised " for use by B.O.A.C. on priority freight and mail flights. The grand total of Mosquito production reached 7,781 aircraft, 6,710 of which were built during the war.

BRIEF TECHNICAL DETAILS

(B. Mk. XVI):
Engines: Two 1,290 h.p. Rolls-Royce Merlin 73 inlines.
Span: 54 ft. 2 in.
Length: 40 ft. 6 in.
Height: 12 ft. 6 in.
Weight Empty: 15,510 lb.
Loaded: 19,093 lb.
No. in crew: Two.
Max. Speed: 408 m.p.h. at 26,000 ft.
Service Ceiling: 37,000 ft.
Normal Range: 1,370 miles.
Armament: Up to 4,000 lb. of bombs.

(N.F. Mk. XIX):
Engines: Two 1,635 h.p. Rolls-Royce Merlin 25 inlines.
Span: 54 ft. 2 in.
Length: 41 ft. 10¾ in.
Height: 15 ft. 3½ in.
Weight Empty: 14,000 lb.
Loaded: 19,600 lb.
No. in crew: Two.
Max. Speed: 378 m.p.h. at 13,200 ft.
Service Ceiling: 34,500 ft.
Max. Range: 1,830 miles.
Armament: Four 20 mm. Hispano cannon.

Mosquito B. Mk. XVI

Mosquito F.B. Mk. VI

Mosquito F.B. Mk. XVIII/*I.W.M.*

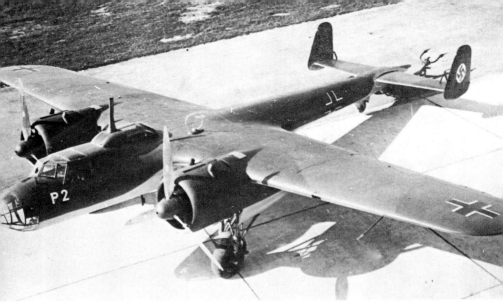

Do 17P-2

Dornier Do 17 and Do 215

Country of origin: **GERMANY**
Purpose: **Medium bomber and reconnaissance.**

Makers: **Dornier-Werke G.m.b.H.**
In operational use: **1939/45.**

The Dornier Do 17, the famous " Flying Pencil " or " Eversharp ", made its first flight in 1934 and was intended as a fast mail-carrier for Deutsche Luft Hansa. Rejected by that airline after three machines (all with single fins) had been completed, it was taken up as a high speed bomber by the German Air Ministry the following year and made a spectacular public début, now with a twin tail assembly, at Zurich in the 1937 International Military Aircraft Competitions. By this time, bomber squadrons of the Luftwaffe were already being equipped with the first two production models, the Do 17E and F, and in 1938 both of these versions were seeing service in the Spanish Civil War. Also in 1938 the next major series, the Bramo 323-powered Do 17M-1, entered production, closely followed by the reconnaissance Do 17P with BMW 132N engines. After small numbers of the Do 17S (reconnaissance) and Do 17U (pathfinder) had been built with DB 600A inline powerplants, a return to the radial Bramo 323 was made in 1939 with the Do 17Z. On the outbreak of war the Luftwaffe had in service the Do 17M and Z bombers, and the Do 17P and a handful of Do 17Fs for reconnaissance.

Before the outbreak of the Second World War, in 1937, Yugoslavia had been a customer for earlier models of the Do 17; it was the interest later shown by that country in the Do 17Z which gave rise to the designation Do 215, allotted for no apparent reason to the Do 17Z aircraft sent to Yugoslavia for demonstration purposes. In the event, none of this type were sold in that part of the world, although a couple were delivered, curiously enough, to Russia. The type did, however, go into Luftwaffe service, in relatively small numbers, as the Do 215A and B.

> **BRIEF TECHNICAL DETAILS**
> **(Do 17Z-2):**
> *Engines:* Two 1,000 h.p. Bramo 323P radials.
> *Span:* 59 ft. 1 in.
> *Length:* 52 ft. 0 in.
> *Height:* 15 ft. 1 in.
> *Weight Empty:* 11,484 lb.
> *Loaded:* 18,832 lb.
> *No. in crew:* Four or five.
> *Max. Speed:* 263 m.p.h. at 16.400 ft.
> *Service Ceiling:* 26,740 ft.
> *Max. Range:* 1,860 miles.
> *Armament:* Six 7.9 mm. MG 15 machine guns; up to 2,200 lb. of bombs.

Do 217K-2

Dornier Do 217

Country of origin: **GERMANY**   *Makers:* **Dornier-Werke G.m.b.H.**
Purpose: **Bomber and night fighter.**   *In operational use:* **1940/45.**

The Dornier Do 217 was a progressive development of the Do 17, and bore a distinct outward resemblance to the " in-between " Do 215.   The unarmed first Do 217 prototype flew in August 1938 and crashed a month later—an inauspicious start not at all in keeping with the aircraft's later career.   The first major production versions were the Do 217E-0 and E-1, powered by BMW 801A radial engines; these and later E sub-types began to appear in Luftwaffe squadrons in 1941, being used for " legitimate " bombing, torpedo-carrying and other anti-shipping duties, and reconnaissance.   The last of this series, the Do 217E-5, was equipped to carry the Hs 293 glider bomb, as were certain later bomber variants.   The Do 217K, which was the next purely bomber version to go into production, featured an enlarged and deepened nose section; and the K-2 an extended-span wing of 81 ft. 4½ in.   Meanwhile, as a precaution against possible shortage of BMW powerplants, an inline-engined version of the Do 217 had been developed; as the Do 217M-1, with 1,750 h.p. DB 603A motors, this entered service alongside the K-1, to which it was otherwise generally similar. The top speed of the M-1 was 348 m.p.h., and the maximum bomb load was increased to 8,820 lb.   The versatility of the basic Do 217 design was emphasised by its extensive use, in modified form, for night fighter duties.   With a re-designed " solid " nose containing four 20 mm. cannon and four 7.9 mm. machine guns, and an additional ventral 13 mm. gun, a large number of E-2 bombers were converted to night fighters during 1942.   These were designated Do 217J-1 and J-2, the former also carrying a small bomb load, the latter having no bomb bay but incorporating radar equipment.   Many Do 217M bombers were similarly converted to Do 217N night fighters.   Some 1,700 Do 217s of all variants were built for the Luftwaffe, a small number of Do 217Js being supplied to Italy.

```
BRIEF TECHNICAL DETAILS
    (Do 217E-1):
Engines: Two 1,600 h.p. BMW 801A
    radials.
Span: 62 ft. 4 in.
Length: 55 ft. 9¼ in.
Height: 16 ft. 4 in.
Weight Empty: 18,940 lb.
        Loaded: 33,730 lb.
No. in crew: Four.
Max. Speed: 326 m.p.h. at 17,200 ft.
Service Ceiling: 29,850 ft.
Max Range: 1,500 miles.
Armament: One 15 mm. MG 151 and
    five 7.9 mm. MG 15 machine guns.
    Up to 6,600 lb. of bombs.
```

55

P-70/U.S.A.F.

Douglas P-70, A-20 Havoc and Boston

Country of origin: **U.S.A.**
Purpose: **Attack bomber, night intruder and night fighter.**

Makers: **Douglas Aircraft Company. Inc.**
Other U.S. designations: **P-70, F-3, BD.**
In operational use: **1941/45.**

Although its wartime career was less spectacular than, say, those of the Mosquito or Ju 88, the Havoc was nevertheless extremely rugged, versatile and dependable, and was very much a " pilot's aeroplane ". Its origins go back to the Douglas Model 7A, a pre-war private venture ordered, in much-modified form as the DB-7, by the French government as a day bomber. The first flight in this form was made on 17th August, 1939, and by the end of that year a substantial number had been despatched to the French, although comparatively few were actually operational before the fall of France in the spring of 1940. The balance of the French consignment, together with a few Belgian DB-7s, were taken over by the R.A.F. as the Boston I (for training duties) and Boston II. Many of the latter were converted during 1940 for night fighting and intruder missions. being renamed Havoc. Variants included the Havoc I and IV (intruder), Havoc III (fighter), and the searchlight-nosed Turbinlite Havoc. The glazed nose of the Havoc II was replaced by a British-designed "solid" one bearing twelve .303 machine guns. The R.A.F. also ordered, for the day bomber role, a quantity of Boston IIIs. The first aircraft of this design to be ordered by the U.S.A.A.F. were 63 A-20s; these never served as bombers, 60 of them being converted later to P-70 night fighters (briefly known as Nighthawks) and the remaining three to F-3 photo-reconnaissance aircraft. The A-20A which followed (143 built) corresponded, except in armament and equipment detail, with the Boston III; a few of these were supplied as the BD-1 to the U.S. Navy, and a further 17, re-engined, emerged later as A-20Es. The first major U.S. production versions were the A-20B and A-20C; 999 of the former were completed, with 1,690 h.p. Double Cyclones, and .50 guns figuring in the armament for the first time. The U.S. Navy received eight A-20Bs as the BD-2. The A-20C, generally similar to the Boston III, entered production in 1941 and reached a total of 948, many of which were ultimately to serve with the Soviet Air Force. For the first time, with the A-20C, the Havoc was enabled to carry an external 2,000 lb. torpedo, and the Russians particularly made good use of this capability. Thirteen A-20Cs were converted as P-70A-1 night fighters. The A-20D version was cancelled, and the XA-20F project, with a 37 mm. nose gun and mid-upper and lower turrets, was a re-worked A-20A which provided data for later Havocs. Thus the next—and, as it happened, the principal—production model was the A-20G, of which 2,850 examples were finally completed. The majority of the early Gs found their way to Russia where, with somewhat modified nose gunnery, they were widely used for the ground attack rôle. Nor-

Boeing-built Boston III

mal A-20G configuration included uprated engines, a nose armament of four 20 mm. cannon and two .50 guns, or six .50 guns, one .50 gun ventrally and another in the aft cockpit for rearward defence. Later G models featured a Martin turret in place of the rear cockpit gun, and a dorsal turret became a feature of all later Havocs. A batch of 26 A-20Gs were converted to P-70A-2 night fighters. In 1944 the A-20G was followed into production by the A-20H (1,700 h.p. Double Cyclones), the 412 aircraft of this type that were completed serving alongside earlier versions with the U.S. forces in the United Kingdom, Middle East and Pacific theatres. A "lead ship" development was the A-20J, 450 of which were converted from A-20Gs with a one-piece Perspex nose, and the final production model, the A-20K of which 413 were built, reverted entirely to the bomber role for which the aircraft had originally been designed. A batch of 46 A-20J and K aircraft were converted to photographic reconnaissance aircraft under the designation F-3A. Production of the A-20 terminated in September 1944 after a total of 7,385 aircraft had been completed. Nearly 3,000 of these saw service in Russia, 455 were supplied to the R.A.F., 28 to the Netherlands Government and 31 to Brazil. Final R.A.F. versions were the Boston IV and V, corresponding to the A-20J and A-20K respectively; eleven of the latter were handed over to the R.C.A.F. during the final stages of the war.

BRIEF TECHNICAL DETAILS
(A-20G):
Engines: Two 1,600 h.p Wright R-2600-23 Double Cyclone radials.
Span: 61 ft. 4 in.
Length: 48 ft. 0 in.
Height: 17 ft. 7 in.
Weight Empty: 17,200 lb.
         Loaded: 24,000 lb.
No. in crew: Three.
Max. Speed: 317 m.p.h. at 10,000 ft
Service Ceiling: 25,000 ft.
Normal Range: 1,025 miles.
Armament: Nine .50 machine guns or five .50 and four 20 mm. cannon; up to 2,000 lb. of bombs internally and a further 2,000 lb. externally.

A-20J

R4D-4/U.S. Navy

Douglas C-47 Skytrain and C-53 Skytrooper

Country of origin: **U.S.A.**
Purpose: **Passenger and freight transport, ambulance and glider tug.**
Makers: **Douglas Aircraft Company, Inc.**

Other U.S. designations: **C-48, -49, -50, -51, -52, -68, -84 and -117; R4D.**
In operational use: **1941/45.**

The name Dakota, bestowed by the R.A.F. on its own examples of this most famous of all transport aeroplanes, is the one by which the DC-3 has since become popularly known in nearly every part of the world. The first of a long line of Douglas Commercials, the DC-1, was produced in 1932 to a specification issued by TWA (Transcontinental & Western Air, Inc.), and its clean lines, comfortable interior and excellent performance set a standard that was to be followed in many later designs. The DC-1 proved so successful during its flight tests (first flight was made on 1st July 1933) that it was never put into production—instead, with detail improvements, it was developed into the DC-2, and TWA ordered a fleet of 25, later increasing this figure to 40. The DC-2 was an immediate success, and by the end of 1935 Douglas were turning out one every three days, building altogether 138 of these aircraft. The DC-3, which flew for the first time on 18th December, 1935, was a development of the DC-2 with a crew of three and accommodation for 21 passengers, half as many again as the DC-1. It was also the first aeroplane to be designed to provide sleeping berths, the DST (Douglas Sleeper Transport) version having provision for 14 sleeping passengers. Larger than the DC-2, the DC-3 was three feet longer, had a ten-foot greater span and could accommodate 3,000 lb. more payload; this figure was later increased, as was the passenger accommodation to 28. Alternate models were powered by Twin Wasp or Cyclone engines, and were known respectively as the DC-3A and DC-3B.

Prior to the adoption of the DC-3 by the U.S. armed forces, a small batch of DC-2s were acquired, being designated C-32 and -34 by the Army and R2D-1 by the Navy. These were followed by several aircraft which contained features

XC-47C experimental floatplane

of both the DC-2 and DC-3: the Cyclone-powered C-38 (personnel) and C-39 (cargo), and the C-41 (personnel) with Twin Wasps. These all had DC-3 outer wing sections "married" to a DC-2 fuselage and centre-section. The two principal military versions of the DC-3, however, were the C-47 Skytrain and the C-53 Skytrooper, from which the U.S. Navy R4D counterpart differed in minor detail only; all were Twin Wasp-powered. The C-53, as its name implied, was primarily a troop-carrier, and had the normal DC-3 floor and entry door; it entered service in October 1941. Following in January 1942, the C-47 could be fitted either as a trooper, with folding benches, or as a heavy freighter with a reinforced floor and landing gear and a large cargo-loading door on the port side. Both were also adaptable to the role of glider tug. The C-49 (Navy R4D-2) was similar to the above versions except for a Cyclone powerplant, but was not produced in the same quantities. In addition to those built for military service, a number of airline DC-3s were taken over by the U.S. Air Transport Command under the designations C-68 and C-84. More than 1,200 C-47s and C-53s were supplied under Lend-Lease to the Royal Air Force, and the type was the mainstay of both American and British transport units throughout World War 2. It played important parts in every theatre of combat, from the Southern Pacific to the Normandy landings, and was in considerable demand as an ambulance and glider tug as well as in the transport role. Total military production reached 10,123 machines and included such experimental models as the C-47C with twin Edo floats and the XCG-17 which, with its engines removed, was successfully tested as a glider. The fame of the DC-3 continued undiminished after the cessation of hostilities, and the type is still providing widespread and worthwhile service throughout the world today.

BRIEF TECHNICAL DETAILS (C-47):

Engines: Two 1,200 h.p. Pratt & Whitney R-1830 Twin Wasp radials.
Span: 95 ft. 0 in.
Length: 64 ft. 5½ in.
Height: 16 ft. 11 in.
Weight Empty: 16,976 lb.
    Loaded: 29,000 lb. (max.).
No. in crew: Four.
Max. Speed: 230 m.p.h. at 8,800 ft.
Service Ceiling: 24,100 ft.
Normal Range: 1,350 miles.
Armament: None.

C-54G/U.S.A.F.

Douglas C-54 Skymaster

Country of origin: **U.S.A.**
Purpose: **Transport and glider tug.**
Makers: **Douglas Aircraft Company, Inc.**

Other U.S. designations: **R5D.**
In operational use: **1942/45.**

The Douglas Skymaster was one of the mainstays of United States transport squadrons during most of World War 2; subsequently, of course, it has become even more widely known as the DC-4, the forerunner of a long line of four-motor Douglas Commercial transports. The original DC-4 was built, in 1938, as a 52-seater to U.S. airline requirements. As modified before entering civil production, the DC-4 was a 40/42-seater, but work on an early batch was slowed down during 1941 pending adaptation to U.S.A.A.F. military transport requirements. As the 26-seater C-54, it was then ordered in substantial numbers for the Army; the first production C-54 flew early in 1942 and the type was beginning to enter service by the end of that year. Later the Skymaster was to be selected as the principal type for transatlantic personnel and freight carriage. A small number were supplied under Lend-Lease to R.A.F. Transport Command, who used them on ferry routes to the Far East; these aircraft were returned to America after the war. After the initial batch of C-54s, the principal service versions (U.S. Navy equivalents in brackets) were the C-54A (R5D-1), C-54B (R5D-2), C-54D (R5D-3), C-54E (R5D-4) and C-54G (R5D-5). The C-54C was a " one-off " conversion as a V.I.P. transport for the use of President Roosevelt and his staff. In addition to its transport duties, the Skymaster was often called upon as a glider tug. Limited production of the military model was continued for a time after VJ day, though most of those produced post-war were naturally for the commercial airliner market.

BRIEF TECHNICAL DETAILS
(C-54A):
Engines: Four 1,350 h.p. Pratt & Whitney R-2000-7 Twin Wasp radials.
Span: 117 ft. 6 in.
Length: 93 ft. 10 in.
Height: 27 ft. 6¼ in.
Weight Empty: 37,300 lb.
Loaded: 65,800 lb.
No. in crew: Six.
Max. Speed: 275 m.p.h. at 14,000 ft.
Service Ceiling: 22,500 ft
Max. Range: 3,900 miles.
Armament: None.

60

SBD-3

Douglas SBD Dauntless

Country of origin: **U.S.A.**
Purpose: **Light bomber and reconnaissance.**
Makers: **Douglas Aircraft Company, Inc.**

Other U.S. designations: **A-24.**
In operational use: **1941/45.**

Conceived in 1939, the Dauntless design was already obsolescent by the time of Pearl Harbour; yet, in the absence of a suitable replacement, it became the backbone of the Pacific air war and rendered excellent service as a bomber, dive bomber, scout and reconnaissance aircraft. Its ability to absorb considerable punishment was evidenced by the fact that the Dauntless had the lowest loss rate of any U.S. Pacific carrier type. The Dauntless was a development of the XBT-1 and -2 designs by Northrop, which company was absorbed by Douglas in 1937, and was originally given the torpedo bomber designation XBTD-1. After some modification, including the installation of a 1,000 h.p. Cyclone engine, it entered production as the SBD-1 for the U.S. Marine Corps in the summer of 1939; 57 of this model were built. These were followed by 87 SBD-2 for the Navy, featuring an autopilot and revised fuel and armament installations. At about this time the Army also began to take an interest in the Dauntless, procuring 78 of the first 252 SBD-3s and redesignating them A-24. A further 170 A-24A and 615 A-24B followed, corresponding to the Navy's SBD-4 and -5; modifica-

tions in the former were of a minor nature, but the SBD-5 had a more powerful Cyclone and was equipped with radar. Production of the Dauntless finally ceased on 22nd July, 1944, by which time a total of 5,936 had been built. During a long and valiant service this aircraft performed well a wide range of duties beyond its original specification; latterly it was equipped with depth charges for anti-submarine work, and it was also one of the first U.S. aircraft to carry rocket projectiles. In January 1945, a batch of nine SBD-5s were supplied to the Fleet Air Arm, but these were never used operationally.

BRIEF TECHNICAL DETAILS (SBD-5):
Engine: One 1,200 h.p. Wright R-1820-60 Cyclone radial.
Span: 41 ft 6 in.
Length: 33 ft. 0 in.
Height: 12 ft. 11 in.
Weight Empty: 6,533 lb.
Loaded: 9,352 lb.
No. in crew: Two.
Max. Speed: 252 m.p.h. at 13,800 ft.
Service Ceiling: 24,300 ft.
Max. Range: 1,115 miles.
Armament: Two .50 and two .30 machine guns; two 100 lb., or one 500 lb. or 1,000 lb. bomb, or two 250 lb. depth charges.

Fairey Albacore

Country of origin: **GREAT BRITAIN**
Purpose: **Torpedo bomber.**
Makers: **Fairey Aviation Co. Ltd.**

Specification: **S.41/36.**
In operational use: **1940/44.**

The Fairey Albacore was intended to enter service as a replacement for its famous forebear, the Swordfish (page 68). In the event, the worth of the Swordfish was such that it remained in service alongside, and eventually outlasted, the later design. Nevertheless the Albacore proved to be a very useful aeroplane, and in mid-1942, when its career was at its peak, no fewer than fifteen squadrons were equipped with the type. The design of the Albacore included several improvements over that of the Swordfish, notably a much more powerful engine, an enclosed crew cabin and hydraulic flaps. The prototype (L 7074) flew for the first time on 12th December, 1938, and after a second prototype had been completed production of 98 aircraft began in 1939. The first of these entered F.A.A. service in March 1940, and for the first year of its career the Albacore was operated from shore bases only. Its duties at this time included anti-shipping patrols, minelaying and night bombing. Its first carrier-borne operation—and the first occasion on which it used torpedos—was from H.M.S. *Formidable* in March 1941 at the Battle of Cape Matapan. Albacores were subsequently flown successfully from carriers on convoy escort in the Baltic and on anti-submarine missions in the Mediterranean and Indian Ocean. Other land-based operations included artillery spotting, and target-marking with flares during the North African campaign. Production ceased in 1943 after 803 Albacores had been built, but by the end of that year all but two squadrons had been re-equipped with Barracudas or American Avengers. One of these squadrons, however, handed on their Albacores to the R.C.A.F., by whom they were employed in the D-day landings of June 1944.

BRIEF TECHNICAL DETAILS:
Engine: One 1,065 h.p. Bristol Taurus II or 1,130 h.p. Taurus XII radial.
Span: 50 ft. 0 in.
Length: 39 ft. 9½ in.
Height: 15 ft. 3 in.
Weight Empty: 7,250 lb.
 Loaded: 10,460 lb.
No. in crew: Two or three.
Max. Speed: 161 m.p.h. at 4,500 ft.
Service Ceiling: 20,700 ft.
Normal Range: 930 miles.
Armament: One .303 Browning and two .303 Vickers machine guns; six 250 lb. or four 500 lb. bombs or one 1,610 lb. (18-in.) torpedo.

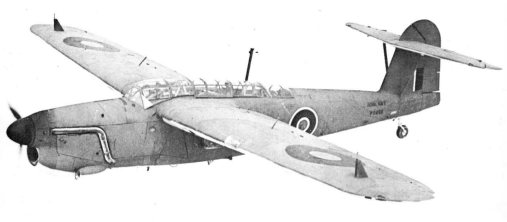

Barracuda Mk. II/I.W.M,

Fairey Barracuda

Country of origin: **GREAT BRITAIN**
Purpose: **Torpedo bomber and reconnaissance.**
Makers: **Fairey Aviation Co. Ltd.**

Specification: **S.24/37.**
In operational use: **1943/45.**

Although design of the Barracuda was begun in 1937, the aircraft did not enter F.A.A. service until six years later. Following the abandonment of the Rolls-Royce Exe engine for which it was planned, the Fairey Type 100 (as the aircraft was first known) was adapted to take a Merlin 30 powerplant, and the prototype (P 1767) flew on 7th December, 1940. Concentration of early wartime efforts on a few selected and proven types delayed the Barracuda's production until May 1942, but deliveries of the Mk. I commenced the following September. The 25 Mk. Is were succeeded by a large number of Mk. IIs, produced by Fairey, Boulton Paul, Blackburn and Westland, and incorporating a later Merlin engine. After twelve months of service, Barracudas went into action during the Salerno landings in September 1943, but their big day was 3rd April, 1944, when 42 of them, with a large fighter escort from half a dozen aircraft carriers, attacked the battleship *Tirpitz* in Kaafjord on the north coast of Norway; further attacks on the ship were maintained by F.A.A. Barracudas throughout that summer. The final wartime version was the torpedo-reconnaissance Mk. III, generally similar to its predecessor but carrying an A.S.V. Mk. X scanner in a housing beneath the rear fuselage. The Griffon-powered Mk. V (the IV was not produced) arrived too late for its intended role in the Pacific theatre, and was used mainly on post-war training duties. Total Barracuda production during the war reached 2,582 aircraft. The type was the Royal Navy's first monoplane torpedo bomber, and throughout its career was hung about with as wide a variety of "stores" as any aircraft—bombs, mines, depth charges, torpedos, lifeboats, even containers to carry four " passengers " under its wings. It was also equipped with RATO gear to assist its operation from smaller carriers.

BRIEF TECHNICAL DETAILS (Mk. II):
Engine: One 1,640 h.p. Rolls-Royce Merlin 32 inline.
Span: 49 ft. 2 in.
Length: 40 ft. 6 in.
Height: 15 ft. 5 in.
Weight Empty: 9,350 lb.
Loaded: 13,916 lb.
No. in crew: Three.
Max. Speed: 228 m.p.h. at 1,750 ft.
Service Ceiling: 16,600 ft.
Normal Range: 686 miles.
Armament: Two .303 Vickers ' K ' machine guns; six 250 lb. bombs, four 450 lb. depth charges or one 1,620 lb. torpedo.

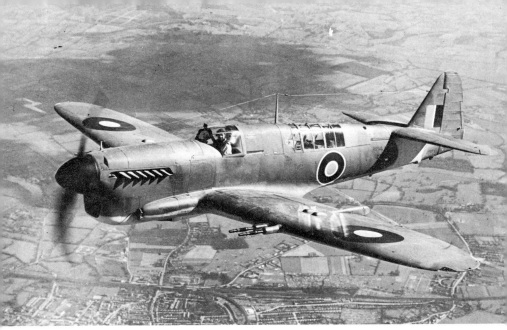

Firefly F. Mk. I

Fairey Firefly

Country of origin: **GREAT BRITAIN**
Purpose: **Carrier-borne fighter and reconnaissance.**
Makers: **Fairey Aviation Co. Ltd.**

Specification: **N.5/40.**
In operational use: **1943/45.**

Designed to follow the Fulmar (opposite) into naval service, the Fairey Firefly was one of a small band of World War 2 aircraft to employ a more or less elliptical wing shape. Its Griffon engine, installed for the first time in a fighter designed for the Fleet Air Arm, brought a much better performance than that of the Fulmar, and the design of the Firefly also made it a much easier machine to handle, both in the air and on the flight deck. Four prototypes were built, the first of these (Z 1826) flying for the first time on 22nd December, 1941. The initial production order was for 200 Firefly Mk. I, though this subsequently developed into a much larger total. Faireys built 297 F. Mk. I, and a further 132 of this version were completed by General Aircraft Limited. Deliveries of the F.I. began in March 1943, the type going into operational service in October of that year, and these were followed by 376 fighter/reconnaissance F.R. Mk. I. A lengthened nose characterised the night-flying N.F. Mk. II, but only 37 of these were completed before their role was assumed by F.R. Is converted as N.F. I. One of the Firefly's operations was a photographic reconnaissance of the German battleship *Tirpitz* which led to the final attack and sinking of this important warship. It was chiefly active, during the war years, in the Pacific theatre, and one of its biggest successes was the attack on Japanese-held oil refineries in Sumatra. Altogether the Firefly had a 13-year service career, though most of this was post-war. By mid-1946 most squadrons equipped with the early models had disbanded and production had turned to the Mk. IV; with this and later variants, the Fleet Air Arm continued to use Fireflies until as recently as 1956.

BRIEF TECHNICAL DETAILS
(F. Mk. I):
Engine: One 1,730 h.p. Rolls-Royce Griffon IIB or 1,990 h.p. Griffon XII inline.
Span: 44 ft. 6 in.
Length: 37 ft. 7¼ in.
Height: 13 ft. 7 in.
Weight Empty: 9,750 lb.
    Loaded: 14,020 lb. (max.)
No. in crew: Two.
Max. Speed: 316 m.p.h. at 14,000 ft.
Service Ceiling: 28,000 ft.
Max. Range: 1,070 miles.
Armament: Four 20 mm. cannon; two 1,000 lb. bombs or eight 60 lb. R.Ps. optional.

Fairey Fulmar

Country of origin: **GREAT BRITAIN**   *Specification:* **O.8/38.**
Purpose: **Carrier-borne fighter.**   *In operational use:* **1940/45.**
Makers: **Fairey Aviation Co. Ltd.**

First announced in action in September 1940, after it had been in service for three months, the Fulmar was a most useful addition to Fleet Air Arm strength, bringing to that service the eight-gun fighter armament already enjoyed by the Royal Air Force.   Developed from the Fairey P.4/34 aircraft of 1937, which it closely resembled, the Fulmar prototype (N 1854) flew on 4th January, 1940, and the type went quickly into production.   First deliveries of the Fulmar Mk. I, of which 250 were built, began to enter service from June 1940 until the following year, when the Mk. II (1,300 h.p. Merlin 30 and tropical equipment) replaced it on the production lines; 350 of the latter version were completed.   By mid-1942 there were 14 squadrons equipped with the Fulmar, and during its career it performed a variety of duties including reconnaissance, escort, convoy protection and night intrusion.   In addition to its valuable firepower the Fulmar possessed excellent manoeuvrability, performance and endurance; its only shortcoming was the relatively low speed, due to the additional all-up weight imposed by the carrier equipment and the second crew member.   Despite this penalty it gave a good account of itself against all opposition, and was particularly successful against the Italians.   During 1943 it began to be replaced by the Seafire (page 153), but remained in service in diminishing numbers until 1945, turning its hand in these latter years to yet another role—that of night fighter. The Fulmar was employed in Europe and the Middle and Far East during its wartime career, and although produced in comparatively small numbers was a most useful piece of Fleet Air Arm equipment.

> **BRIEF TECHNICAL DETAILS (Mk. I):**
> *Engine:* One 1,080 h.p. Rolls-Royce Merlin VIII inline.
> *Span:* 46 ft. 4½ in.
> *Length:* 40 ft. 3 in.
> *Height:* 10 ft. 8 in.
> *Weight Loaded:* 9,800 lb.
> *No. in crew:* Two.
> *Max. Speed:* 280 m.p.h.
> *Service Ceiling:* 26,000 ft.
> *Normal Range:* 800 miles.
> *Armament:* Eight .303 Browning machine guns.

Above: de Havilland Mosquito B35/TT35/*Stuart Howe*
Right: Fairey Swordfish/*Stuart Howe*

Blackburn-built Swordfish III with A.S.V. Mk. X radar

Fairey Swordfish

Country of origin: **GREAT BRITAIN**
Purpose: **Torpedo bomber and reconnaissance.**
Makers: **Fairey Aviation Co. Ltd.**

Specification: **S.15/33.**
In operational use: **1939/45.**

Universally known as the " Stringbag ", the Fairey Swordfish had nearly a decade of distinguished service with the Royal Navy, finally outliving its intended replacement, the Albacore (page 62). Derived from the private-venture Fairey T.S.R.1, the prototype of the Swordfish (K 4190) was first known as the T.S.R.2 and made its initial flight on 17th April, 1934, powered by a 690 h.p. Pegasus III M.3 engine. The first contract, for 86 Swordfish Mk. I, was placed in April 1935 and the type entered F.A.A. service in July 1936. At the outbreak of World War 2, thirteen front-line squadrons were equipped with Swordfish, and during the war years a further twelve were formed. Later variants were the Mk. II (Pegasus III M.3 or 750 h.p. Pegasus 30), featuring a strengthened lower wing to take eight R.Ps., and the Mk. III, which introduced A.S.V. Mk. X radar in a ventral fairing; both of these appeared in 1943. Some conversions as Mk. IV for Canadian use had the crew positions totally enclosed. Total Swordfish production was 2,391 machines; 1,700 by Blackburn and 691 by Fairey. In its torpedo bombing role, the Swordfish took part in many memorable events of the war: the decimation of the Italian Fleet at Taranto in November 1940, the Battle of Cape Matapan in March 1941, the crippling of the *Bismarck*, the "Channel Dash" of the German pocket battleships in February 1942, and a long record of shipping destruction from bases in Malta. As the war progressed, the Swordfish went on to such duties as convoy escort and anti-submarine patrols. Its flying qualities, which were legion, are illustrated by the story of one aircraft, so badly damaged by A.A. fire as to be virtually a monoplane, which nevertheless flew back successfully from the Western Desert to Great Britain for repair.

> **BRIEF TECHNICAL DETAILS (Mk. I):**
> *Engine:* One 690 h.p. Bristol Pegasus III M.3 radial.
> *Span:* 45 ft. 6 in.
> *Length:* 35 ft. 8 in.
> *Height:* 12 ft. 4 in.
> *Weight Empty:* 4,700 lb.
>   *Loaded:* 7,510 lb.
> *No. in crew:* Two or three.
> *Max. Speed:* 138 m.p.h. at 5,000 ft.
> *Service Ceiling:* 19,250 ft.
> *Normal Range:* 546 miles.
> *Armament:* Two .303 machine guns; one 1,610 lb. torpedo, one 1,500 lb. mine or equivalent load of bombs. (Mk. II: eight 60-lb. R.P. in place of torpedo or bombs.)

Fiat B.R. 20 Cicogna *(Stork)*

Country of origin: **ITALY**   *Makers:* **Aeronautica d'Italia S.A. (Fiat).**
Purpose: **Medium bomber.**   *In operational use:* **1940/44.**

A bomber design which appeared in 1936, the Fiat B.R.20 was sent to Spain during the Civil War in support of General Franco's insurgents, and in limited numbers the type was supplied to the Japanese Army Air Force. Shortcomings revealed in combat in these early years were to some extent ironed out in the later B.R.20M version, and between 100 and 150 B.R.20s were in Regia Aeronautica service when Italy entered the war. In October 1940 a force of 75 B.R.20s was flown to Brussels, from which base a few night raids were made on the United Kingdom; these aircraft were withdrawn, however, after some three months to reinforce the Italian air assault on Greece. In the autumn of 1942 a further B.R.20 force was dispatched to the Russian front to support the Luftwaffe, and at this period also Cicognas were used on anti-resistance campaigns in the Balkans. Losses were heavy, and by the time that the Italian Government surrendered in 1943 only a handful of B.R.20s survived. Total Cicogna production, including the improved B.R.20 *bis,* amounted to about 600 machines.

> **BRIEF TECHNICAL DETAILS (B.R.20M):**
>
> *Engines:* Two 1,000 h.p. Fiat A.80 RC 41 radials.
> *Span:* 70 ft. 8½ in.
> *Length:* 53 ft. 0½ in.
> *Height:* 15 ft. 7 in.
> *Weight Empty:* 14,300 lb.
>   *Loaded:* 22,220 lb.
> *No. in crew:* Four.
> *Max. Speed:* 255 m.p.h. at 13,450 ft.
> *Service Ceiling:* 23,600 ft.
> *Max. Range:* 1,860 miles.
> *Armament:* Four 7.7 mm. Breda-SAFAT machine guns; up to 3,520 lb. of bombs.

Fiat C.R. 42/*Aviation Photo News*

Messerschmitt Bf 109E/*Aviation Photo News*

Curtiss P-40N Warhawk/Arthur Pearcy

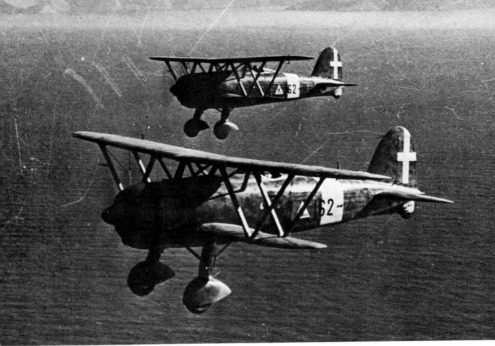

Italian Air Ministry

Fiat C.R. 42 Falco *(Falcon)*

Country of origin: **ITALY**   *Makers:* **Aeronautica d'Italia S.A. (Fiat).**
Purpose: **Fighter.**   *In operational use:* **1940/45.**

During the 1930s the Fiat company's Divisione Aviazione produced a string of attractive biplane designs in the C.R. series, among which may be remembered the C.R.30, C.R.32, C.R.33 and C.R.40. All of them had excellent performance and high manoeuvrability; the aerobatic teams of C.R.32s in particular were a highlight of many an air display of the period and this type also fought in the Spanish Civil War. From this lineage there appeared, in 1936, the C.R.41 biplane fighter. Powered by a 900 h.p. Gnôme-Rhône 14 radial engine, the C.R.41 did not enter series production, although it had quite a fine performance; it was, however, used to good effect in the design and development of Fiat's last C.R. biplane, the C.R.42, also a single-seat fighter. Built in 1939, the prototype C.R.42 retained the general—almost traditional—structural appearance of its progenitors, whilst incorporating the latest technical improvements and employing more up to date materials. The C.R.42 remained in active service throughout the war, in a variety of roles which included escort, night fighter and fighter-bomber in addition to the original role of interceptor. As a fighter-bomber, it could carry a pair of 220 lb. bombs on underwing racks. A floatplane version, the I.C.R.42, and a DB 601-powered development, the C.R.42B, were produced in 1940 and 1941 respectively. Altogether some 1,781 C.R.42s of all types were built before production terminated in 1942, and flew with the air forces of Belgium, Sweden and Hungary as well as with the Regia Aeronautica.

BRIEF TECHNICAL DETAILS:
Engine: One 840 h.p. Fiat A.74 RC 38 radial.
Span: 31 ft. 9¾ in.
Length: 27 ft. 1¼ in.
Height: 11 ft. 9 in.
Weight Empty: 3,784 lb.
  Loaded: 5,049 lb.
No. in crew: One.
Max. Speed: 267 m.p.h at 17,485 ft.
Service Ceiling: 32,472 ft.
Normal Range: 480 miles.
Armament: Two 12.7 mm. Breda-SAFAT machine guns. Two 220 lb. bombs optional.

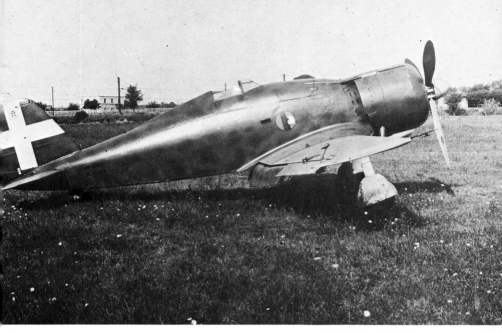

Fiat G.50 Freccia *(Arrow)*

Country of origin: **ITALY**   *Makers:* **Aeronautica d'Italia S.A. (Fiat).**
Purpose: **Fighter.**   *In operational use:* **1940/45.**

A single-seat fighter which first flew on 26th February, 1937, the Freccia went through the testing-ground of the Spanish Civil War during the following year. Knowledge accumulated as a result of this experience was incorporated in the modified G.50*bis* which was first flown in the autumn of 1940, one modification being the substitution of an open cockpit in place of the enclosed canopy fitted to the G.50 (*cf.* also the Macchi C.200, page 115). One Regia Aeronautica group was equipped with the G.50 when Italy entered the war on 10th June, 1940, and these were supplemented soon afterwards by the arrival of production G.50*bis* aircraft.   A total of 450 of the latter version were built, some of these and some of the 280 G.50s also being exported. An attractive aeroplane, bearing some resemblance to its contemporary, the Macchi C.200 Saetta, the Freccia suffered from the common problem of underpowering and its performance never matched that of Allied or German fighters of the same period. The basic soundness of the design was however illustrated by the subsequent development of the G.50 into the G.55 Centauro. A tandem-seat trainer version (100 built) was designated G.50B.

BRIEF TECHNICAL DETAILS
(G.50*bis*):
Engine: One 840 h.p. Fiat A.74 RC 38 radial.
Span: 35 ft. 2 in.
Length: 25 ft. 7 in.
Height: 9 ft. 9 in.
Weight Empty: 4,320 lb.
    Loaded: 5,285 lb.
No. in crew: One.
Max. Speed: 293 m.p.h. at 14,760 ft.
Service Ceiling: 35,100 ft.
Normal Range: 420 miles.
Armament: Two 12.7 mm. Breda-SAFAT machine guns.

Kawasaki Type 5 Model IB (Ki-I00-IB)/*Paul Terian*

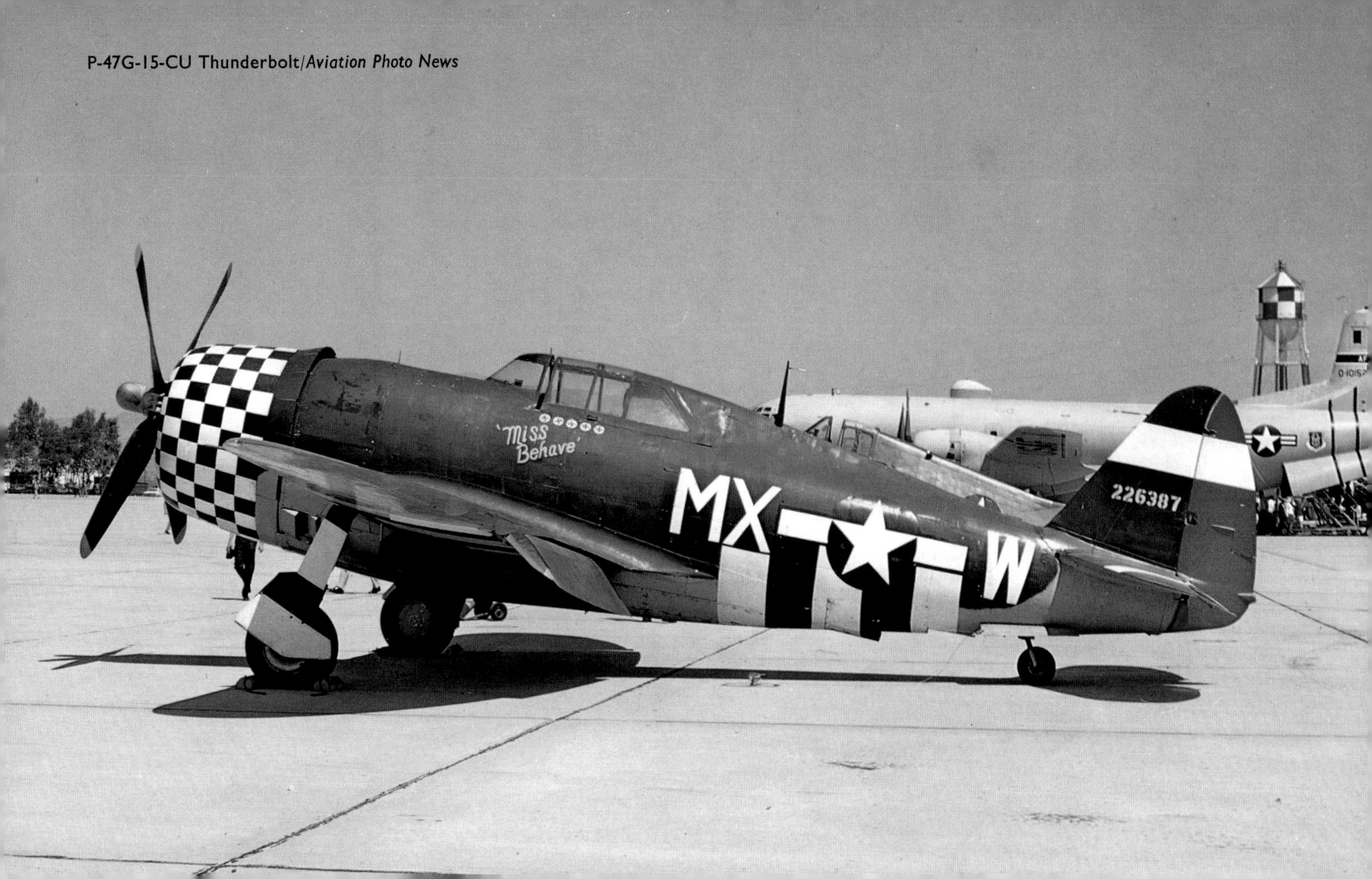

P-47G-15-CU Thunderbolt/*Aviation Photo News*

Fi 156C-1, Finnish Air Force/*Eino Ritaranta*

Fieseler Fi 156 Storch *(Stork)*

Country of origin: **GERMANY**
Purpose: **General communications and reconnaissance.**

Makers: **Gerhard Fieseler Werke G.m.b.H.**
In operational use: **1939/45.**

Designed in 1935 and first flown the following year, the Fieseler Storch went straight into quantity production for the Luftwaffe as the Fi 156A-1. The Fi 156B was a proposed civil counterpart which did not materialise, and production continued with the C series during 1939. The Fi 156 was used throughout the war in a multitude of roles, among which were those of staff transport (Fi 156C-1), short-range reconnaissance (Fi 156C-2), ambulance (Fi 156D) and army co-operation (various models). The experimental Fi 156E featured a special caterpillar-type landing gear for rough-strip operations. In view of the emphasis placed on the production of front-line aircraft, the Fieseler aircraft factories were primarily concerned with contracts for the Fw 190 interceptor,

and construction of the Fi 156 was put in the hands of German-controlled factories at Puteaux in Occupied France and Mraz in Czechoslovakia. At Puteaux, the Morane-Saulnier company developed for a while an enlarged version, the Fi 256, which could carry five passengers, but this was essentially a civil project and was ultimately abandoned. Total wartime production of the Storch amounted to 2,549 aircraft, of which many served with the air arms of Germany's allies as well as with the Luftwaffe.

BRIEF TECHNICAL DETAILS
(Fi 156C-3):
Engine: One 240 h.p. Argus As 10C inline.
Span: 46 ft. 9 in.
Length: 32 ft. 5¾ in.
Height: 9 ft. 10 in.
Weight Empty: 2,050 lb.
　　　　Loaded: 2,910 lb.
No. in crew: Two.
Max. Speed: 109 m.p.h. at sea level.
Service Ceiling: 15,090 ft.
Normal Range: 236 miles.
Armament: One 7.9 mm. MG 15 machine gun in rear cabin.

Fw 189A-1

Focke-Wulf Fw 189

Country of origin: **GERMANY**
Purpose: **Reconnaissance, liaison and training.**

Makers: **Focke-Wulf Flugzeugbau G.m.b.H.**
In operational use: **1940/45.**

The purposes for which the Fw 189 was originally designed were those of close support and light bomber, and the first prototype flew at the beginning of 1938. Various modifications, particularly to the central crew nacelle, were made to the second and third machines, the latter being fitted out for reconnaissance and liaison duties; and with the adoption of the Henschel Hs 129 (see page 206) for the specialist ground attack role, it was as a reconnaissance aircraft that the Fw 189 eventually entered production for the Luftwaffe in 1939. The type entered squadron service (Fw 189A-1) towards the end of 1940. Production continued, through the generally similar Fw 189A-2 and A-3 sub-types, until 1944, during which time 846 aircraft of all versions were built. The type was most extensively used on the Russian front, although it was encountered in most other theatres of the European war as well. Although admirably fitted for short range reconnaissance functions—the view from the extensively glazed crew nacelle was excellent—the performance of the Fw 189 was not dazzling, and it was something of a "sitter" for intercepting fighters. For this reason it became relegated, as the war progressed, to less hazardous second-line duties such as communications, casualty evacuation and training.

BRIEF TECHNICAL DETAILS
(Fw 189A-1):
Engines: Two 450 h.p. Argus As 410A-1 inlines.
Span: 60 ft. 5 in.
Length: 39 ft. 4 in.
Weight Empty: 5,930 lb.
Loaded: 8,700 lb.
No. in crew: Three.
Max. Speed: 221 m.p.h. at 8,530 ft.
Service Ceiling: 27,550 ft.
Normal Range: 430 miles.
Armament: Two 7.9 mm. MG 17 and two 7.9 mm. MG 15 muachine gns. Two 110 lb. bombs optional.

Above: Westland Lysander/*March/Molyneux*

Right: Bf 109G-2/*Aviation Photo News*

Focke-Wulf Fw 190

Country of origin: **GERMANY**
Purpose: **Fighter and ground attack.**

Makers: **Focke-Wulf Flugzeugbau G.m.b.H.**
In operational use: **1941/45.**

Widely regarded by both sides as probably the best fighter which Germany produced during the Second World War, the Fw 190 flew in prototype form on 1st June 1939 as a " second string " to the Messerschmitt Bf 109. Despite some mistrust by the Reichsluftministerium of air-cooled radial engines, the BMW 139-powered early prototypes underwent very successful flight trials and the Fw 190 became Germany's first radial-engined monoplane fighter. Its subsequent achievements should certainly have allayed any doubts the RLM may have had, although they were cautious in their early use of the type and it was not seen over the United Kingdom until August 1941. The original production series (Fw 190A) were fitted with the more powerful BMW 801 engine, the sub-types differing principally in firepower. The next major production series was the Fw 190D, the " long-nosed " model powered by the Junkers Jumo 213 engine, which was introduced into service in 1943. The installation of the liquid-cooled Jumo inline engine brought several structural alterations to the Fw 190 airframe, although the annular radiator duct of the Jumo preserved the " radial " engined appearance. Standard wings and tailplane of the A series were retained, but the fuselage was lengthened to 33 ft. 11 in., and the fin slightly widened. Provision was made, in the Fw 190D-12 and -13, for mounting a 30 mm. MK 108 cannon in the engine Vee to fire through the airscrew boss.

The installation of MW50 power boost in the engine stepped up the performance, the Fw 190D-12 having a maximum speed of 453 m.p.h. at 37,000 feet. Further development of the Jumo-powered D series thereafter continued under the new designation of Ta 152 (see page 197). There was no Fw 190E and the Fw 190F was developed from the A, with additional armour and no outer wing guns, for ground attack duties. The Fw 190G was a fighter-bomber, normally capable of carrying one 1,100 lb. or 2,200 lb. bomb slung under the centre fuselage.

BRIEF TECHNICAL DETAILS
(Fw 190A-8):
Engine: One 2,100 h.p. (with boost) BMW 801D-2 radial.
Span: 34 ft. 5¼ in.
Length: 29 ft. 0 in.
Height: 13 ft. 0 in.
Weight Empty: 7,000 lb.
Loaded: 9,750 lb.
No. in crew: One.
Maximum Speed: 408 m.p.h. at 20,600 ft.
Normal Range: 500 miles.
Service Ceiling: 37,400 ft.
Armament: Four 20 mm. MG 151 cannon and two 13 mm. MG 131 machine guns.

Focke-Wulf Fw 200C Condor

Country of origin: **GERMANY**
Purpose: **Long range maritime reconnaissance bomber**

Makers: **Focke-Wulf Flugzeugbau G.m.b.H.**
In operational use: **1939/45.**

Although originally a commercial aircraft, converted to military use, it was as a maritime patrol bomber that the Fw 200 Condor made its mark during the Second World War. In this capacity, acting in co-operation with U-boat packs, it formed one of the most effective Luftwaffe combinations of the war, and many a convoy was to rue the moment it first spied a Condor above the horizon. The prototype Fw 200 commercial transport first flew in 1937, followed by a few Fw 200As and the first major production version, the Fw 200B. Work on a bomber conversion began in 1939 at the request of the Japanese Army Air Force, who were interested in such a project. This version introduced more powerful engines and was designated Fw 200C; war had broken out, however, before the first one was ready, and the project was promptly adopted by the Luftwaffe for the sea-going reconnaissance role. Meantime, the airline Fw 200Bs and the few pre-production C-0s were pressed into service as transports. Production continued until early 1944 through sub-types C-1, -2, -3, -4 and -6, a total of 263 Condors of all versions being the final figure. Towards the end of the war, when the Fw 200's marauding tactics had been largely mitigated, several Condors were again diverted to transport duties, for the use of Hitler and his staff. A projected development, the Fw 300, with enlarged wing span and inline engines of greater power, did not progress beyond the design stage.

**BRIEF TECHNICAL DETAILS
(Fw 200C-3):**
Engines: Four 1,000 h.p. Bramo 323R-2 radials.
Span: 108 ft. 3 in.
Length: 78 ft. 3 in.
Height: 23 ft. 4 in.
Weight Empty: 31,020 lb.
   Loaded: 49,940 lb.
No. in crew: Eight.
Max. Speed: 240 m.p.h. at 13,000 ft.
Service Ceiling: 28,700 ft.
Max. Range: 3,950 miles.
Armament: One 20 mm. MG FF cannon and five 7.9 mm. MG 15 machine guns. Normal bomb load 3,300 lb.

Gladiator Mk. II

Gloster Gladiator

Country of origin: **GREAT BRITAIN**
Purpose: **Fighter.**
Makers: **Gloster Aircraft Co. Ltd.**

Specification: **F.7/30.**
In operational use: **1939/41.**

A development of the Gauntlet, which it closely resembled apart from its enclosed cockpit and more powerful engine, the Gladiator was the last biplane fighter to serve with the R.A.F. and was originally produced as a private venture. In July 1935, little less than a year after the first prototype (K 5200) had flown, 23 Gladiator Is were ordered by the Air Ministry; a further order for 186 followed two months later, and by the Spring of 1940 production was complete, including an additional batch of 60 aircraft built for the F.A.A. as Sea Gladiators. The latter were powered by the Mercury VIIIA engine, as were the Gladiators Mk. II, which also incorporated certain other refinements. The Gladiator entered service with the R.A.F. in January 1937 and the Sea Gladiator with the Royal Navy in February 1939. In addition to the 60 Sea Gladiators built as such, a further 38 were converted from R.A.F. machines. By 1939 and 1940 respectively these aircraft had largely been replaced by more modern types, but served in small numbers in and around Europe and in the Battle of Britain, not to mention the epic defence of Malta.

BRIEF TECHNICAL DETAILS (Mk. I):
Engine: One 840 h.p. Bristol Mercury IX radial.
Span: 32 ft. 3 in.
Length: 27 ft. 5 in.
Height: 10 ft. 4 in.
Weight Empty: 3,476 lb.
Loaded: 4,750 lb.
No. in crew: One.
Max. Speed: 253 m.p.h. at 14,500 ft.
Service Ceiling: 33,000 ft.
Normal Range: 410 miles.
Armament: Four .303 Browning machine guns.

Gloster Meteor

Country of origin: **GREAT BRITAIN**
Purpose: **Fighter.**
Makers: **Gloster Aircraft Co. Ltd.**

Specification: **F.9/40.**
In operational use: **1944/45.**

Britain's first—and the Allies' only—jet fighter to see action during World War 2, the Gloster Meteor first entered service during the last year of hostilities, though it had been developing since the early days of the war. Making every use of experience gained with the Gloster G.40 single-jet aeroplane built to Spec. E.28/39, which flew in May 1941, the Meteor design by W. G. Carter and his team employed a twin-engined layout to ensure sufficient thrust from this new form of propulsion. By September 1941 contracts had been placed for eight prototypes and a modest production run of 20 Meteor Mk. Is. It is not widely known that at this time, and until March 1942, the aircraft was known as the Thunderbolt; the change was subsequently made to avoid confusion with the American P-47 fighter of that name. First flight of the Meteor was made by the fifth prototype (DG 206) on 5th March 1943, this and the second machine being powered by 1,500 lb.s.t. Halford H.1 turbojets, precursors of the de Havilland Goblin later to be employed in the Vampire. One other prototype had Metrovick F.2 engines installed, but the remainder were powered by a variety of developments of the Whittle type engine. The first production Meteor F. Mk. I aircraft was supplied to the United States for study purposes, in exchange for an example of America's first jet-propelled aeroplane, the P-59 Airacomet, and only 16 of the 20 Mk. Is found their way into R.A.F. squadron service. The first of these (1,700 lb.s.t. Welland I) were delivered to No. 616 Squadron in July 1944, and at the end of that month made their first sorties against the V.1 flying bombs. At the beginning of 1945, by which time the Mk. III was also in service, Meteors began to extend their activities to the European continent to counteract the appearance of Germany's jet-propelled Me 262. The final few of the 280 Meteor IIIs built, apart from the additional tankage and modified cockpit, also introduced the lengthened engine nacelles later to become standard on post-war Meteors.

BRIEF TECHNICAL DETAILS (Mk. III):
Engines: Two 2,000 lb.s.t. Rolls-Royce Derwent I turbojets.
Span: 43 ft. 0 in.
Length: 41 ft. 3 in.
Height: 13 ft. 0 in.
Weight Empty: 8,810 lb.
Loaded: 13,300 lb.
No. in crew: One.
Max. Speed: 493 m.p.h. at 30,000 ft.
Service Ceiling: 44,000 ft.
Normal Range: 1,340 miles.
Armament: Four 20 mm. Hispano cannon.

83

Grumman F4F Wildcat

Country of origin: **U.S.A.**
Purpose: **Carrier-based fighter and fighter-bomber.**
Makers: **Grumman Aircraft Engineering Corporation.**

Other U.S. designations: **FM-1 and -2.**
In operational use: **1940/45.**

The tubby Grumman Wildcat was the United States Navy's standard single-seat fighter at the time America entered the war, and, as the Martlet, had been operational with the Fleet Air Arm for more than a year before that. To a Martlet went the distinction of being the first type of American aeroplane in British service to shoot down a German bomber. Developed out of a long line of Grumman biplane naval fighters, the prototype was the XF4F-2, which was powered by a 1,050 h.p. R-1830-66 Wasp and flew for the first time on 2nd September, 1937. After extensive modifications, an order was placed in 1939 for 78 F4F-3s, followed by a contract for 243 F4F-4s and a further quantity of F4F-5s in 1941. Following upon the first U.S. contract, the G-36A export version of the F4F-3 was acquired by the Royal Navy, 85 entering service as the Cyclone-powered Martlet I from October 1940 onwards. These were followed in 1941 by 90 Mk. II and 40 Mk. III, both powered by Twin Wasps, but the former batch incorporating wing folding for carrier stowage. Deliveries to the R.N. continued under Lend-Lease with 220 Martlet IV, 312 Mk. V and 370 Mk. VI. Grumman built 1,971 Wildcats up to May 1943, when construction was transferred to the Eastern Aircraft Division of General Motors. The Eastern Wildcats—some 5,972 in all—were designated FM-1 and FM-2, to which the British Mks. V and VI also corresponded; the FM-2 featured a taller fin and rudder and a slightly longer engine cowling. The British Martlets, which were renamed Wildcats in January 1944, were active from both naval and merchant aircraft carriers in the Atlantic and the Mediterranean, including in their duties convoy protection, anti-submarine and ground support missions. With the U.S. Navy in the Pacific, though often outnumbered by Japanese opposition, the Wildcat established a fine fighting record, despite being made to suffer various aerodynamic penalties.

BRIEF TECHNICAL DETAILS (F4F-3):
Engine: One 1,200 h.p. Pratt & Whitney R-1830-76 Twin Wasp radial.
Span: 38 ft. 0 in.
Length: 28 ft. 10 in.
Height: 11 ft. 11 in.
Weight Empty: 5,342 lb.
Loaded: 7,002 lb.
No. in crew: One.
Max. Speed: 328 m.p.h. at 21,000 ft.
Service Ceiling: 37 500 ft.
Max. Range: 1,150 miles.
Armament: Four .50 machine guns; two 100 lb. bombs optional.

Grumman F6F Hellcat

Country of origin: **U.S.A.**
Purpose: **Carrier-borne fighter.**

Makers: **Grumman Aircraft Engineering Corporation.**
In operational use: **1943/45.**

Following the success of Grumman's earlier Wildcat fighter, itself the descendant of a long line of naval combat aircraft, work was begun in the spring of 1941 to produce an even more refined version. The result of this study, the XF6F-3 Hellcat, made its maiden flight on 26th June, 1942. A logical development of the Wildcat, it was a much more streamlined aircraft despite its greater size and weight, and its performance was considerably better. It succeeded the F4F on Grumman production lines during the latter part of 1942, the first deliveries for service use (the F6F-3) being in January 1943. From then until November, 1945, when Hellcat production was terminated, Grumman factories turned out 12,272 of these aircraft. The chief production versions were the F6F-3 (4,423 built) and F6F-5 (6,436 built). Their first reported action was at Marcus Island with the U.S. Pacific Fleet on 1st September, 1943, though they were also entering Fleet Air Arm service at about the same time. The first F.A.A. Hellcat Is were F6F-3s; 252 of these were supplied, and known for a time by the name Gannet. Later arrivals were F6F-5s (Hellcat II), an improved version: the F.A.A. received 930 of these, later converting about 75 of them to carry wing-mounted radar for night fighting, in parallel with the U.S. Navy's F6F-5Ns. All British Hellcats were returned to the U.S.A. after VJ day. Hitting power was further augmented, in the later war years, by the provision for carrying a pair of 1,000 lb. bombs or rocket projectiles.

BRIEF TECHNICAL DETAILS (F6F-3):

Engine: One 2,000 h.p. Pratt & Whitney R-2800-10 Double Wasp radial.
Span: 42 ft. 10 in.
Length: 33 ft. 6½ in.
Height: 13 ft. 0 in.
Weight Empty: 9,042 lb.
    Loaded: 11,381 lb.
No. in crew: One.
Max. Speed: 376 m.p.h. at 17,300 ft.
Service Ceiling: 38,400 ft.
Normal Range: 1,090 miles.
Armament : Six .50 Browning machine guns.

85

Grumman TBF Avenger

Country of origin: **U.S.A.**
Purpose: **Torpedo bomber.**
Makers: **Grumman Aircraft Engineering Corporation.**

Other U.S. designations: **TBM.**
In operational use: **1942/45.**

One of the most successful torpedo bombers of World War 2—and for many years after—the Grumman Avenger first appeared in its XTBF-1 form in 1941, as a replacement for the Douglas Devastator. It was one of the first U.S. production aircraft to incorporate a power-operated turret, and one of very few which could carry a 22-inch torpedo internally. Although a large machine by carrier standards of the day, the Avenger proved itself to be easily manageable aboard ship, and began to enter service in the spring of 1942; its first reported action was at Midway in June 1942. A year later production of the Avenger was transferred to the Eastern Aircraft Division of General Motors, after Grumman had built 2,290 TBF-1s. Eastern-built Avengers were designated TBM-1 (2,882 of these were completed) and TBM-3 (4,664 completed), and these two basic versions eventually superseded the TBFs in U.S. service. Nearly 1,000 Avengers of various types were supplied from the beginning of 1943 to the Fleet Air Arm. The initial batch of 402 TBF-1s were known, until the American name was standardised in January 1944, as the Tarpon; subsequent deliveries of 334 TBM-1s and 222 TBM-3s were known as the Avenger II and III respectively. Owing to some difficulty in installing British torpedos in the American machines, the Fleet Air Arm Avengers were employed for the most part as " straight " bombers, minelayers or rocket-firing strike aircraft, which tasks they carried out with no small success. Avengers were, incidentally, the first F.A.A. aircraft to attack the Japanese mainland, in July 1945; others were employed against German land targets. The final production model, with improved Double Cyclone engines, was the TBM-4.

BRIEF TECHNICAL DETAILS (TBF-1):

Engine: One 1,850 h.p. Wright R-2600-8 Double Cyclone radial.
Span: 54 ft. 2 in.
Length: 40 ft. 0 in.
Height: 16 ft. 5 in.
Weight Empty: 10,080 lb.
    Loaded: 13,667 lb.
No. in crew: Three.
Max. Speed: 271 m.p.h. at 12,000 ft
Service Ceiling: 23,000 ft.
Normal Range: 1,020 miles.
Armament: Three .50 and two .30 machine guns; up to 2,000 lb. of bombs, one 1,921 lb. torpedo or eight R.P.s.

Halifax Mk. I

Handley Page Halifax

Country of origin: **GREAT BRITAIN**
Purpose: **Heavy bomber.**
Makers: **Handley Page Ltd.**

Specification: **P.13/36.**
In operational use: **1940/45.**

A product of the first limited company incorporated in Great Britain for the manufacture of aircraft, the Halifax was the second of the four-engined "heavies", entering service only a few months behind the Stirling.   It was evolved from the same Specification that produced the Avro Manchester (page 172), and construction of two prototypes began in January 1938.   The first (L 7244) flew in October 1939, and thirteen months later the first Bomber Command Halifax squadron was formed.   Production increased through 1941, and " satellite " factories included English Electric (who built 2,145), Rootes (1,070), Fairey (661) and the London Aircraft Production Group (710).   The sequence began with the Mk. I Series I, and continued through the Series II (higher loaded weight), Series III

Halifax Mk. II Series I

(extra fuel), Mk. II Series I (dorsal turret, no beam guns, 1,390 h.p. Merlin XX), Mk. II Series I Special (nose and dorsal turrets removed), and the Mk. II Series IA (redesigned and longer glazed nose, new dorsal turret, 1,390 h.p. Merlin XXII). Later models of the last-named introduced rectangular fins and rudders, and were followed by the bomber/reconnaissance Mk. V which was generally similar to the Mk. II. In mid-1943 a radial powerplant, retractable tailwheel and a wing extended from the original 98 ft. 10 in, appeared in the Halifax III.

Nearer the end of the war appeared the improved Mks. VI (1,800 h.p. Hercules 100, extra fuel) and VII (Hercules XVI). Some Halifax III, V and VII were equipped for paratrooping, glider towing and agent dropping. Just in service before the war ended, the Mk. VIII was a transport with faired-in gun positions and a detachable 8,000 lb. freight pannier under the fuselage; the final version was the post-war Mk. IX transport. Total Halifax production of 6,176 aircraft included 2,050 Mks. I/II, 2,060 Mk. III, 916 Mk. V, 480 Mk. VI, 395 Mk. VII, over 100 Mk. VIII and the remainder Mk. IX. In addition to its activities in the European theatre with Bomber and Coastal Commands, the Halifax also served with distinction in the Middle East, the only British four-engined bomber to serve there.

BRIEF TECHNICAL DETAILS (Mk. III):
Engines: Four 1,615 h.p. Bristol Hercules XVI radials.
Span: 104 ft. 2 in.   *Length:* 70 ft. 1 in.
Height: 20 ft. 9 in.
Weight Empty: 38,240 lb.
Loaded: 54,400 lb.
No. in crew: Seven.
Max. Speed: 282 m.p.h. at 13,500 ft.
Service Ceiling: 24,000 ft.
Normal Range: 1,030 miles.
Armament: Nine .303 Browning machine guns. Up to 13,000 lb. of bombs.

Halifax B. Mk. VI

Handley Page Hampden

Country of origin: **GREAT BRITAIN**
Purpose: **Medium bomber**
Makers: **Handley Page Ltd.**

Specification: **B.9/32.**
In operational use: **1939/44.**

Easy to fly, faster than the Whitley or Wellington, and possessing a good range with a respectable bomb load, the Handley Page Hampden ought perhaps to have achieved greater renown than it did. Nevertheless, despite a number of shortcomings, it performed useful service and at the outbreak of World War 2 was one of the R.A.F's standard " heavy " bombers, as they were then rated. Handley Page's first monoplane bomber design, the Hampden introduced several novel features, chief among which were its " tadpole " or " frying pan " fuselage—only three feet wide at its fattest point. Only two months after the prototype (K 4240) had flown on 21st June 1936, a production order for 180 Hampdens was placed, with a simultaneous order for 100 Herefords (see page 202). Several modifications, including new Pegasus engines, armament changes and a new transparent Perspex nose, were introduced on the production Hampdens, deliveries of which began in August 1938. By the outbreak of war eight R.A.F. squadrons were equipped with the type, and initially it was employed on daylight operations. One of the Hampden's most serious faults, the lack of adequate defensive firepower, was quickly reflected by heavy losses in these raids, and it was soon switched to the less hazardous business of night bombing. Although a small quantity of Hampdens took part in the first thousand-bomber raid, against Cologne at the end of May 1942, by this time the aircraft was becoming obsolete and it performed its last Bomber Command sortie in the middle of September. It was, however, to take on a new lease of life under the aegis of Coastal Command as a minelayer and torpedo bomber. For the latter role, in which the Hampden had no small success, the torpedo was carried enclosed within a specially deepened bomb bay. Production of the Hampden Mk. I (there were only two Mk. II) included 500 built by Handley Page, 770 by English Electric and 160 by Canadian Associated Aircraft Ltd.; a few Herefords were also re-engined to Hampden standard.

BRIEF TECHNICAL DETAILS (Mk. I):
Engines: Two 965 h.p. Bristol Pegasus XVIII radials.
Span: 69 ft. 2 in. Length: 53 ft. 7 in.
Height: 14 ft. 11 in.
Weight Empty: 11,780 lb.
     Loaded: 18,756 lb.
No. in crew: Four.
Max. Speed: 265 m.p.h. at 15,500 ft.
Service Ceiling: 22,700 ft.
Max. Range: 1,990 miles.
Armament: Six .303 machine guns.
     Up to 4,000 lb. of bombs.

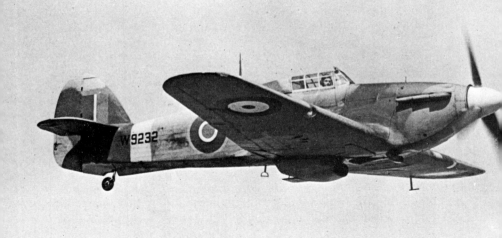

Hawker Hurricane

Country of origin: **GREAT BRITAIN**   *Specification:* **F.36/34.**
Purpose: **Fighter and fighter-bomber.**   *In operational use:* **1939/45.**
Makers: **Hawker Aircraft Ltd.**

The first R.A.F. monoplane fighter, and its first capable of more than 300 m.p.h., the Hurricane proved throughout the war to be a highly adaptable and versatile aeroplane. In the Battle of Britain it equipped more than 60 per cent of Fighter Command squadrons; it shot down nearly half the total of enemy aircraft destroyed in the first year of war; in the Western Desert it was an effective light bomber and tank-buster; at sea it was a valuable convoy protector; in the Far East it served as a night fighter; and in Russia it did sterling work with the Soviet forces. Sydney Camm's design of the Hurricane began early in 1934, and an order for one aircraft was placed on 21st February 1935. This prototype (K 5083) flew on 6th November the same year, working up to a speed of 315 m.p.h. during trials. In June 1936 a production order for 600 was placed and the name Hurricane adopted; the first production Mk. I (Merlin II engine) entered service with No. 111 Squadron in December 1937, and by the outbreak of war nearly 500 were in service with eighteen squadrons. During the Battle of Britain, their speed being slightly inferior to that of the Bf 109E, Hurricanes concentrated mainly on the interception of raiding bombers. In mid-1940 production turned to the Mks. IIB (twelve .303 machine guns) and IIC (four 20 mm. cannon), these versions reaching the squadrons during 1941. In October 1941 " Hurribomber " versions of the IIB and IIC made their appearance, carrying two 250 lb. bombs underwing, and in mid-1942 there appeared the Mk. IID, with wings modified to support a pair of 40 mm. cannon for ground attack missions. Although its speed was reduced to 286 m.p.h., and each shot with the 40 mm. guns pulled the aircraft's nose down 5 degrees so that the target had to be re-aligned before the next, the Hurricane IID was nevertheless employed with no small success in the anti-tank role. In March 1943 the Hurricane IV (1,620 h.p. Merlin 24 or 27) entered service, and the following September saw rocket-carrying versions of the IIB, IIC and IV go into action.

The Sea Hurricane IA, popularly known as the " Hurricat ", was a converted Hurricane I, fitted with catapult gear for launching from C.A.Ms. (Catapult Aircraft Merchantmen); at least 800 conversions to Sea Hurricane IA were ordered. It appeared in 1941 with the Merchant Ship Fighter Unit, following Winston Churchill's order for an aircraft to protect convoys from the marauding German Fw 200C Condors. There were no facilities for these to regain ship

Sea Hurricane Mk. IA on board a C.A.M. ship/I.W.M.

Hurricane Mk. IIC/I.W.M.

91

Gloster-built Mk. IIB for Soviet Air Force

once they had been launched: the pilot had either to make for a shore base, if within range, or ditch near the convoy and be picked up; later IAs, however, were helped by the addition of two auxiliary fuel tanks. They performed valuable service on Baltic convoys and in the Mediterranean, but had largely disappeared by 1943. The chief Fleet Air Arm version was the Sea Hurricane IB, equipped with normal arrester gear for carrier operation, which became operational in 1942. The Mk. IC was similar with a four-cannon armament, as was the Mk. IIC, except for a Merlin XX powerplant.

The Hurricanes supplied to Russia were modified as two-seat ground attack aircraft with tandem cockpits, serving with the French " Normandie " squadron operating with the Russian forces.

Hurricane production was delegated to the Gloster Aircraft Co., the Austin Motor Co. and the Canadian Car and Foundry Co., who built 2,750, 300 and 1,451 respectively, the Canadian versions being designated Mks. X, XI, XII and XIIA and powered by Packard-built Merlin engines. Sea Hurricane conversions were carried out by General Aircraft Ltd. and Austin Motors Ltd. Hawker production of Hurricanes amounted to over 10,030 aircraft, bringing the grand production total to 14,533 machines.

BRIEF TECHNICAL DETAILS
(Mk. IIB):

Engine: One 1,280 h.p. Rolls-Royce Merlin XX inline.
Span: 40 ft. 0 in.
Length: 32 ft. 3 in.
Height: 13ft. 1 in.
Weight Empty: 5,640 lb.
        Loaded: 8,250 lb.
No. in crew: One.
Max. Speed: 339 m.p.h. at 22,000 ft.
Service Ceiling: 36,000 ft.
Normal Range: 470 miles.
Armament: Twelve .303 Browning machine guns. Two 250 lb. or 500 lb. bombs and/or eight R.P.

Hurricane Mk. V

Tempest F. Mk. V

Hawker Tempest

Country of origin: **GREAT BRITAIN**   Specification: **F.10/41.**
Purpose: **Fighter and fighter-bomber.**   In operational use: **1944/45.**
Makers: **Hawker Aircraft Ltd.**

Proposals for a Mk. II version of the Typhoon (page 94), incorporating superior cockpit view and tail assembly, an improved Sabre engine driving a 4-blade airscrew, and a thin elliptical wing, were submitted to the Ministry of Aircraft Production in August 1941. Whilst it was under discussion, a Centaurus-powered Tornado prototype was completed, but with the cancellation of the Tornado the Centaurus programme was transferred to the Typhoon; the Bristol engine would not fit into the Typhoon I, so it graduated to the Mk. II project. Hawkers had already been asked to construct two prototypes, one with the Sabre II and one with a Rolls-Royce Griffon, and to avoid confusion the name Tempest was adopted for the new venture. In June 1942 the Air Ministry proposed six prototypes: one with the Sabre IV (Tempest Mk. I); two with the Centaurus (Mk. II); two with the Griffon (Mks. III and IV); and one with the Sabre II (Mk. V). However, Hawkers decided to concentrate on the Mks. I, II and V. The prototypes of these three versions made their respective maiden flights on 24th February 1943, 28th June 1943 and 2nd September 1942. As the Sabre II was already tried and tested, the Tempest V was the first to go into production—and, as it turned out, the only version to see war service. Eight hundred and five Mk. Vs were completed, the first entering service in January 1944. Although the Tempest followed the Typhoon's train-busting trail across Europe, it is probably best remembered for its work against the V.1 flying bombs over Southern England and the Channel, when in the three months June-September 1944 Tempest squadrons disposed of 638 of these devices. With the 2nd Tactical Air Force in Europe, the Tempest's excellent performance enabled it to destroy the very creditable total of 20 Me 262s. The Tempest II (2,500 h.p. Centaurus V or VI) entered production in August 1944, and 450 were eventually built, but they did not reach R.A.F. squadrons until three months after the end of the war. They were followed by 142 Tempest VI (2,700 h.p. Sabre VA).

BRIEF TECHNICAL DETAILS (Mk. V):
Engine: One 2,420 h.p. Napier Sabre IIB inline.
Span: 41 ft. 0 in.
Length: 33 ft. 8 in.
Height: 16 ft. 1 in.
Weight Empty: 9,250 lb.
        Loaded: 11,540 lb.
No. in crew: One.
Max. Speed: 435 m.p.h. at 17,000 ft.
Service Ceiling: 36,500 ft.
Max. Range: 1,530 miles.
Armament: Four 20 mm. Hispano cannon; two 1,000 lb. bombs or eight R.P.

93

Hawker Typhoon

Country of origin: **GREAT BRITAIN**
Purpose: **Fighter and ground attack.**
Makers: **Hawker Aircraft Ltd.**

Specification: **F.18/37.**
In operational use: **1941/45.**

Although not particularly successful in the interceptor role for which it was originally conceived, the Typhoon subsequently became probably the best ground attack aeroplane on either side during the Second World War. Design began in March 1937, and on 30th August 1938 an order was placed for four prototypes—two " Type N " (Napier Sabre) and two " Type R " (Rolls-Royce Vulture)—subsequently named Typhoon and Tornado. The Tornado became a victim of the Vulture cutback, and only one, apart from the two prototypes, was completed. The prototype Typhoon (P 5212) made its maiden flight on 24th February 1940, but the first Typhoon IA did not fly until 26th May 1941. The IA (twelve .303 machine guns) began to join R.A.F. squadrons in July 1941. Meanwhile, in October 1940, the Air Ministry had asked for the urgent production of a fighter to counter the " tip and run " raids by Fw 190s, which were outrunning the Spitfire. The Typhoon had the necessary speed, and Hawkers quickly produced the Mk. IB, armed with four 20 mm. cannon, which entered service in September 1941. During the remainder of that year, and through 1942, the new " Tiffy " did useful work against the Fw 190, and was the first to shoot down the new Me 210; it also began steadily to increase its activities abroad, making low level attacks on Channel shipping and ground targets in Europe. Proof of its genuine low level flying lay in the twig-bedecked wings of many of the returning aircraft. The Typhoon's range was augmented by external tanks, and later began to carry two 1,000 lb. bombs—the heaviest load of any single-engined aircraft at that time— or eight rocket projectiles. By D-day, the R.A.F. had 26 Typhoon IB squadrons; they made possible in no small measure the break-through to the Rhine, and on one day—7th August, 1944— Typhoons alone destroyed 135 enemy tanks. " Cab-rank " attacks, by waves of Typhoons constantly in the air waiting to be given a target, became a commonplace. Production, most of which was handled by the Gloster Aircraft Co. Ltd., totalled 3,330 aircraft, of which all but the first few hundred were the Mk. IB.

BRIEF TECHNICAL DETAILS (Mk. IB):
Engine: One 2,200 h.p. Napier Sabre IIA inline.
Span: 41 ft. 7 in.
Length: 31 ft. 11 in.
Height: 15 ft. 3½ in.
Weight Empty: 8,840 lb.
Loaded: 11,250 lb.
No. in crew: One.
Max. Speed: 417 m.p.h. at 20,500 ft.
Service Ceiling: 35,200 ft.
Max. Range: 980 miles.
Armament: Four 20 mm. Hispano cannon; two 500 lb. or 1,000 lb. bombs or eight R.P.

Heinkel He 111

Country of origin: **GERMANY**
Purpose: **Medium bomber.**

Makers: **Ernst Heinkel A.G.**
In operational use: **1939/45.**

The Heinkel He 111 was designed, ostensibly as a civil transport, in 1935, but in 1936 the He 111B was delivered to the Luftwaffe and by the following year it had joined in the Spanish Civil War. Succeeding the B series were the DB 600-powered He 111D and the Jumo 211-engined He 111E. The He 111P (DB 601) was the next major version, entering service some six months before the outbreak of the Second World War. The He 111P first introduced the asymmetrically-placed "bubble" housing the nose machine gun that was a trade mark of all later He 111s. Despite a wide variety of P sub-types, production of this series was not extensive, and in 1939 it began to be superseded by the more promising Jumo-powered He 111H. The bomber's successful evasion of the second-rate Spanish opposition had led the Luftwaffe to bank on sending it against Britain with little or no protective escort; but in the Battle of Britain the He 111 took a considerable hammering. Panic build-up of armour and guns did little to alleviate matters, and the He 111 was diverted to such less hazardous duties as night bombing, minelaying and torpedo-carrying—proving quite successful at the last-named. By the middle of the war the He 111 was obsolescent, but the lack of success of its potential replacements, notably the He 177 (see page 97), necessitated keeping it in production well into 1944. Versions produced during this time included the He 111H-6, H-16, H-20 and H-23—the last of these reverting to the transport role as a paratroop carrier. He 111s were also used for such lesser duties as the carriage of Hs 293 and FZG-76 flying bombs and for glider towing. In the latter category was the "Siamese" He 111Z Zwilling (Twin), twelve of which were produced. This consisted of two He 111H-6 aircraft, joined wing to wing by a new "centre section" bearing a fifth Jumo 211 and spanning 115 ft. 6 in. overall.

BRIEF TECHNICAL DETAILS
(He 111H-6):
Engines: Two 1,340 h.p. Junkers Jumo 211F-2 inlines.
Span: 74 ft. 1¾ in. Length: 54 ft. 5½ in.
Height: 13 ft. 9 in.
Weight Empty: 14,400 lb.
  Loaded: 25,000 lb.
No. in crew: Five.
Max. Speed: 258 m.p.h. at 16,400 ft.
Service Ceiling: 25,500 ft.
Max. Range: 1,740 miles.
Armament: One 20 mm. MG FF cannon, five 7.9 mm. MG 15 and one 7.9 mm. MG 17 machine guns. Up to 5,510 lb. of bombs.

He 115C-1/H. J. Nowarra

Heinkel He 115

Country of origin: **GERMANY**
Purpose: **Reconnaissance and anti-shipping.**

Makers: **Ernst Heinkel A.G.**
In operational use: **1939/45.**

Designed in 1937, the first prototype Heinkel He 115V1, bearing the civil registration D-AEHF, set up on 20th March, 1938, eight world speed records for its class by achieving a speed of 204.93 m.p.h. over 1,000 km. and 2,000 km. courses with various payloads.   These attempts were rewarded by orders for Heinkel to supply a number of aircraft of the type for the use of the Norwegian and Swedish air forces, this export version being designated He 115A-2. Meanwhile, the He 115A-0, He 115A-1 and He 115B were put into product-

ion for the German Naval air arm, and by the outbreak of the Second World War a number of He 115s were already in service, employed primarily on sea-going reconnaissance duties. Later missions of the He 115, including the He 115C and E which followed the B into production, included torpedo bombing and mine laying, and this aircraft was in fact the first to be adapted to carry the new magnetic sea mine.   In co-operation with U-boat squadrons, He 115s were active in harassing convoys in the English Channel when the Battle of Britain was at its peak.   A total of over 300 He 115s were built.

BRIEF TECHNICAL DETAILS
(He 115B):

Engines: Two 900 h.p. BMW 132N radials.
Span: 75 ft. 10 in.
Length: 57 ft. 0 in.
Height: 23 ft. 4 in.
Weight Empty: 14,748 lb.
       Loaded: 22,928 lb.
No. in crew: Four.
Max. Speed: 196 m.p.h. at 11,150 ft.
Service Ceiling: 17,060 ft.
Normal Range: 1,305 miles
Armament: Two 7.9 mm. MG 15 machine guns. Up to 2,200 lb. of bombs, mines or torpedos.

Captured He 177A-5 in British markings /I.W.M.

Heinkel He 177 Greif *(Griffin)*

Country of origin: **GERMANY**   *Makers:* **Ernst Heinkel A.G.**
Purpose: **Heavy bomber.**   *In operational use:* **1942/45.**

In 1938 the German Air Ministry called for a multi-range heavy bomber suited to anti-shipping operations. Heinkel's design featured many advanced proposals, including coupled engines—two mounted side by side, and driving a single propeller shaft, in each nacelle—and remote-control gun positions. The latter notion was soon abandoned in favour of manned turrets, and this and heavier structural alterations (arising out of attempts to stress this huge aircraft for *dive* bombing!) made considerable inroads upon the He 177's original optimistic performance estimate. The idea and design work behind the He 177 were good, but there its merits ended. Troublesome in the extreme, and heartily disliked by its crews, it was pushed into operational service before half its worst vices had been overcome. No other heavy bomber was produced by Germany during the Second World War, though whether the career of the He 177 had any influence on subsequent heavy bomber policy is a matter for conjecture. The first prototype, powered by two 2,600 h.p. DB 606 (coupled DB 601) motors, made its maiden flight in November 1939 and was soon in trouble from engine heating; the second and fourth machines broke up in the air; the engines of the fifth caught fire and crashed the aircraft; and similar troubles with later prototypes rapidly, though justifiably, earned the He 177 the unwelcome nickname of " Flaming Coffin ". Yet, despite its untrustworthy powerplants and other shortcomings, work proceeded on the pre-production 177A-0 and production 177As. Recommended engine modifications, which would probably have solved many of the aircraft's initial problems, were unaccountably ignored until several hundred aircraft had been completed and put into service, by which time more had been lost through engine fires than in combat. The twin-finned He 177B-5 entered priority production in May 1944, but two months later this was stopped and the few B series aircraft completed never saw service. Altogether, over 1,000 He 177s of all variants were built.

BRIEF TECHNICAL DETAILS
(He 177A-5):
Engines: Two 2,950 h.p. Daimler-Benz
   DB 610A (coupled DB 605A) inlines
   in annular cowlings.
Span: 103 ft. 2 in.   *Length:* 72 ft. 0 in.
Height: 21 ft. 10 in.
Weight Empty: 37,000 lb.
   Loaded: 68,500 lb. (max.)
No. in crew: Six.
Max. Speed: 295 m.p.h. at 17,000 ft.
Service Ceiling: 26,500 ft.
Range: 2,260 miles.
Armament: Two 20 mm. MG 151 cannon, three to five 13 mm. MG 131 and one 7.9 mm. MG 81 machine guns. Up to 13,225 lb. of bombs.

97

II-2, two-seat version/*via Jean Alexander*

Ilyushin II-2

Country of origin: **RUSSIA**   *Design bureau:* **S. V. Ilyushin.**
Purpose: **Ground attack.**   *In operational use:* **1941/45.**

Perhaps the most famous aircraft to appear in the ranks of the Red Air Force during World War 2, the II-2 introduced a new word into the parlance of ground attack and close support operations: *Shturmovik*. This aeroplane was specifically designed for such missions, and made its service début in 1941 as a single-seater. It was well armed—two 20 mm. cannon and two 7.62 mm. machine guns—and well armoured, with plating behind, beneath and each side of the pilot. Despite this protection, however, the II-2 proved vulnerable to attack from the rear, and in 1942 a new version appeared in which the cockpit enclosure was lengthened to accommodate a second crew member operating an additional 12.7 mm. gun for rearward defence.

This modification proved eminently successful, and the II-2 finished the war with the lowest attrition rate of any Russian aircraft, not to mention an excellent record of ground strafing, " train-busting " and similar missions —in which, incidentally, it was one of the first wartime aircraft to make use of the rocket projectile. The data refer to the two-seat version.

BRIEF TECHNICAL DETAILS:
Engine: One 1,600 h.p. Mikulin AM-38F inline.
Span: 47 ft. 10 in.
Length: 38 ft. 0 in.
Weight Loaded: 12,250 lb.
No. in crew: Two.
Max. Speed: 257 m.p.h. at 6,560 ft.
Armament: Two 20 mm. cannon, one 12.7 mm. and two 7.62 mm. machine guns; up to 880 lb. of bombs or eight 56 lb. R.Ps.

Ilyushin Il-4

Country of origin: **RUSSIA**
Purpose: **Long range medium bomber.**

Design bureau: **S.V. Ilyushin.**
In operational use: **1941/45.**

This aircraft, a standard medium bomber type of the Red Air Force throughout World War 2, was a development of the DB-3 (alias ZKB-26) which appeared in 1936. During that year the DB-3 was successful in establishing a number of height-with-load records in its class, and was subsequently ordered into large scale production. The most widely used wartime version was that originally known as the DB-3F, to which the data below apply; thanks to their excellent range, aircraft of this type achieved the distinction of being the first Soviet aircraft to bomb Berlin. Although it was produced originally as a straight-forward bomber, the Il-4 subsequently achieved almost equal success as a torpedo bomber, particularly in the Baltic area. The final service version, despite the higher power of its M-82 engines (1,600 h.p. each), had a rather lower performance than its predecessor, but was capable of carrying a greatly enhanced bomb load (up to a maximum of 5,950 lb.). Alternative loads included a 2,200 lb. sea mine or a 2,070 lb. 18-in. torpedo. Armament was increased to one 12.7 mm. Beresin and four 7.62 mm. guns. The Il-4 remained in service after the end of the war, though in its latter days it was primarily employed on aircrew training or glider towing.

BRIEF TECHNICAL DETAILS:

Engines: Two 1,100 h.p. M-88 radials.
Span: 70 ft. 2 in.
Length: 47 ft. 6 in.
No. in crew: Three or four.
Max. Speed: 265 m.p.h. at 20,000 ft.
Service ceiling: 30,700 ft.
Max. Range: 2,500 miles.
Armament: Three 7.62 mm. machine guns and up to 4,400 lb. of bombs or one 18-in. torpedo.

Junkers Ju 52/3m

Country of origin: **GERMANY**
Purpose: **General purpose transport and glider tug.**

Makers: **Junkers Flugzeug und Motorenwerke A.G.**
In operational use: **1939/45.**

The first Ju 52 was a single-engined freighter, appearing in 1930. The more familiar trimotor Ju 52/3m appeared two years later, when large numbers were built for Deutsche Luft Hansa and foreign civil operators, particularly in South America. They were first put to use by the new Luftwaffe as bombers when they formed the core of the "heavy" squadrons, and they were initially used in this role in the Spanish Civil War. However, with the arrival of more specialised bombing types, the Ju 52/3m was soon discarded as a bomber and turned into a military transport. Although it was a "sitter" for fighters, and its losses were heavy, the Ju 52/3m was otherwise very successful in its new role and took part in invasions and advances by the Wehrmacht in many theatres of war, including Libya, Crete and the Low Countries. In April 1940 it figured in the first large-scale use of air transport in a war when it took part in the invasion of Norway.

"Iron Annie", as the Ju 52/3m was popularly known, remained in quantity production almost to the end of hostilities despite the emergence of several potential replacements. Among these were Junkers' own Ju 252, built only in small numbers, and Ju 352, both of which are mentioned on page 207. Total production of the type, including a number built under licence in Spain, reached 3,500 aircraft. They still serve on transport duties with the Spanish Air Force, and a few served briefly, in the immediate post-war years, with British European Airways.

BRIEF TECHNICAL DETAILS:
Engines: Three 830 h.p. BMW 132T radials.
Span: 95 ft. 10 in.
Length: 62 ft. 0 in.
Height: 14 ft. 10 in.
Weight Empty: 14,325 lb.
　　Loaded: 24,200 lb. (max. overload).
No. in crew: Two or three (plus up to 18 troops).
Max. Speed: 165 m.p.h. at sea level.
Service Ceiling: 18,000 ft.
Normal Range: 800 miles.
Armament: One 13 mm. MG 131 and two 7.9 mm. MG 15 machine guns.

Ju 87D-1/Archiv Schliephake

Junkers Ju 87

Country of origin: **GERMANY**
Purpose: **Dive bomber and ground attack.**

Makers: **Junkers Flugzeug und Motorenwerke A.G.**
In operational use: **1939/45.**

Releasing its bombs from a near-vertical dive, its Jumo engine screaming like a banshee, the psychological effect created by this ugly, awkward, vulture-like aeroplane succeeded in weaving around it a reputation far in excess of its actual powers. Commonly called the Stuka—an abbreviation of the term " Sturz-kampfflugzeug " applied to all dive bombers—the Ju 87 was, technically, not a particularly good aeroplane: it was slow, cumbersome, and wide open to fighter attack. Nevertheless, in the early stages of the war it was remarkably successful, screaming and bombing its way through Poland, France and the Low Countries against little or no opposition. In the Battle of Britain, however, against sterner resistance from R.A.F. fighters, large numbers were shot down. The Ju 87V1, featuring a twin-fin tail unit, flew in 1935 with a Rolls-Royce Kestrel powerplant, followed in 1936 by the single-finned Ju 87V2 with a Jumo engine. Within another year, the Ju 87A had entered production for the Luftwaffe, giving way in turn to the improved Ju 87B (1,100 h.p. Jumo 211) in 1938. The B series remained in quantity production for some two years, during which time large numbers were supplied to Germany's allies as well as to the Luftwaffe. The designation Ju 87C applied to a handful of Ju 87Bs converted for the never-finished carrier " Graf Zeppelin ". Meanwhile, the availability of the improved Jumo 211J had led the Junkers designers to modify the Ju 87 with a view to utilising this engine. The result appeared in 1940 in the form of the Ju 87D—still ugly, but much more refined aerodynamically, with cleaner cockpit and cowling lines. The Ju 87D-3 and D-4, with various alternative underwing gun packs, marked the first specialised use of the type in the ground attack role. The Ju 87G (the F was not produced) was an anti-tank conversion of the long-span D-5, with two 37 mm. underwing cannon; the Ju 87H was a two-seat trainer. Like other early Luftwaffe aircraft, the Ju 87 was compelled to serve long after it had become obsolete, because of the non-arrival of a successful replacement. Remaining in production until late 1944, something like 5,000 examples of the various sub-types were built.

BRIEF TECHNICAL DETAILS
(Ju 87D-1)
Engine: One 1,400 h.p. Junkers Jumo 211J-1 inline.   *Span:* 45 ft. 3¼ in.
Length: 37 ft. 8¾ in. *Height:* 12 ft. 9 in.
Weight Empty: 6,085 lb.
    Loaded: 12,600 lb.
No. in crew: Two.
Max. Speed: 255 m.p.h. at 13,500 ft.
Service Ceiling: 24,000 ft.
Normal Range: 620 miles.
Armament: Two 7.9 mm. MG 81 and two 7.9 mm. MG 17 machine guns. Up to 3,960 lb. of bombs or additional underwing MG 81 or MG 151 cannon.

101

Ju 88D-0/*Archiv Schliephake*

Junkers Ju 88

Country of origin: **GERMANY**
Purpose: **Bomber, fighter, ground attack and reconnaissance.**

Makers: **Junkers Flugzeug und Motorenwerke A.G.**
In operational use: **1939/45.**

Conceived in 1935 in response to an official requirement for a high-speed medium bomber, the Junkers Ju 88 was to become the most versatile and widely produced German bomber of World War 2. Although far from being the only German aeroplane to perform tasks for which it was not originally intended, few were " misemployed " with such success. The prototype Ju 88V1 flew just before Christmas 1936, only eleven months after design work commenced, being powered by a pair of 900 h.p. DB 600 inline engines in annular cowlings. The next year or two saw the completion of further prototypes and–as with many other Luftwaffe aircraft of this period—a World record or two by the new aeroplane. Production of the first bomber series commenced in 1938, and Ju 88A-1s, together with the few A-0 pre-production machines, were in service at the outbreak of war. With two 1,200 h.p. Jumo 211B engines, the Ju 88A-1 had a top speed of 286 m.p.h. and a normal bomb load of 3,960 lb., most of which was carried externally. The A-1, the generally-similar A-2 and the A-3 trainer all had a wing span of 59 ft. 10¾in., but this and several other details were modified, in the light of operational experience, in the Ju 88A-4. The span was increased by six feet, considerable extra gunnery was installed, the bomb load was almost doubled; and in 1942 the A-4/R adopted the 1,410 h.p. Jumo 211J as its powerplant. Many later A sub-types were completed, including the A-5 (produced *before* the A-4 but having the same wing and bomb load), the A-8 with balloon-cable gear, the A-12 dual control trainer, the A-13 ground attack and the A-17 torpedo bomber. Parallel with production of the A series, Junkers developed the Ju 88B around a pair of Jumo 213As; this series did not achieve full production, though the new nose of the B-1 was reflected in the later Ju 188, for which another B sub-type acted as prototype. In order to maintain performance of the Ju 88 against that of later designs, Junkers engineers began an extensive reorientation in the middle war years, from which emerged the Ju 88S bombers. Powered by two BMW 801G radial engines of 1,700 h.p. each, the S-1 featured a smoothly-rounded nose, no " gondola ", and drastically-reduced bomb load and defensive armament; the S-2 and S-3 were generally similar except for engine and gunnery changes and a bulged bomb bay in the S-2. Altogether more than 9,000 bomber versions of the Ju 88 were built.

Parallel with the development of the Junkers Ju 88 as a medium bomber, the type was also being adapted to a variety of other roles, particularly those of night fighter, close support and reconnaissance. Approximately 6,000 non-bomber versions of the Ju 88 were built, and the length and diversity of this aeroplane's career make an interesting comparison with the British de Havilland Mosquito. The first Ju 88 fighter to enter series production was the Ju 88C, comparable with the A bomber and powered by Jumo 211 inline or BMW 801 radial motors. The Ju 88C-1 featured the shorter-span wing of the early As, but from the C-2 onwards the extended wing of the Ju 88A-4 was employed. The early Cs carried a crew of three and an armament, in a " solid " nose, of three 7.9 mm. machine guns and one 20 mm. cannon, with two further 20 mm. cannon in a detachable mounting below the nose. Provision was made for 1,100 lb. of bombs internally, which could be replaced by an extra fuel tank. From the C was developed the Ju 88G, a specialist night fighter carrying an additional crew member, which entered service in 1944. Another " parallel " to the A-4 bomber appeared as the long range reconnaissance Ju 88D-1, with fuel and cameras in the bomb bay and further fuel in underwing drop tanks. Altogether, nearly 2,000 D-1, -2 and -3 aircraft were built. Another long range model was the Ju 88H, both the H-1 (reconnaissance) and the H-2 (fighter) having a 58 ft. fuselage. Several Ju 88H aircraft ended their days as the lower half of a " Mistel " composite, with a Bf 109 or Fw 190 fighter on top of the fuselage. The ubiquitous A-4 lent itself to yet another specialised development in the Ju 88P anti-tank aircraft which carried a heavy calibre cannon (two smaller ones in the case of the P-2) in a special housing under the fuselage. The final photographic reconnaissance variant, the Ju 88T, was a development of the S bomber.

With total production, of all types, reaching more than 15,000 aircraft, whose duties included bombing, dive bombing, minelaying, torpedo-carrying, photographic reconnaissance, day fighter, night fighter, ground attack and operational trainer, the Junkers Ju 88 was one of the truly outstanding aeroplanes on either side during World War 2.

BRIEF TECHNICAL DETAILS

(Ju 88A-4/R):
Engines: Two 1,410 h.p. Junkers Jumo 211J-1 inlines in "radial" cowlings.
Span: 65 ft. 10½ in.
Length: 47 ft. 1½ in.
Height: 15 ft. 11 in.
Weight Empty: 18,965 lb.
    Loaded: 26,700 lb.
No. in crew: Four.
Max. Speed: 273 m.p.h. at 17,500 ft.
Service Ceiling: 27,880 ft.
Normal Range: 1,550 miles.
Armament: Various combinations of 20 mm. MG FF cannon, 13 mm. MG 131 and 7.9 mm. MG 81 machine guns. Up to 3,960 lb. of bombs.

(Ju 88C-6):
Engines: Two 1,410 h.p. Junkers Jumo 211J inlines in "radial" cowlings.
Span: 65 ft. 10½ in.
Length: 47 ft. 1½ in.
Height: 16 ft. 7½ in.
Weight Empty: 18,871 lb.
    Loaded: 26,125 lb.
No. in crew: Three.
Max. Speed: 311 m.p.h. at 19,685 ft.
Service Ceiling: 32,480 ft.
Max. Range: 2,130 miles.
Armament: Three 20 mm. MG FF and two 20 mm. MG 151 cannon, one 13 mm. MG 131 and three 7.9 mm. MG 17 machine guns.

Ju 88S-1

Junkers Ju 188

Country of origin: **GERMANY**
Purpose: **Bomber and reconnaissance.**

Makers: **Junkers Flugzeug und Motorenwerke A.G.**
In operational use: **1942/45.**

The Junkers Ju 188 was a logical " stretch " of the basic Ju 88, and was first flown in prototype form in the latter half of 1940. It was characterised by its large, bulbous " glasshouse " of a nose and its new pointed-tip wing spanning 72 ft. 2 in. In 1941 the first major version, the Ju 188E-1, entered production; powered by two 1,700 h.p. BMW 801G radial motors and carrying up to 6,600 lb. of bombs, it was in operational service the following year together with its reconnaissance counterpart, the Ju 188F, which was similar. Following these came the Ju 188A, which had been awaiting the availability of the powerplant originally intended, the 1,776 h.p. Junkers Jumo 213A. Apart from the engine change and a reduced bomb load, the Ju 188A-1 and A-2 were largely similar to the E series although slightly faster. An experimental bomber development of the A model was the Ju 188C, featuring a remote-control tail turret containing two 13 mm. MG 131 machine guns; although this model did not achieve production status, a development of it was built in small numbers as the Ju 188G. The Ju 188D was a fully-armed reconnaissance counterpart to the Ju 188A bomber; the Ju 188H a further reconnaissance project, based on the G, which did not materialise. Other developments that were soon abandoned were the Ju 188M, for long-range reconnaissance, the night fighter Ju 188R and the photographic Ju 188T. The last operational version, the Ju 188S, was a fast, high-altitude bomber with quite an impressive performance. Possessing a pressurised and more streamlined crew cabin, and powered by two 1,750 h.p. Jumo 213E engines, the Ju 188S had a service ceiling above 38,000 feet and was unarmed, relying on its high speed (nearly 430 m.p.h.) to evade pursuit. The Ju 188S was also adapted for low-level work, one version of the S-1 having a ventrally-mounted 50 mm. BK 5 cannon for ground attack missions.

BRIEF TECHNICAL DETAILS
(Ju 188A-1):
Engines: Two 1,776 h.p. Junkers Jumo 213A inlines in radial cowlings.
Span: 72 ft. 2 in.
Length: 49 ft. 0 in.
Height: 17 ft. 8 in.
Weight Loaded: 31,970 lb.
No. in crew: Four.
Max. Speed: 325 m.p.h. at 20,500 ft.
Service Ceiling: 33,000 ft.
Max. Range: 1,550 miles.
Armament: One 20 mm. MG 151 cannon, two 13 mm. MG 131 and two 7.9 mm. MG 81 machine guns. Up to 3,000 lb. of bombs.

104

Ju 290A-5/*Archiv Schliephake*

Junkers Ju 290

Country of origin: **GERMANY**
Purpose: **Maritime patrol bomber and transport.**

Makers: **Junkers Flugzeug und Motorenwerke A.G.**
In operational use: **1941/45.**

The Junkers Ju 290 was a progressive development of the pre-war Ju 90 civil transport, and was occasionally referred to by the alternative designation of Ju 90S. First flown in 1941, the prototype Ju 290V1 was the Ju 90V7 re-engined with four BMW 801 motors. Proposed as a successor to the Fw 200C, the Ju 290 did not in fact achieve this distinction, although it was encountered operationally in some numbers over the Mediterranean and the Atlantic. As an anti-shipping aircraft it could carry a range of weapons, including a pair of Henschel Hs 293 glider bombs. Somewhat under-powered for a heavy bomber, it was later switched to reconnaissance and transport duties. The Ju 290A-1 served first in the transport role, a number being converted in 1943 for reconnaissance; other A sub-types were also used on seagoing duties, including U-boat co-operation missions. In the transport role the Ju 290 could accommodate about 40 fully-armed troops. The Ju 290B was a more heavily armed bomber project with a strengthened fuselage and modified nose; the Ju 290C was similar, but with a powerplant of BMW 801E engines, and was another transport-reconnaissance variant. The Ju 290D long range bomber did not enter production, and the Ju 290E was a later night bomber development based on the 290C.

> **BRIEF TECHNICAL DETAILS**
> **(Ju 290A-8):**
> *Engines:* Four 1,600 h.p. BMW 801L-2 radials.
> *Span:* 138 ft. 0 in.
> *Length:* 92 ft. 6 in.
> *Weight Loaded:* 88,000 lb.
> *No. in crew:* Four to six.
> *Max. Speed:* 280 m.p.h. at 18,000 ft.
> *Service Ceiling:* 19,700 ft.
> *Max. Range:* 3,785 miles.
> *Armament:* Three 20 mm. MG 151 cannon and two 7.9 mm. MG 81 machine guns.

105

Kawanishi NIK2-J Shiden
(Violet Lightning)

Country of origin: **JAPAN**
Purpose: **Fighter and fighter-bomber.**

Designers: **Kawanishi Kokuki K.K.**
In operational use: **1944/45.**

Possessing a somewhat unusual background for a land-based fighter (it was developed from the N1K1 *Rex* floatplane—page 209), the Shiden in its final service form was one of the best Japanese naval fighters of the war. Its success, however, was not achieved without some early setbacks. Design work began in November 1942; by the end of July 1943 four prototypes had been completed, and by the end of 1943 it was in production as the N1K1-J. Known to the Allies as *George* 11, the N1K1-J was met in growing numbers in most Pacific theatres from the early part of 1944. Kawanishi and Himeji combined to produce 1,007 machines of this model, with one of three standard armaments: two 7.7 mm. fuselage guns and four 20 mm. cannon (two in, two under, the wings) in the N1K1-J; the four cannon only in the -Ja; and four cannon within the wings of the -Jb. Later modifications included a ventral bomb attachment, and a few aircraft were experimentally equipped with a booster rocket. Meanwhile, the parent company had recast and simplified the original design, resulting in the excellent N1K2-J Shiden-Kai (*George* 21) which possessed, as did many Japanese fighter aircraft, an extremely rapid climb rate and first-class manoeuvrability. It employed only two-thirds as many constructional parts as the N1K1-J, reducing all-up weight by nearly 500 lb., and differed considerably in appearance from its predecessor. The latter's mid-wing gave way to a low-mounted one, the fuselage was streamlined and extended, and the fin and rudder re-shaped. Orders for a small prototype batch—the first of which flew on 31st December 1943—quickly materialised, but, despite the sharing of production among eight different assembly plants, B-29 raids on Japanese industrial targets restricted the number of Shiden-Kais completed to 428. Other projected fighter developments had not attained production status before Japan surrendered, though a few N1K2-K two-seat trainers were completed.

BRIEF TECHNICAL DETAILS (NIK2-J):

Engine: One 1,990 h.p. Nakajima Homare 21 radial.
Span: 39 ft. 4 in.
Length: 30 ft. 8 in.
Height: 13 ft. 0 in.
Weight Empty: 5,858 lb.
       Loaded: 9,039 lb.
No. in crew: One.
Max. Speed: 369 m.p.h. at 18,370 ft.
Service Ceiling: 35,300 ft.
Normal Range: 1,066 miles.
Armament: Four 20 mm. cannon; two 550 lb. bombs optional.

Kawasaki Ki.45 Toryu (Dragon Slayer)

Country of origin: **JAPAN**
Purpose: **Night fighter and ground attack.**

Designers: **Kawasaki Kokuku Kogyo K.K.**
In operational use: **1942/45.**

The Ki.45—code name *Nick*—was one of the most successful aircraft to be employed on night fighting duties by the Japanese Army Air Force. Its origins can be traced back to the Ki.38 design produced by Kawasaki at the J.A.A.F's request in 1937, although so many modifications were called for by the Army that the revised design was re-titled Ki.45. Six prototypes of the latter were completed and tested, during which difficulties were encountered with the undercarriage mechanism and disappointing results achieved with the Ha. 20B engines originally chosen to power the aircraft. In the spring of 1940 the J.A.A.F. decided to install the more reliable Ha.25 in three of the prototypes. Although tests with these and subsequent Ha.25-powered machines were not entirely satisfactory, with further modifications the type finally entered production in October 1941 as the Ki.45-KAI, officially rated as a " heavy " fighter. The higher-powered Ha.102 engine, evolved from the Ha.25, seemed to offer better performance results, and from mid-1942 this was installed as the standard powerplant in production Ki.45s. The Toryu carried a formidable armament, and various permutations of gunnery were employed, one version mounting a 75 mm. cannon for shipping attacks; most models included 37 mm. cannon. An improved model, with uprated engines, was begun in 1942 under the designation Ki.45-II; this subsequently developed into the Ki.96 single-seat heavy fighter, a promising project which was, however, eventually abandoned—although components of it were later utilised in the Ki.102 *Randy* attack aircraft (page 211). The Toryu was widely used in the south-west Pacific and in the defence of the Japanese mainland, and was one of the types used for suicide attacks employed in the later war years. Total production, including prototypes, amounted to 1,698 machines.

> **BRIEF TECHNICAL DETAILS**
> **(Ki.45-KAIc):**
> *Engines:* Two 1,080 h.p. Mitsubishi Ha.102 Type I radials.
> *Span:* 49 ft. 5¼ in.
> *Length:* 36 ft. 1 in.
> *Height:* 12 ft. 1¾ in.
> *Weight Empty:* 8,818 lb.
>   *Loaded:* 12,125 lb.
> *No. in crew:* Two.
> *Max. Speed:* 340 m.p.h. at 22,965 ft.
> *Service Ceiling:* 32,810 ft.
> *Max. Range:* 932 miles.
> *Armament:* One 37 mm. and two 20 mm. cannon.

Kawasaki Ki.61 Hien *(Swallow)*

Country of origin: **JAPAN**
Purpose: **Fighter and fighter-bomber.**

Designers: **Kawasaki Kokuku Kogyo K.K.**
In operational use: **1942/45.**

Due to the complete absence of inline-engined fighters in J.A.A.F. service, and the extensive numbers in which it was first met, the Ki.61 (*Tony*) fighter was at first believed to be a licence-built version of the Messerschmitt Bf 109. Captured examples soon disproved this belief, although the Ha.40 engine with which the Hien was powered was a lightweight Japanese adaptation of the German DB601, and the fighter initially made extensive use of the Mauser MG151 cannon. The first of a dozen Ki.61 prototypes was flown in December 1941, and as the Ki.61-I the type went into production shortly afterwards; it began to reach J.A.A.F. squadrons in the late summer of 1942. Armament was steadily improved on successive production batches, but with the failure of supplies of the German guns Japanese-built 20 mm. cannon were introduced with the Ki.61-Ic. The Ki.61-Id had 30 mm. wing guns. Successive Ki.61-1 models remained in production until early 1945, but meanwhile, in the autumn of 1942, development had begun of the Ki.61-II. Powered by the 1,500 h.p. Ha.140, this model featured a larger wing and modified cockpit canopy; powerplant difficulties, however, limited the number completed to eight. A complete redesign was undertaken for the Ki.61-II-KAI, and 99 of these were built as Ki.61-IIa and -IIb. The Ki.61-III project, featuring a cut-down rear fuselage with an all-round vision cockpit canopy, did not achieve production status, being superseded by the Ki.100 project described on page 211. Total Ki.61-I and -II production amounted to 2,753 aircraft.

> **BRIEF TECHNICAL DETAILS**
> **(Ki.61-Ic):**
> *Engine:* One 1,175 h.p. Kawasaki Ha.40 Type 2 inline.
> *Span:* 39 ft. 4 in.
> *Length:* 29 ft. 4 in.
> *Height:* 12 ft. 1¾ in.
> *Weight Empty:* 5,798 lb.
> *Loaded:* 7,650 lb.
> *No. in crew:* One.
> *Max. Speed:* 348 m.p.h. at 16,400 ft.
> *Service Ceiling:* 32,800 ft.
> *Max. Range:* 1,185 miles.
> *Armament:* Two 20 mm. cannon and two 12.7 mm. machine guns; two 550 lb. bombs optional.

Lavochkin LaGG-3

Country of origin: **RUSSIA**
Purpose: **Fighter and fighter-bomber.**

Design bureau: **S.A. Lavochkin.**
In operational use: **1941/45.**

When it first made its appearance this aircraft was known under the earlier Russian designation system as the I-22, in which form it made its maiden flight on 30th March 1939. In somewhat modified form it entered production in 1940 as the LaGG-1, the new designation signifying the collaboration with Lavochkin of Gorbunov and Gudkov in the aircraft's design. Production of the LaGG-1 was comparatively limited, however, and after further structural and control refinements—and the testing of a new prototype, the I-301—it was superseded on the assembly lines in 1941 by the improved LaGG-3, remaining in production until mid-1942. Of all-wood construction, the LaGG-3 was an extremely rugged machine, but was not too manoeuvrable and was somewhat underpowered, although still considered superior to its running mate, the MiG-3. It saw widespread service in the early and middle war years before giving way to the later La-5. A variety of standard armaments could be installed, one version being fitted with three 12.7 mm. and two 7.62 mm. guns to act as fighter escort to the Il-2 Shturmovik.

BRIEF TECHNICAL DETAILS:
Engine: One 1,100 h.p. Klimov M-105 inline.
Span: 32 ft. 1¾ in.
Length· 29 ft. 1¼ in.
Height: 8 ft. 10 in.
Weight Empty: 5,776 lb.
  Loaded: 7,032 lb.
No. in crew: One.
Max. Speed: 348 m.p.h. at 16,400 ft.
Service Ceiling: 29,530 ft.
Normal Range: 404 miles.
Armament: One 20 mm. ShVAK cannon, one 12.7 mm. Beresin and two 7.62 mm. ShKAS machine guns; up to 484 lb. of bombs or six R.Ps.

Lavochkin La-5 and La-7

Country of origin: **RUSSIA**
Purpose: **Fighter and fighter-bomber,**

Design bureau: **S.A. Lavochkin.**
In operational use: **1942/45.**

The La-5 resulted from the decision, late in 1941, to improve the performance of the LaGG-3 by installing the more powerful 1,600 h.p. ASh-82A radial engine, and in this form the machine was first flown in the early part of 1942. Tests being satisfactory, the La-5 was quickly placed in production, and the early machines retained the cockpit and rear fuselage construction of the earlier fighter. The design earned Lavochkin the title of Hero of Socialist Labour, and the La-5 made its operational debut at the Battle of Stalingrad in October 1942. Further structural improvements, including a higher-powered version of the ASh-82 and the cutting down of the rear fuselage to improve all-round view from the cockpit, produced the La-5FN in 1943; this version fought in the Battle of Kursk, and was produced in fairly substantial quantities. There also flew in 1943 a further development of the La-5AV, the La-7, which featured a 1,775 h.p. ASh-82FN radial motor and an additional 20 mm. ShVAK cannon; with only slightly higher all-up weight than the La-5FN, the La-7 had a maximum speed of 413 m.p.h. Variants of the La-7 which were not produced in great quantity included the two-seat La-7U reconnaissance and liaison aircraft of 1944 and an interceptor version with a small rocket motor to boost combat speed. An even more refined development was the La-9, whose 1,870 h.p. ASh-82FNV engine raised the maximum speed to 428 m.p.h. at sea level: very few of these become operational before the war ended, but, with the ultimate development, the La-11, they remained in postwar Russian service for several years.

BRIEF TECHNICAL DETAILS (La-5FN):
Engine: One 1,640 h.p. Shvetsov ASh-82FN radial.
Span: 32 ft. 1¾ in.
Length: 27 ft. 10¾ in.
Height: 9 ft. 3 in.
Weight Empty: 6.085 lb.
  Loaded: 7,406 lb.
No. in crew: One.
Max. Speed: 402 m.p.h. at sea level.
Service Ceiling: 36,000 ft.
Max. Range: 528 miles.
Armament: Two 20 mm. ShVAK cannon; 330 lb. of bombs optional.

Lockheed A-28, A-29 and Hudson

Country of origin: **U.S.A.**
Purpose: **Maritime patrol bomber and reconnaissance.**

Makers: **Lockheed Aircraft Corporation.**
Other U.S. designations: **AT-18, PBO-1.**
In operational use: **1939/45.**

The first U.S. aeroplane to see operational service during World War 2, this military development of the Lockheed Model 14 commercial airliner served with the U.S., British, Canadian, Australian, New Zealand, Dutch and Chinese air forces in every theatre of the war. It was originally developed to British requirements, and the first order for 200 (later increased to 350) was placed in June 1938 by the British Purchasing Commission on behalf of the R.A.F., who gave it the name Hudson. The first R.A.F. Hudson I flew on 10th December, 1938, and this version was in service with Coastal Command by the following summer. In addition to over 800 Hudsons purchased by the U.K., some 1,170 more were supplied under Lend-Lease, bringing the total to just over 2,000. Among the achievements of Coastal Command Hudsons were the guiding of the Royal Navy to the German prison ship *Altmark* in February 1940, and the first sinking of a U-boat with rocket projectiles in May 1943. Substantial quantities of this aeroplane were also delivered during 1942 and 1943 to the U.S. forces; most of these were either A-28 (1,050 or 1,200 h.p. Pratt & Whitney Twin Wasps) or A-29 (1,200 h.p. Wright Cyclones) models, the U.S. Navy's PBO-1 corresponding to the A-29. Production ceased with the last U.S.A.A.F. delivery on 30th June, 1943. During the later war years, as more modern types became available, this adaptable machine continued to perform valuable service on such duties as troop transport, training, target towing and air-sea rescue. The AT-18, of which 217 were built, was a target tug equivalent of the A-29A; the AT-18A (83 built) had the dorsal turret removed and was equipped as a navigation trainer.

BRIEF TECHNICAL DETAILS (A-29):
Engines: Two 1,200 h.p. Wright R-1820-87 Cyclone radials.
Span: 65 ft. 6 in.
Length: 44 ft. 4 in.
Height: 11 ft. 10½ in.
Weight Empty: 12,825 lb.
Loaded: 20,500 lb.
No. in crew: Five.
Max. Speed: 253 m.p.h. at 15,000 ft.
Service Ceiling: 26,500 ft.
Max. Range: 2,800 miles.
Armament: Five or seven .30 machine guns; up to 1,400 lb. of bombs.

Lockheed C-56 Lodestar

Country of origin: **U.S.A.**
Purpose: **Transport.**
Makers: **Lockheed Aircraft Corporation.**

Other U.S. designations: **C-57, -59, -60 and -66;
R5O.**
In operational use: **1941/45.**

Although it was never employed in anything like the proportions of the Douglas Skytrain or the Curtiss Commando, the Lodestar nevertheless performed valuable service throughout World War 2 as an executive aircraft, cargo and paratroop transport, ambulance, glider tug and flying laboratory. Like its contemporaries it had its origins in a pre-war commercial airliner, the Lockheed Model 18 Lodestar, and many of the early examples employed were actually civil machines acquired and adapted for military service. All of the C-56 series, through to the C-56E, were thus acquired; the sole C-56A differed in having Hornet engines, and all could accommodate 18 passengers except the C-56E, which was normally a 22-seater. There were only seven effective C-57s, designated C-57B, which were 18-seat troopers; the acquisition of civil models as C-57As was cancelled, and the three C-57C and one C-57D were test aircraft. Ten C-59s and 36 C-60s were again civil conversions. Military production of the Lodestar centred on the C-60A, 325 of which were built as standard Army/Navy paratroop transports; an order for 691 C-60C, an improved version, was subsequently cancelled. The U.S. Navy counterparts to the C-56, C-59, C-60 and C-60A were designated R5O-1, -2, -5 and -6; the R5O-3 and -4 were respectively four- and seven-seat executive aircraft. One further civil Lodestar was impressed for military service as the C-66. A number of C-56, C-59 and C-60 Lodestars were supplied to the R.A.F. as the Lodestar I, IA and II, equipping four Transport Command squadrons in the Middle East for ambulance and general transport duties. With the increase in the numbers of mass-produced military transports available towards the end of the war, many of the requisitioned airliner models were returned to their civil owners, and very few of these conversions remained in service beyond the end of 1944.

Lockheed P-38 Lightning

Country of origin: **U.S.A.**
Purpose: Long range fighter and fighter-bomber.

Makers: **Lockheed Aircraft Corporation.**
Other U.S. designations: **F-4 and F-5.**
In operational use: **1941/45.**

Although produced in less numbers than other front-line U.S. fighters of World War 2, the Lightning performed a wide variety of missions in every theatre, and destroyed more Japanese aircraft in the Pacific than any other fighter. Its design began in 1937, to a specification issued in the previous year; the XP-38 flew on 27th January, 1939, but crashed a fortnight later during a landing. Despite this unfortunate start, an order ensued for 13 YP-38 test aircraft, considerably redesigned with 1,150 h.p. Allisons and improved armament. Two contracts, worth 673 aircraft, were placed before mid-1940, and by mid-1941 the YP-38 batch was being followed by 30 P-38 production aircraft. The XP-38A, P-38B and C projects did not materialise, but delivery of 36 P-38D began in August 1941. Succeeding versions of the Lightning included 210 P-38E (modified armament); 527 P-38F (1,325 h.p. Allison, first version with underwing racks for fuel tanks, torpedos or 1,000 lb. bombs); 1,082 P-38G (further engine change); 601 P-38H (1,425 h.p. Allison, armament changes and provision for two 1,600 lb. underwing bombs); 2,970 P-38J (further engine and gunnery changes); 3,923 P-38L (introducing underwing R.P. racks); and finally the radar-carrying two-seat P-38M night fighter, which went into service during the closing stages of the Pacific war. Total Lightning production was 9,923, of which over 1,000 were converted into photographic reconnaissance aircraft having a battery of cameras (usually five) in place of the nose guns. These included the F-4 (P-38E), F-4A (P-38F), F-5, -5A and -5B (P-38G), F-5C (P-38H), F-5E and -5F (P-38J) and F-5G (P-38L). A number of P-38J and L Lightnings serving in Europe were converted as " lead ships " with a bombardier accommodated in a lengthened Perspex nose; and some P-38F were converted in 1942 as 2-seat combat trainers. The R.A.F., after taking delivery of three of the 143 P-38E-style Lightning Mk. I ordered, rejected the type and subsequently cancelled an order for 524 Mk. II based on the P-38G. These were taken over by the U.S.A.A.F. for its own use.

BRIEF TECHNICAL DETAILS (P-38L):
Engines: Two 1,475 h.p. Allison V-1710-111/113 inlines.
Span: 52 ft. 0 in.
Length: 37 ft. 10 in.
Height: 9 ft. 10 in.
Weight Empty: 12,800 lb.
    Loaded: 17,500 lb.
No. in crew: One.
Max. Speed: 414 m.p.h. at 25,000 ft.
Service Ceiling: 44,000 ft.
Max. Range: 2,260 miles.
Armament: One 20 mm Hispano cannon and four .50 Browning machine guns; up to 4,000 lb. of bombs or ten 5-in. R.P.

Lockheed PV-1 Ventura

Country of origin: **U.S.A.**
Purpose: **Patrol bomber.**
Makers: **Lockheed Aircraft Corporation.**

Other U.S. designations: **B-34, B-37.**
In operational use: **1942/45.**

A military development of Lockheed's Model 18 Lodestar civil transport, the Ventura was originally produced to meet British requirements for a successor to the Hudson. Initial contracts for the type were placed during the summer of 1940, and the first Ventura Is (1,850 h.p. Double Wasp) began to enter Bomber Command service some two years later. During 1943 these were switched to Coastal Command, for whom the later Ventura II and IIA incorporated various armament and equipment changes and were powered by 2,000 h.p. Double Wasps. Some 400 Venturas I and II were supplied to the R.A.F. A version of the Ventura II was adopted, as the B-34, by the U.S.A.A.F. for coastal patrol, advanced training and target towing, and the 200 B-34s built, subsequently improved to B-34A standard, were followed by a further 133 B-34As and 117 navigation trainer B-34Bs. Of the later B-37 (1,700 h.p. Wright Cyclones) only 18 were completed, the remainder of the 550 order being cancelled. The principal production model of the Ventura, however, was the U.S. Navy's PV-1; some 1,600 of this version were completed. The most obvious difference from earlier Venturas lay in the PV-1's slightly lengthened and "solid" machine-gun nose; the bomb bay was modified for the carriage of bombs, depth charges or a single torpedo, and the aircraft's range was improved by increased fuel capacity. The PV-1, which was still in production in 1944, was used largely in the Pacific theatre, where it was ultimately joined by the later PV-2 Harpoon (see page 213). A number of PV-1s also saw R.A.F. service as the Ventura IV and V.

BRIEF TECHNICAL DETAILS
(PV-1):
Engines: Two 2,000 h.p. Pratt & Whitney R-2800-31 Double Wasp radials.
Span: 65 ft. 6 in.
Length: 51 ft. 9 in.
Height: 13 ft. 2 in.
Weight Empty: 20,197 lb.
Loaded: 26,500 lb.
No. in crew: Four.
Max. Speed: 315 m.p.h. at 15,200 ft.
Service Ceiling: 27,500 ft.
Normal Range: 1,100 miles.
Armament: Six .50 machine guns; up to 3,500 lb. of bombs or depth charges or one 22-in. torpedo.

Macchi C.200 Saetta *(Lightning)*

Country of origin: **ITALY**   Makers: **Aeronautica Macchi.**
Purpose: **Fighter.**   In operational use: **1940/45.**

A product of one of Italy's most illustrious designers, Mario Castoldi, the Macchi C.200 Saetta, like the Spitfire, resulted from a racing seaplane ancestry. As with practically every Italian fighter of the period, the design was excellent and the manoeuvrability and general flying characteristics left little to be desired —except a good engine. The poor battle performance of Italian fighters was due to the lack of aero-engines of sufficient merit; tied to the cumbersome, high-drag, underpowered radial engines which were all the Italian industry could offer, early Regia Aeronautica fighters were unable to produce the performance results for which their design rendered them capable. By the time suitable German engines had been imported and incorporated in these airframes, the war was too far advanced for them to play the part they might have done. The Saetta was designed in 1936, flown in 1937 and ordered into immediate production. At the time of Italy's entry into the war the Regia Aeronautica had received 156 Saettas which, with large numbers of the obsolescent Fiat C.R. 42 biplane (see page 72), formed the backbone of the fighter force. Production C.200s, which were employed on all fronts, were designated C.200A1 and A2, the latter having a C.202-type wing strengthened for the carriage of two small bombs for the fighter-bomber role. An interesting feature of the C.200's development was that the enclosed canopy of the early machines was abandoned on later production aircraft in favour of an open cockpit. About one thousand Saettas altogether were built.

BRIEF TECHNICAL DETAILS:
Engine: One 840 h.p. Fiat A.74 RC 38 radial.
Span: 34 ft. 9 in.
Length: 26 ft. 10 in.
Height: 11 ft. 6 in.
Weight Empty: 4,176 lb.
     Loaded: 5,122 lb.
No. in crew: One.
Max. Speed: 312 m.p.h. at 14,760 ft.
Service Ceiling: 29,190 ft.
Normal Range: 354 miles.
Armament: Two 12.7 mm. Breda-SAFAT machine guns. Two 220 lb. or 352 lb bombs optional.

C.202 Serie III/Italian Air Ministry

Macchi C.202 Folgore *(Thunderbolt)*

Country of origin: **ITALY**   *Makers:* **Aeronautica Macchi.**
Purpose: **Fighter.**   *In operational use:* **1941/45.**

The Macchi C.202 marked the beginning of the phase when, with the availability of high-powered, low-drag liquid cooled Daimler-Benz engines from Germany, Italian fighters attempted to overtake the performance capabilities of their contemporaries. To a large extent this effort was unsuccessful, and really first class performers did not begin to materialise in quantity until Italy's part in the war was nearly over. Nevertheless the advent of the German power-plants provided a very welcome shot in the arm for the Regia Aeronautica's fighter aircraft of the earlier war years. The first DB 601 was supplied to the Macchi company in 1940 and was immediately installed in a standard C.200 Saetta airframe, being flown in that form in August the same year. Flight tests with this machine were highly satisfactory, and parallel with the decision to licence-build the German engine in Italy the DB 601-powered Saetta was put into production under the new designation C.202. Saetta production lines were adapted to the construction of the new fighter and the Folgore entered squadron service in 1941. Armament was progressively improved in the new machine and the general performance was much closer to, though still somewhat below, the best of the opposing Allied fighters. The combination of the C.202 airframe with the DB 605 engine eventually gave rise to the C.205 Veltro which is described on page 214.

BRIEF TECHNICAL DETAILS:
Engine: One 1,200 h.p. licence-built Daimler-Benz DB 601A inline.
Span: 34 ft. 9 in.
Length: 29 ft. 0½ in.
Height: 9 ft. 10 in.
Weight Empty: 4,850 lb.
    Loaded: 6,056 lb.
No. in crew: One.
Max. Speed 369 m.p.h. at 17,056 ft.
Service Ceiling: 34,500 ft.
Normal Range: 475 miles.
Armament: Two 12.7 mm. and two 7.7 mm. Breda-SAFAT machine guns

B-26G

Martin B-26 Marauder

Country of origin: **U.S.A.**
Purpose: **Medium bomber.**
Makers: **Glenn L. Martin Co.**

Other U.S. designations: **JM-1.**
In operational use: **1942/45.**

The Marauder had a somewhat chequered career: in its early days " Widow Maker " was one of the least unpleasant names bestowed on it, and its continued production was in jeopardy at least four times. It had its faults, but in the hands of an experienced pilot was, as it later proved successfully, an excellent weapon, and by the end of the war in Europe Marauders had a lower attrition rate than any other U.S. aircraft. Designed in the early part of 1939, the Marauder was rewarded by an order for 1,100 " off the drawing board " in September of that year. There was, consequently, no XB-26, the first flight being made on 25th November, 1940, by the first of 201 B-26s, powered by two 1,850 h.p. Double Wasp motors. Most of the 139 B-26As which followed had later model—though similar horsepower—engines, but by Pearl Harbour only one U.S. unit was equipped with the type. Three Marauders were sent at this time to the R.A.F. for evaluation, and these were the predecessors of 52 Marauder Is (B-26A), 19 Mk. IA (B-26B), 100 Mk. II (B-26C) and 350 Mk. III (B-26F and G) eventually supplied to the R.A.F. and the South African Air Force, and which were operational from 1943 onwards. Several variations of engine, bomb load, armament and other equipment were found among the 1,883 B-26Bs completed, and tail defence was improved by a twin-gun turret; some of the later B series, with twelve .50 guns, were almost as heavily armed as the B-17 Fortress, and other were completed as B-26Cs, of which model 1,235 were built. The U.S. Navy took on some Marauders for target towing and reconnaissance as the JM-1 and -1P; their later JM-2s were a few of the 57 TB-26Gs produced for the same role in the U.S.A.A.F. Some early B-26 bombers were also converted as AT-23 trainers. The XB-26D, XB-26E and XB-26H were " one-off " research aircraft. Final Marauders were the B-26F (300 built) and B-26G (893 built). Altogether 5,157 Marauders were completed.

BRIEF TECHNICAL DETAILS (B-26G):
Engines: Two 1,920 h.p. Pratt & Whitney R-2800-43 Double Wasp radials.
Span: 71 ft. 0 in.
Length: 56 ft. 1 in.
Height: 20 ft. 4 in.
Weight Empty: 25,300 lb.
    Loaded: 38,200 lb. (max.).
No. in crew: Seven.
Max. Speed: 283 m.p.h. at 5,000 ft.
Service Ceiling: 19,800 ft.
Normal Range: 1,100 miles.
Armament: Eleven .50 machine guns; up to 4,000 lb. of bombs.

117

Messerschmitt Bf 109

Country of origin: **GERMANY**   *Makers:* **Messerschmitt A.G.**
Purpose: **Fighter.**   *In operational use:* **1939/45.**

Professor Willi Messerschmitt joined the Bayerische Flugzeugwerke in 1927, and in 1932, when that company became insolvent, formed the Messerschmitt A.G. to take over its interests.   In 1934, his first design, the Bf 108, appeared; this four-seat cabin monoplane is described on page 216.   The first high-powered inverted Vee liquid-cooled engines, the Junkers Jumo and the Daimler-Benz DB 600, were being developed at about this time, and under the cloak of civilian usage a modified Bf 108 airframe, using the new engine, became in effect a small scale prototype for a fighter.   The first prototype Bf 109 (695 h.p. Rolls-Royce Kestrel) flew in September 1935, followed in 1936 and 1937 by subsequent prototypes fitted with the 610 h.p. Jumo 210A. The Bf 109 followed the familiar civil prototype-record breaker-Spanish War train of development common to so many other German aircraft of the period; Bf 109s won three contests in the military aircraft competitions at Zurich in 1937 and on 11th November that year a machine with a specially boosted DB 601 of 1,650 h.p. set up a new World Air Speed Record of 379.4 m.p.h. which stood for two years.   Meantime, the Bf 109B-1 (635 h.p. Jumo 210D) had entered production to equip the Condor Legion in the Spanish Civil War, being joined later by the Bf 109C.   Experience in this campaign led to further variations, particularly in armament, and in 1939, discarding the Bf 109D after only a small production batch, the Bf 109E entered quantity production, powered by the 1,100 h.p. DB 601A and armed with two 20 mm. cannon and two 7.9 mm. machine guns.   Soon replacing all earlier Bf 109s in Luftwaffe service, the Bf 109E remained the standard single seat fighter for the first three years of the war.   Heavy losses in the Battle of Britain and elsewhere, however, forced the German authorities to con- sider the adaptation of the Bf 109 as a defensive fighter rather than an offensive one.   The result was the Bf 109F (1,200 h.p. DB 601N), which featured a much refined and more streamlined airframe and reduced armament—one 20 mm. cannon and two 7.9 mm. machine guns. (After introduction of the later G

Bf 109G-2s

series, the Fs were adapted to carry underwing R.Ps. and retained in service in the ground attack role.) The next development, the Bf 109G "Gustav", first reported in the summer of 1942 in Russia and North Africa, was thereafter used extensively in all theatres until the capitulation, and was eventually produced in greater numbers than all the other Bf 109 versions put together. The Bf 109G-1 (1,475 h.p. DB 605A) had a pressurised cockpit and an armament of one 20 mm. cannon and two 7.9 mm. machine guns. The DB 605D engine, giving 1,800 h.p. with boost, was fitted to the G-5, which also introduced a modified fin and rudder; the G-6 was more heavily armed, with an engine-mounted 30 mm. MK 108 cannon, two 13 mm. nose machine guns and two 20 mm. cannon in underwing containers. Some G-6s were used as rocket-firing ground attack aircraft. The Bf 109G-8 was a photo-reconnaissance variant with reduced armament, and the designation Bf 109G-12 covered certain G-1 airframes modified as trainers with two-seat cockpits. Later variants included the Bf 109H, a long-span high altitude project which did not enter service (being discarded in favour of the Ta 152H); the Bf 109K, which was generally similar to the G except for minor structural changes, and which saw limited service; and the Bf 109L, a G-type airframe with Junkers Jumo 213 engine and greater span, a project which was unfinished when the war ended. One other interesting variant, which did not see service, was the Bf 109T, a special deck-landing model with increased wing area, adapted from a Bf 109E in 1940.

Bf 109s, originally supplied from Germany in 1937 and subsequently built by the Hispano company, have remained in service to the present day with the Spanish Air Force—now powered, ironically enough, by the very brand of engine that helped shoot them out of the sky in 1940—the Rolls-Royce Merlin!

> **BRIEF TECHNICAL DETAILS**
> **(Bf 109G-10):**
> *Engine:* One 1,800 h.p. (with boost) Daimler-Benz DB 605D inline.
> *Span:* 32 ft. 8½ in.
> *Length:* 29 ft. 4 in.
> *Height:* 7 ft. 8 in.
> *Weight Empty:* 4,330 lb.
>   *Loaded:* 7,700 lb.
> *No. in crew:* One.
> *Max. Speed:* 428 m.p.h. at 24,250 ft.
> *Service Ceiling:* 41,200 ft.
> *Normal Range:* 350 miles.
> *Armament:* One 30 mm. MK 108 cannon firing through the spinner (optional), two 13 mm. MG 131 machine guns on top of the cowling.

Messerschmitt Bf 110

Country of origin: **GERMANY**
Purpose: **Day and night fighter, fighter-bomber.**

Makers: **Messerschmitt A.G.**
In operational use: **1939/45.**

Although in early encounters with British fighters the Bf 110 did not show up too well, it was in continuous service throughout the war, and production ran through six series from B to G. In its various roles, the Bf 110 was extensively used and was a more competent aircraft than many gave it credit for; production was in fact increased following the failure of the later Messerschmitt Me 210, and had it not become such a maid-of-all-work it would probably have had a distinguished career in one of the roles for which it was better suited. It was the first twin-engined military aeroplane designed by Willi Messerschmitt, and was originally projected in 1934, the prototype flying on 12th May, 1936. Some delay occurred in acquiring engines of adequate power, and by the time these were available the Bf 110 was too late for the Spanish Civil War in which many of its contemporaries gathered valuable operational experience. The Bf 110C joined the Luftwaffe early in 1939 and first saw action in Poland, where it served in the ground attack role in support of the invading force. Its first brush with the R.A.F. was against Wellingtons over the Heligoland Bight on the 14th December 1939, but it did not encounter our fighters until the Battle of Britain in the following year, when it was found wanting in several respects. As a result, many Bf 110Cs were adapted to other duties, including bomber interception and glider towing. The Bf 110D-1 was intended as a long range fighter with greatly increased fuel tankage, but did not remain in service long. The Bf 110E was the first major version to figure as a bomber, offensive load of the E-2 reaching a maximum of 4,410 lb; the photo-reconnaissance E-3 was similar except for a reduced armament. The early F series, apart from having higher powered (1,300 h.p.) DB 601s, was again similar, but from the F-4 onwards the Bf 110's potential as a night fighter began to blossom. With the G series, the type reverted temporarily to the fighter-bomber role in 1943, but the G-4 and later models resumed the night fighting mantle in a vain attempt to stem the increasing Allied bomber offensive over Germany.

BRIEF TECHNICAL DETAILS
(Bf 110G-4):
Engines: Two 1,475 h.p. Daimler-Benz DB 605B inlines.
Span: 53 ft. 4¾ in.
Length: 41 ft. 6¾ in.
Height: 13 ft. 1¼ in.
Weight Empty: 11,220 lb.
    Loaded: 20,700 lb.
No. in crew: Three.
Max. Speed: 342 m.p.h. at 22,900 ft.
Service Ceiling: 26,000 ft.
Max. Range: 1,305 miles.
Armament: Two 30 mm. MK 108 and two 20 mm. MG 151 cannon, and two 7.9 mm. MG 81 machine guns.

Me 163B-1 in the Deutsches Museum, Munich

Messerschmitt Me 163B Komet

Country of origin: **GERMANY**
Purpose: **Ultra-short range interceptor.**

Makers: **Messerschmitt A.G.**
In operational use: **1944/45.**

Most unconventional of the reaction-propelled aircraft to go into service with the Luftwaffe in World War 2, the Me 163 was an ultra-short range home defence fighter in which everything was sacrificed to the ability to get up to, and attack, marauding Allied bombers in the shortest possible time. Weight was saved in every possible direction, including the undercarriage, which was jettisoned immediately after take-off. The duration was short—only about 10 minutes on full power—but the Komet could climb to 30,000 feet in 2½ minutes. Due no doubt to the radical nature of its design, and certainly aggravated by professional disagreements among its sponsors, development of the Me 163 was uncommonly troublesome, and although the aircraft made its first powered flight in August 1941 the first Luftwaffe test group was not formed until late in 1944, equipped with the Me 163B-1 (the Me 163A being an unpowered version produced in limited numbers for training purposes). The great speed, climbing and turning performance of the Komet necessitated the forming of new tactics both by its own pilots and those of its adversaries, but among the former the Me 163 rapidly acquired the reputation of being a death-trap. Living rather too literally up to its name, the Komet would often touch down with such force on its landing skid as to ignite any residue of fuel and explode in a ball of fire. More Me 163s were in fact lost in this way than in actual operations. At the time of the capitulation over 350 Me 163s had been built, and projects were in hand for a larger and higher-powered Me 163C. The Me 163D project, with normal retractable undercarriage and greater endurance, was later redesignated Me 263, but did not progress beyond the flight test stage.

BRIEF TECHNICAL DETAILS:
Engine: One 3,750 lb.s.t. Walter HWK 109 liquid rocket motor.
Span: 30 ft. 7 in.
Length: 18 ft. 8 in.
Height: 9 ft. 0 in.
Weight Empty: 4,200 lb.
  Loaded: 9,500 lb.
No. in crew: One.
Max. Speed: 596 m.p.h. at 30,000 ft.
Service Ceiling: 54,000 ft.
Armament: Two 30 mm. MK 108 cannon.

Me 210A-1

Messerschmitt Me 210 and Me 410 Hornisse (*Hornet*)

Country of origin: **GERMANY**
Purpose: **Fighter-bomber and reconnaissance.**

Makers: **Messerschmitt A.G.**
In operational use: **1941/45.**

Fritz Wendel, chief test pilot of the Messerschmitt A.G., said of the Me 210 that it had all the least desirable attributes an aeroplane could possess, and rated it second only to the He 177 (page 97) as the Luftwaffe's greatest failure of the war. Even the redesigned Me 410 "did not fulfil all our hopes". The Me 210, a clean-looking design resembling the de Havilland Mosquito, was first reported in late 1941 on the Russian front, but was not encountered in Western Europe until one was shot down by a Typhoon over the South coast in the summer of 1942. The first production version, the Me 210A, was powered by two 1,395 h.p. DB 601F inlines, these being replaced in the Me 210C by DB 605Bs. Many attempts were made, with different fuselage lengths and various tail arrangements, to reduce the aircraft's shortcomings, but with little avail. In spite of its vices the aircraft was pressed into service as a fighter, ground attack and reconnaissance type, but after a large number of fatal crashes even the RLM was obliged to admit its unsuitability and withdraw it from production. After extensive re-designing, and with twin DB 603s as the new powerplant, the aircraft re-emerged in the latter part of 1942 as the Me 410 Hornisse. The Me 410A was placed in production and began to enter service early in 1943, the principal sub-types being the A-1 fighter-bomber, with provision for a 4,400 lb. bomb load, the A-1/U2 and A-2 "heavy" fighters with two extra 20 mm. guns or one 50 mm. BK 5 cannon in the bomb bay, and the reconnaissance A-3 with cameras and additional fuel in the bomb bay. Total Me 410 production was 1,913 aircraft; together with the Me 210 (325 built), it was used on a far wider scale than its merits really deserved.

BRIEF TECHNICAL DETAILS
(Me 410A-1/U2):

Engines: Two 1,720 h.p. Daimler-Benz DB 603A inlines.
Span: 53 ft. 7¾ in.
Length: 40 ft. 11½ in.
Height: 14 ft. 0½ in.
Weight Empty: 13,550 lb.
        Loaded: 23,500 lb.
No. in crew: Two.
Max. Speed: 388 m.p.h. at 21,980 ft.
Service Ceiling: 32,800 ft.
Armament: Four 20 mm. MG 151 cannon, two 13 mm. MG 131 and two 7.9 mm. MG 17 machine guns.

Me 262 V3

Messerschmitt Me 262A Sturmvogel (Stormbird)

Country of origin: **GERMANY**
Purpose: **Fighter and fighter-bomber.**

Makers: **Messerschmitt A.G.**
In operational use: **1944/45.**

Messerschmitt A.G. were asked in 1938 to design a vehicle around the new turbojet engines then being developed by Junkers and BMW. This they completed the following year, and early in 1940 were authorised to construct a small batch of prototypes. For various reasons the early jet engines were unsuited to the aircraft, and official enthusiasm wavered, but in July 1942, with the emergence of Jumo engines of 1,850 lb. s.t., the Me 262 began to show its true promise as a fighter. The RLM, however, remained convinced that they could win the war with conventional fighters and gave the Me 262 a very low development priority. Despite the success of flight trials and the enthusiasm of his advisers, Hitler refused to sanction quantity production until November 1943, when after a personal demonstration he decided against overwhelming advice to the contrary to go ahead with the type as a bomber. Series production of the Me 262A-1 Schwalbe (*Swallow*)—as a fighter—began in May 1944, but when Hitler discovered this a month or two later he immediately ordered the conversion of those so far built into bombers. The Me 262A-2 Sturmvogel, as the bomber version was known, was fitted to carry two 1,100 lb. bombs or one 2,200 lb.—a factor which immediately cut its speed to a point within reach of Allied piston-engined fighters. This typical piece of Hitlerian pig-headedness cost the Luftwaffe valuable months, when they might have been employing the Me 262 as a fighter, in converting it to a role for which it was quite unsuited.

Ironically, as the result of the war became more and more certain, Hitler gave the Me 262—as a defensive fighter—utter priority over all other aircraft production in Germany; yet of over 1,400 produced, probably only 200 or so were actually operational against the Allies. Other variants built or projected included the Me 262B-1 dual control trainer, the B-2 night fighter, the Me 262C rocket-boosted fighter and the Me 262D and E rocket-armed bomber interceptors.

BRIEF TECHNICAL DETAILS
(Me 262A-1):
Engines: Two 1,980 lb.s.t. Junkers Jumo 004B turbojets.
Span: 40 ft. 11½ in.
Length: 34 ft. 9½ in.
Height: 12 ft. 7 in.
Weight Empty: 9,741 lb.
   Loaded: 14,101 lb.
No. in crew: One.
Max. Speed: 540 m.p.h. at 19,684 ft.
Max. Range: 652 miles.
Service Ceiling: 37,565 ft.
Armament: Four 30 mm. MK 108 cannon.

123

Me 323E-1

Messerschmitt Me 321 Gigant *(Giant)* and Me 323

Country of origin: **GERMANY**   *Makers:* **Messerschmitt A.G.**
Purpose: **Heavy transport.**   *In operational use:* **1942/45.**

One of the largest aeroplanes of the Second World War, with a wing span greater even than the Bv 222 six-engined flying boat, the Messerchmitt Me 321 transport glider was designed towards the end of 1940 and the first prototype tested in March 1941. At that time the only aircraft capable of towing it into the air was the Junkers Ju 90—powered, incidentally, with American engines. Later on, groups of three Bf 110s were used to get the Gigant off the ground, with some further assistance from auxiliary take-off rockets fitted to the glider. Eventually, the problem of a tug powerful enough to tow the Me 321 was solved by the evolution of the composite Heinkel He 111Z (see page 95).

Meanwhile, development of a powered version of the glider was proceeding. The great size and weight of this machine needed plenty of power to get it off the ground, and early trials with four Jumo 211 engines installed did not meet with unqualified success. Finally, an installation of six Gnôme-Rhône motors, developing altogether nearly 6,000 horsepower, was adopted. The powered glider, which first flew late in 1941, was allocated the new designation Me 323. It subsequently proved one of the most successful German transports of the war—though it needed a strong pilot to fly it ! Principal sub-types of the Me 323 were the D and E; and combined production of the Me 321 and Me 323 reached a figure of some 200 aircraft.

> **BRIEF TECHNICAL DETAILS**
> **(Me 323E):**
>
> *Engines:* Six 990 h.p. Gnome-Rhone 14N radials.
> *Span:* 181 ft. 0 in.
> *Length:* 93 ft. 4 in.
> *Weight Empty:* 61,700 lb.
>   *Loaded:* 96,000 lb.
> *No. in crew:* Five to seven (plus up to 130 troops or 21,500 lb. of freight).
> *Max. Speed:* 136 m.p.h. at sea level.
> *Normal Range:* 685 miles.
> *Armament:* Five 13 mm. MG 131 machine guns.

A5M2b/I.W.M.

Mitsubishi A5M

Country of origin: **JAPAN**   Designers: **Mitsubishi Jukogyo K.K.**
Purpose: **Carrier-borne fighter.**   In operational use: **1941/42.**

Although it had been phased out of production in 1940 and was obsolescent by the time Japan entered World War 2, this dumpy little aeroplane remained standard J.N.A.F. fighter equipment for most of the first year of the war. It was, in fact, the Japanese Navy's first operational monoplane fighter, and was first flown in prototype form on 4th February 1935, powered by a 550 h.p. Naka-jima Kotobuki 5 radial engine. The inverted-gull wing of this prototype was replaced, on the second machine, by a "straight" one, and the powerplant became the 560 h.p. Kotobuki 3; a further engine change saw the 585 h.p. Kotobuki 2 installed in the first production version, the A5M1. The A5M2a and the A5M2b followed it in 1937, the latter experimenting with an enclosed cockpit position which, in service, did not find favour and was omitted from subsequent production models. After the experimental A5M3 (690 h.p. Hispano-Suiza inline engine) came the A5M4, which was the version standard at the time of Pearl Harbour; a trainer variant of this was known as the A5M4-K. Total production of the A5M series (*Claude* in the Allied coding system) was close on 1,000 aircraft, of which 200 were completed by the Sasebo and Watanabe concerns.

> **BRIEF TECHNICAL DETAILS (A5M4):**
> Engine: One 710 h.p. Nakajima Koto-buki 41 radial.
> Span: 36 ft. 1 in.
> Length: 24 ft. 9½ in.
> Height: 10 ft. 6 in.
> Weight Empty: 2,681 lb.
>   Loaded: 3,684 lb.
> No. in crew: One.
> Max. Speed: 273 m.p.h. at 9,840 ft.
> Service Ceiling: 32,150 ft.
> Max. Range: 746 miles.
> Armament: Two 7.7 mm. machine guns; two 66 lb. bombs optional.

Captured A6M2 flown by the Allied Tactical Air Intelligence Unit/I.W.M.

Mitsubishi A6M Zero-Sen

Country of origin: **JAPAN**
Purpose: **Fighter and fighter-bomber.**

Designers: **Mitsubishi Jukogyo K.K.**
In operational use: **1941/45.**

If the world at large recalls little else of Japan's weapons of the Second World War, it has undoubtedly heard of the Zero fighter. This aeroplane's reputation in Far Eastern circles was almost as great as that of the Spitfire or the Fw 190 in Europe—and with justification, for at the time of its introduction it was superior by far to all other Japanese Navy fighters and many of the Army machines then in service. Although, as the war progressed, modifications and improvisations became necessary to maintain the Zero's position as a front-line fighter, a tremendous production programme ensured that substantial numbers were constantly available as carrier-based and land-based fighters, fighter-bombers, dive bombers and suicide aircraft. (The Zero was, in fact, the first Japanese aircraft to be deliberately used in anti-shipping suicide attacks.)

The Zero-Sen—or *Zeke*, to give it its Allied code name—owed its inception to a 1937 specification issued by the Japanese Navy, a specification so demanding that Mitsubishi were the only company willing to try and meet it. Intended as a replacement for the A5M (page 125) and designed by a team under the leader-

A6M3

A6M5

ship of Jiro Horikoshi, the prototype Zero made its maiden flight on 1st April 1939 powered by the lightweight 780 h.p. Mitsubishi Zuisei 13 radial engine. Two prototypes, designated A6M1, were completed, and both had been accepted by the J.N.A.F. before the end of 1939. In January 1940 the third machine was flown, designated A6M2 by virtue of its new powerplant, the 925 h.p. Nakajima Sakae 12 radial, and later that year a small batch of A6M2s were successfully employed in China. This version, the A6M2 Model 11, totalled 64 aircraft, but major production was reserved for the A6M2 Model 21, which featured folding wingtips for carrier stowage. About two-thirds of the ultimate production of 740 Model 21s (which was shared with Nakajima) were already in service when Japan entered the war. During 1942, 508 examples of a two-seat training variant, the A6M2-K, were manufactured by the Hitachi and Sasebo factories. Meanwhile there had appeared the A6M3 Zero, powered by the 1,130 h.p. Sakae 21. Although this model possessed improved speed and range, other shortcomings revealed during tests led to the clipping of 1 ft. 8 in. (i.e., the folding portion) off each wingtip before, as the A6M3 Model 32, it entered production. Variously code-named *Hap* and *Hamp*, before its identity was established as a Zero variant (*Zeke* 32), this type became operational in 1942 and 343 examples were finally built by the parent company. A further 560 A6M3 Model 22, employing the normal full-span wing, were also completed by Mitsubishi.

By 1943, however, a much-improved performance was clearly needed, and the A6M5 Model 52—which ultimately accounted for more than half the overall Zero production—was produced to meet this demand. The short-span wing of the *Zeke* 32 was utilised, but with its tips rounded off, and the Sakae 21 engine was modified to boost the top speed to 358 m.p.h. Various refinements of this model were the A6M5a, '5b and '5c, with differing degrees of firepower, armour protection and other features. A trainer version, the A6M5-K, did not pass beyond the pre-production stage. The Sakae 32-powered A6M6 did not come up to expectations, but a further adaptation of the A6M5 produced the A6M7, which entered production, as the European war ended, for the dive bomber role. Difficulties over the supply of Sakae engines finally enabled Mitsubishi, late in 1944, to introduce their own 1,560 h.p. Kinsei 62 engine in what was destined to be the last Zero variant, the A6M8; but, although it was planned to build many thousands of this version, only the two prototypes were ever flown. Total Zero production, excluding 327 *Rufe* floatplanes (page 219), was 10,611 aircraft, of which Mitsubishi built 3,879 and Nakajima 6,215.

BRIEF TECHNICAL DETAILS (A6M5b):
Engine: One 1,130 h.p. Nakajima Sakae 21 radial.
Span: 36 ft. 1 in.
Length: 29 ft. 9 in.
Height: 9 ft. 2 in.
Weight Empty: 4,175 lb.
    Loaded: 6,047 lb.
No. in crew: One.
Max. Speed: 351 m.p.h. at 19,685 ft.
Service Ceiling: 35,100 ft.
Max. Range: 975 miles.
Armament: Two 20 mm. cannon, one 12.7 mm. and one 7.7 mm. machine gun; up to 700 lb. of bombs optional.

G3M3/H. J. Nowarra

Mitsubishi G3M

Country of origin: **JAPAN**   *Designers:* **Mitsubishi Jukogyo K.K.**
Purpose: **Medium bomber.**   *In operational use:* **1941/45.**

When Japan entered World War 2 the G3M formed the backbone of the J.N.A.F. medium bomber force, over 250 examples then being in service. Although it was supplemented in later years by more modern designs, the G3M (code name *Nell*) soldiered on until the capitulation, being principally employed, in the closing stages, on transport work. Arising out of various experimental designs produced in the early and middle 1930s, the first prototype (G3M1), powered by two 600 h.p. Hiro Type 91 radial motors, made its maiden flight in July 1935. Three further prototypes with similar powerplants were completed before a change was made to the 825 h.p. Kinsei 2 engine which offered an improved performance. Only 21 G3M1 were completed with this powerplant, however, before the 840 h.p. Kinsei 3 was introduced into production aircraft; then from the 56th production aircraft the Kinsei 45 was adopted and the aircraft was re-designated G3M2. A small number of G3M1 machines, converted as ten-passenger transports, were given the new designation L3Y1. Total production of the G3M series, which reached 1,100 machines, included the Kinsei 42-powered G3M2b, the transport G3M2d (L3Y2) and the final bomber, the G3M3 with 1,300 h.p. Kasei 51s. Although production of the *Nell* was already being phased out at the beginning of the war in favour of the G4M *Betty* (opposite), the type saw widespread service throughout the war years. One of its first successful actions was the sinking of H.M. Ships *Prince of Wales* and *Repulse* on 10th December 1941.

BRIEF TECHNICAL DETAILS (G3M2):
Engines: Two 1,000 h.p. Mitsubishi Kinsei 45 radials.
Span: 82 ft. 0¼ in.
Length: 53 ft. 11¾ in.
Height: 11 ft. 11¾ in.
Weight Empty: 11,442 lb.
Loaded: 17,637 lb.
No. in crew: Seven.
Max. Speed: 238 m.p.h. at 9,840 ft.
Service Ceiling: 29,890 ft.
Armament: One 20 mm. cannon and two 7.7 mm. machine guns; up to 2,200 lb. of bombs or one 1,760 lb. torpedo.

Mitsubishi G4M

Country of origin: **JAPAN**   *Designers:* **Mitsubishi Jukogyo K.K.**
Purpose: **Medium bomber.**   *In operational use:* **1941/45.**

Although, numerically, the G4M (*Betty*) was one of the Japanese Navy's principal wartime bombers, its excellent range was achieved only at the expense of adequate protection for its crew and fuel load.   In consequence it was somewhat vulnerable to attack, and losses were high.   The design was begun late in 1937 as a successor to the G3M2, and the prototype G4M1 bomber flew in October 1939.   In the same month, however, the J.N.A.F. caused it to be put into production, in suitably modified form as the G6M1, as an escort fighter; but comparatively few were completed before this venture was abandoned as impracticable, and the aircraft concerned eventually became trainers or transports.   In April 1941 the G4M1 finally entered production, and by Pearl Harbour nearly 200 were in service.   The G4M1 was often flown without its bomb doors, giving it a curiously deformed look amidships.   It was widely used at the beginning of the Pacific war, on torpedo as well as normal bombing duties, but the much-improved G4M2 prototype made its first flight in November 1942.   During 1943, the G4M1 was diverted to transport, reconnaissance, training and similar duties and was replaced in bomber squadrons by the G4M2. These were followed, from the summer of 1944, by the Kasei 25-powered G4M2a. Subsequent experiments included the high-altitude G4M2b (Kasei 27), G4M2c (Kasei 25b), and the turbojet testbed G4M2d.   Limited production was undertaken of the G4M2e, specially modified to carry the Ohka suicide aircraft (page 165), and a pair of G4M2s brought the Japanese surrender delegation to Ie Shima on 19th August 1945.   Other projects included the G7M1 Taizan (*Great Mountain*), abandoned in 1944 in favour of the somewhat similar G4M3: this had a shorter range, and more protection for crew and fuel. Sixty G4M3a and G4M3b were completed; the turbo-supercharged G4M3d came too late for operational service. Total G4M bomber production amounted to 2,479 machines.

BRIEF TECHNICAL DETAILS
(G4M2a):
Engines: Two 1,850 h.p, Mitsubishi Kasei 25 radials.
Span: 81 ft. 8 in.
Length: 64 ft. 4¾ in.
Height: 13 ft. 5¾ in.
Weight Empty: 18,449 lb.
   Loaded: 27,557 lb.
No. in crew: Seven.
Max. Speed: 272 m.p.h. at 15,090 ft.
Service Ceiling: 29,360 ft.
Normal Range: 2,262 miles.
Armament: Four 20 mm. Type 99 cannon and one 7.7 mm. Type 97 machine gun; up to 2,200 lb. of bombs or one 1,764 lb. torpedo.

Ki-21-IIb

Mitsubishi Ki.21

Country of origin: **JAPAN**   *Designers:* **Mitsubishi Jukogyo K.K.**
Purpose: **Medium bomber.**   *In operational use:* **1941/45.**

Although it was obsolescent well before the end of the war the Ki. 21 *Sally*
remained a pillar of the Japanese Army Air Force bomber squadrons throughout
hostilities, and at the time of Pearl Harbour was their standard bomber type.
Its prolonged usefulness was no doubt attributable to the original Army specification issued in February 1936, which was a most exacting one by Japanese
standards of that time.   Mitsubishi completed five Ki. 21 prototypes, each with
a different arrangement of armament but each powered by a pair of 850 h.p.
Kinsei Ha. 6 radial engines; the first prototype was flown early in 1937.   The
design was accepted, subject to being re-engined with the Nakajima Zuisei Ha. 5,
and went into series production as the Ki. 21-Ia in the autumn of 1937, entering
service early the following year.   By the end of 1938 Nakajima had joined the
production team with the more refined
Ki. 21-Ib, which featured increases in
bomb load and defensive armament;
and training and transport variants were
also evolved.   The Ki. 21-IIa, the
major service version, was developed
in 1939/40, principal changes being the
higher-powered Ha. 101 engines and a
wider span tailplane,   and the later
Ki. 21-IIb introduced a dorsal gun
turret.   The final projected version,
the Ki. 21-III, was ultimately abandoned
in favour of the Ki. 67 *Peggy* (page 132),
and production of the Ki. 21 ceased in
September 1944 after the completion
of more than 1,800 machines.

> **BRIEF TECHNICAL DETAILS**
>   **(Ki. 21-IIb):**
> *Engines:* Two 1,490 h.p. Mitsubishi
>   Ha. 101 radials.
> *Span:* 72 ft. 9¾ in.
> *Length:* 52 ft. 6 in.
> *Height:* 15 ft. 11 in.
> *Weight Empty:* 13,382 lb.
>   *Loaded:* 21,407 lb.
> *No. in crew:* Seven.
> *Max. Speed:* 297 m.p.h. at 13,120 ft.
> *Service Ceiling:* 32,800 ft.
> *Normal Range:* 1,350 miles.
> *Armament:* One 12.7 mm. and five
>   7.7 mm. machine guns, and up to
>   2,200 lb. of bombs.

130

Mitsubishi Ki.46

Country of origin: **JAPAN**   *Designers:* **Mitsubishi Jukogyo K.K.**
Purpose: **Reconnaissance.**   *In operational use:* **1941/45.**

The Ki. 46 (*Dinah*) was by far the most important reconnaissance type used by the Japanese air forces and was also, aerodynamically, one of the most perfect machines produced by any of the combatants in World War 2. With a fully adequate powerplant its performance was so far ahead of the early Allied fighters that it was able to dispense with the single defensive gun originally carried. The prototype (which first flew in November 1939) and early production Ki.46-I aircraft were powered by the 850 h.p. Ha. 26-I engine, giving the relatively modest top speed of 312 m.p.h. at 26,250 ft. These were, however, soon replaced by the Ha. 102 which offered a vastly superior performance. The Ki. 46-II (with the Ki. 46-II-KAI trainer) was the principal operational variant, and such was the success achieved with this aircraft that at one stage of the war a technical mission from Germany seriously considered the prospects of licence production. A further version, the Ki.46-IIIA, appeared in the early spring of 1943, 654 examples of which were eventually completed. The Ki.46-IIIA featured a redesigned all-glazed nose section, giving a completely unbroken top line to the fuselage, and carried considerably more fuel. Maximum range of this version was 2,485 miles, and its 1,500 h.p. Ha.112-II engines boosted the top speed to 397 m.p.h. Other variants of the Dinah included the Ki.46-III-KAI interceptor ("solid" nose, armament of one 37 mm. cannon and two 20 mm. or 12.7 mm. guns) and the generally similar Ki.46-IIIB for ground attack. Production of all versions totalled 1,738 aircraft, including three Ki.46-IVA machines which were based on the -IIIA with exhaust turbines added to the engines. The Ki.46-IVB, a parallel version for ground attack, did not materialise.

BRIEF TECHNICAL DETAILS
(Ki.46-II):
Engines: Two 1,050 h.p. Mitsubishi Ha. 102 radials.
Span: 48 ft. 2¾ in.
Length: 36 ft. 1 in.
Height: 10 ft. 10 in.
Weight Empty: 7,149 lb.
    Loaded: 11,133 lb.
No. in crew: Two.
Max. Speed: 375 m.p.h. at 19,000 ft.
Service Ceiling: 35,170 ft.
Max. Range: 1,535 miles.
Armament: One 7.7 mm. machine gun.

131

Mitsubishi Ki.67 Hiryu
(Flying Dragon)

Country of origin: **JAPAN**   *Designers:* **Mitsubishi Jukogyo K.K.**
Purpose: **Medium bomber.**   *In operational use:* **1944/45.**

Although the Hiryu, or *Peggy*, was only in full operational service for the last ten or eleven months of the war, during that time it proved to be by far the Army's best bomber, and also appeared as a torpedo-bomber, reconnaissance aircraft, suicide bomber and interceptor. Its design began in 1941, and the first prototype flew in January 1943. Successful though the initial tests were, further improvements on subsequent prototypes meant that by the spring of 1944 only 21 aircraft had been completed. By then, however, the urgent needs of the Japanese air forces could be denied no longer, and the Hiryu entered series production. Comparatively few Ki.67-Ia were completed before being superseded by the Ki.67-Ib, which continued in production to the end of the war. Curiously, the first Ki.67s to enter service did so, in October 1944, with Navy units, and several were fitted with improvised torpedo shackles for anti-shipping missions. Three other manufacturers—Kawasaki, Nippon and Rikugun—were drawn into the production team, but only completed just over 100 aircraft between them; thus, of the overall production of approximately 700 machines, the bulk were completed by the parent company. The Ki.67 was additionally employed as a ground attack and suicide aircraft, and various other versions were projected or built. These included a parent aircraft for an experimental guided missile; an engine testbed for developed versions of the Ha.104; and an escort fighter (Ki.69 and Ki.112). Experiments with a 75 mm. cannon in the Ki.104 'heavy fighter' project led to 44 examples of the Ki.109 being completed in 1944/45 for interception of high-flying Superfortress bombers, but this venture was not particularly successful.

BRIEF TECHNICAL DETAILS
(Ki.67-Ib):
Engines: Two 2,000 h.p. Mitsubishi Ha. 104 radials.
Span: 73 ft. 9¾ in.
Length: 61 ft. 4¼ in.
Height: 15 ft. 9 in.
Weight Empty: 19,068 lb.
      Loaded: 30,346 lb.
No. in crew: Six to eight.
Max. Speed: 334 m.p.h. at 19,980 ft.
Service Ceiling: 31,070 ft.
Max. Range: 2,360 miles.
Armament: One 20 mm. cannon and four 12.7 machine guns; up to 1,760 lb. of bombs normally or one 1,760 lb. torpedo.

B6N1

Nakajima B6N Tenzan
(Heavenly Mountain)

Country of origin: **JAPAN**
Purpose: **Torpedo bomber and reconnaissance.**

Designers: **Nakajima Hikoki K.K.**
In operational use: **1944/45.**

Although it did not enter fully operational service until the summer of 1944, the Nakajima Tenzan (*Jill* in the Allied code naming system) rapidly became the principal torpedo bombing type of the Japanese Naval Air Force. It owed its inception to the need for a replacement of the ageing B5N2 *Kate*, and was first flown in prototype form in March 1942. The powerplant chosen for the first production model, the B6N1, was the 1,870 h.p. Mamoru II radial. Despite a series of troubles experienced with this engine, 498 B6N1s were completed; in the B6N2, however, the Kasei 25 proved a far more satisfactory installation and production of this version amounted to 770 aircraft, bringing the grand total to 1,268. In addition to its secondary employment on reconnaissance duties, the Tenzan was also one of the leading Japanese aircraft types to be utilised in the Kamikaze suicide attacks on Allied shipping in the Pacific zone.

BRIEF TECHNICAL DETAILS (B6N2):
Engine: One 1,850 h.p. Mitsubishi Kasei 25 radial.
Span: 48 ft. 10¼ in.
Length: 35 ft. 7½ in.
Height: 12 ft. 5½ in.
Weight Empty: 6,636 lb.
    Loaded: 12,466 lb. (max.).
No. in crew: Three.
Max. Speed: 299 m.p.h. at 16,076 ft.
Service Ceiling: 26,660 ft.
Max. Range: 900 miles.
Armament: Two 7.7 mm. machine guns; one 1,764 lb. torpedo or six 220 lb. bombs externally.

H. J. Nowarra

Nakajima C6N Saiun *(Painted Cloud)*

Country of origin: **JAPAN**
Purpose: **Long range reconnaissance and torpedo bomber.**

Designers: **Nakajima Hikoki K.K.**
In operational use: **1944/45.**

The Saiun (code name *Myrt*) was the first Japanese aircraft to be specifically designed from the outset for ship-borne reconnaissance, and proved itself in service to be a conspicuously successful machine. Only a comparatively small number (498) had been completed by VJ day, and the type did not make its operational debut until the end of the war was in sight, but the performance of the Saiun was sufficiently good to enable a modified version, the two-seat C6N1-S with two 20 mm. cannon added to its armament, to act as night fighter against the high-flying B-29 Superfortresses attacking targets in Japan. In an effort to bring the Saiun into service quickly, no fewer than 23 prototypes were built to shorten the period of development testing, and many of these were completed before the end of 1943; production aircraft began to be delivered to the J.N.A.F. in August 1944, although some of the prototype machines had been pressed into operational service some two months previously. Other variants of the Saiun included the C6N1-B torpedo bomber version and the C6N2 with the Homare 24 engine of which two prototypes only were completed. A further projected development, which did not achieve fruition, was the C6N3, which was to have been powered with the supercharged 2,000 h.p. Homare NK9L-L engine.

BRIEF TECHNICAL DETAILS (C6N1):

Engine: One 1,990 h.p. Nakajima Homare 21 radial.
Span: 41 ft. 0 in.
Length: 36 ft. 7 in.
Height: 13 ft. 0 in.
Weight Empty: 6,411 lb.
  Loaded: 9,920 lb.
No. in crew: Three.
Max. Speed: 379 m.p.h. at 20,000 ft.
Service Ceiling: 35,235 ft.
Max. Range: 3,306 miles.
Armament: One 7.9 mm. machine gun.

JINI-C-KAI

Nakajima JIN Gekko *(Moonlight)*

Country of origin: **JAPAN**
Purpose: **Night fighter, reconnaissance and light bomber.**

Designers: **Nakajima Hikoki K.K.**
In operational use: **1943/45.**

Born in peacetime as a fighter, the J1N1 (*Irving*) entered production in wartime as a reconnaissance aircraft and was finally pressed into service as a defensive fighter—and was ultimately one of the best night fighters the Japanese industry produced. Work on the design began in 1938 to a Navy specification for a long range escort fighter, and the prototype J1N1 made its maiden flight in May 1941. Flight testing revealed several factors against its suitability as a fighting aircraft but in July 1942 it was ordered into production for the reconnaissance role, making its debut in this form as the J1N1-C early in 1943. Shortly afterwards operational necessity overrode other considerations and several J1N1-C aircraft were converted, with revised armament, for emergency use as night fighters. These were followed by a few turret-mounting J1N1-F aircraft and later by the J1N1-S Gekko, built from the outset for night fighting; some of the latter bore primitive A.I. radar in the closing stages of the war, among the first Japanese aircraft to do so. Total production of the J1N1, including prototypes, amounted to 479 machines; some of these were employed on bombing duties, for which they could accommodate an offensive load up to 2,432 lb.

BRIEF TECHNICAL DETAILS (JINI-S):
Engines: Two 1,130 h.p. Nakajima Sakae 21 radials.
Span: 55 ft. 8½ in.
Length: 39 ft. 11½ in.
Height: 13 ft. 1¼ in.
Weight Empty: 10,697 lb.
Loaded: 15,983 lb.
No. in crew: Two.
Max. Speed: 315 m.p.h. at 19,030 ft.
Serice Ceiling: 30,580 ft.
Max. Range: 1,584 miles.
Armament: Four 20 mm. Type 99 cannon.

Ki-27a/H. J. Nowarra

Nakajima Ki.27

Country of origin: **JAPAN**
Purpose: **Fighter and fighter-bomber.**

Designers: **Nakajima Hikoki K.K.**
In operational use: **1940/44.**

A standard J.A.A.F. fighter type from the middle of 1937 until it was succeeded by the Ki.43 Hayabusa towards the end of 1942, the Ki.27 (*Nate*) was one of the most important Japanese aircraft of the early war years. Over the three years in which it remained in steady production, 3,386 Ki.27a and Ki.27b versions were built, a far greater number than that for any other pre-war Japanese design. The Ki.27 was also noteworthy for being Japan's first monoplane fighter with a low wing, and its first to have an enclosed cockpit. The first of the three Ki.27 prototypes was flown on 15th October 1936, powered by a 650 h.p. Nakajima Ha.1a radial motor; after a further batch of ten aircraft for evaluation, the Ki.27a entered production during 1937, and before that year was out was in service in Manchuria. In 1939 the Ki.27b followed it into production, being used on quite a wide scale in China before Japan's entry into World War 2. Subsequently it appeared in many actions in the Philippines and other south-west Pacific theatres. The Ki.27b featured a more streamlined cockpit and several other refinements, both internal and external. Three examples of an improved Ki.27-KAI were completed in 1940, but owing to the programme for the new Ki.43 this model was not proceeded with. Some Ki.27 production was undertaken by the Manchurian Aircraft Manufacturing Company in addition to that by the parent firm.

> **BRIEF TECHNICAL DETAILS**
> **(Ki.27b):**
> Engine: One 710 h.p. Nakajima Ha. Ib radial.
> Span: 37 ft. 1½ in.
> Length: 24 ft. 8½ in.
> Height: 9 ft. 2¼ in.
> Weight Empty: 2,447 lb.
>   Loaded: 3,946 lb.
> No. in crew: One.
> Max. Speed: 286 m.p.h. at 16,400 ft.
> Max. Range: 389 miles.
> Armament: Two 7.7 mm. machine guns; 220 lb. of bombs.

Nakajima Ki.43 Hayabusa (*Peregrine Falcon*)

Country of origin: **JAPAN**   *Designers:* **Nakajima Hikoki K.K.**
Purpose: **Fighter.**   *In operational use:* **1941/45.**

Although it was far surpassed in performance by later designs, the Ki.43 Hayabusa (code name *Oscar*) was the most widely produced Japanese Army fighter of the war years, and served throughout hostilities in every Pacific theatre of operations.   Following the construction of three prototypes, the first of which made its maiden flight at the beginning of 1939, and a further modified batch of ten evaluation machines, the Ki.43-Ia went into production early in 1941 and a small number were in service by the time of Pearl Harbour.   Comparatively few of this model were completed,however, before they gave way to the progressively better armed Ki.43-Ib and -Ic. Despite their good manoeuvrability, and their superiority over the Ki.27 which they replaced, the Ki.43-I series were somewhat underpowered, and in February 1942 a handful of prototypes for the Ki.43-IIa were begun, utilising the more powerful Ha.115 engine and incorporating various refinements.   This version was also produced by the Tachikawa company.   In the late summer of 1942 three more prototypes—this time of the Ki.43-IIb—were completed, featuring a shorter " clipped " wing and other

changes; this version entered service in the middle of 1943.   With performance still further improved by the 1,250 h.p. Ha.112, both Nakajima and Tachikawa began to produce the last service model, the Ki.43-IIIa, in December 1944; the final version was the Tachikawa-developed Ki.43-IIIb, the first and only version to include 20 mm. cannon in its armament, but only two of these had been completed by VJ day.   Production of all versions, including 3,200 by Nakajima and 2,629 by Tachikawa, totalled 5,878 aircraft.

BRIEF TECHNICAL DETAILS (Ki.43-IIb):
Engine: One 1,130 h.p. Nakajima Ha. 115 radial.
Span: 35 ft. 6¾ in.
Length: 29 ft. 3 in.
Height: 10 ft. 1½ in.
Weight Empty: 3,812 lb.
     Loaded: 5,320 lb.
No, in crew: One.
Max. Speed: 320 m.p.h. at 19,680 ft.
Service Ceiling: 36,800 ft.
Normal Range: 1,006 miles.
Armament: Two 12.7 mm. Type I machine guns; two 550 lb. bombs optional.

137

Nakajima Ki.84 Hayate *(Gale)*

Country of origin: **JAPAN**
Purpose: **Fighter and dive bomber.**

Designers: **Nakajima Hikoki K.K.**
In operational use: **1944/45.**

Although it did not enter operational service until a year before the end of the war, the Hayate (code name *Frank*) was extensively produced and, despite powerplant troubles, became one of the Allies' most formidable opponents in the Far East.   It was sometimes employed as a dive bomber, in which role it was capable of carrying two underwing bombs up to 550 lb. in size, but it was as a fighter that the Hayate really made its mark.   The prototype flew in March 1943 and in August, fifteen months after the design had been started, the Ki.84-Ia entered series production.   The Ki.84-Ib and -Ic which followed differed in the armament fitted, the latter being fairly heavily equipped for a Japanese fighter with two 30 mm. and two 20 mm. cannon.   Total production of the Ki.84-I series amounted to 3,513 machines, including a batch of 100 completed by the Manchurian Aircraft Manufacturing Co.   The shortage of strategic materials in the final stages of the war led to the investigation of a series of developments and modifications of the original Ki.84, intended to employ wood and/or non-strategic metals in their construction. Among these projects were the Ki.84-II, Ki.106 and Ki.113.   None of these came to fruition, being either abandoned or too late to achieve completion beyond the prototype stage.   The Ki. 84-III, which was to have employed a a 2,000 h.p. supercharged Ha. 45ru engine, was likewise too late for completion before the end of the war, as were the Ki.116, Ki.117 (Ki.84N), Ki.84P and Ki.84R, other engine-change projects.

BRIEF TECHNICAL DETAILS
(Ki.84-Ia):
Engine: One 1,900 h.p. Nakajima Ha. 45/11 Type 4 radial.
Span: 36 ft. 10½ in.
Length: 32 ft. 6½ in.
Height: 11 ft. 1¼ in.
Weight Empty: 5,864 lb.
          Loaded: 7,965 lb.
No. in crew: One.
Max. Speed: 388 m.p.h. at 19,680 ft.
Service Ceiling: 34,450 ft.
Max. Range: 1,815 miles.
Armament: Two 20 mm. Type 5 cannon and two 12.7 Type 103 machine guns; up to 1,100 lb. of bombs.

North American AT-6 Texan

Country of origin: **U.S.A.**
Purpose: **General purpose trainer.**
Makers: **North American Aviation Inc.**

Other U.S. designations: **AT-16, SNJ.**
In operational use: **1941/45.**

Designed in the latter 1930s as a low-cost trainer with the characteristics of a high-speed fighter, the North American Texan or Harvard has since become the " flying classroom " for hundreds of thousands of pilots in some forty countries and still serves in many of them to-day. It was evolved from the fixed-under-carriage BC-1 basic combat trainer produced for the U.S.A.A.C. in 1937, and was first ordered in 1939. Such varied equipment as bomb racks, blind flying instruments, gun cameras, standard cameras, and fixed or flexible guns enabled the Texan to be used as an " all-sorts " trainer; some were ski-fitted for Arctic operations, others employed for target towing, and at least one Texan had a submarine " kill " to its credit. Authorities differ over the precise total built, but it was certainly in the region of 15,000; approximately one third of these found their way to the Royal Air Force with whom, as the Harvard, they served for sixteen years from 1938 to 1955, and the remainder were shared in more or less equal proportions between the U.S.A.F. and the U.S. Navy. In Canada, 1,500 were built by Noorduyn as the AT-16, with minor equipment changes. The differences between the various production models of the Texan were mainly confined to internal equipment or minor changes of powerplant, the most-produced versions being the AT-6A (similar to the Navy SNJ-3), AT-6C (=SNJ-4), AT-6D (=SNJ-5) and the SNJ-6.

> **BRIEF TECHNICAL DETAILS (AT-6C):**
> *Engine:* One 600 h.p. Pratt & Whitney R-1340-AN-1 Wasp radial.
> *Span:* 42 ft. 0 in.
> *Length:* 29 ft. 0 in.
> *Height:* 11 ft. 8½ in.
> *Weight Empty:* 4,158 lb.
> *Loaded:* 5,300 lb.
> *No. in crew:* Two (instructor and pupil).
> *Max. Speed:* 208m.p.h. at 5,000 ft.
> *Service Ceiling:* 21,500 ft.
> *Normal Range:* 750 miles'
> *Armament:* Three .30 machine guns.

139

B-25J

North American B-25 Mitchell

Country of origin: **U.S.A.**
Purpose: **Medium bomber and ground attack.**
Makers: **North American Aviation Inc.**

Other U.S. designations: **F-10, PBJ-1.**
In operational use: **1941/45.**

The Mitchell was ordered "off the drawing board" in September 1939, being a development of North American's NA-40 conceived in 1938. Thus there was no XB-25, and the first of 24 B-25s made its maiden flight on 19th August, 1940, powered by two 1,700 h.p. Cyclone engines. The B-25A which followed was similar except for internal improvements, and 40 of this version were completed. By Pearl Harbour these aircraft were in U.S. service, and production of 119 B-25B (armament changes) was under way. In March 1942, 72 Mitchells were supplied to Russia, the first of a total of 870 eventually despatched to that country. The R.A.F's small batch of Mitchell Is (B-25B) were used primarily for training; later deliveries included 500 Mitchell IIs (B-25C and D) and 314 Mitchell IIIs (B-25J). The B-25C and D were largely similar, apart from engine and some internal changes, though on some of them provision was introduced for six or eight small bombs or one 2,000 lb. torpedo to be carried externally; 1,619 B-25C and 2,290 B-25D were completed, ten Ds being converted in 1943 to F-10 photo reconnaissance trainers. Many Cs and Ds were transferred to the Netherlands, Brazil and Canada, and a large number were also used by the U.S. Navy as the PBJ-1 for anti-submarine duties. The XB-25E and XB-25F were " one-off " research models; the XB-25G and 405 production B-25Gs introduced, from late 1943, the famous 75 mm. cannon carried in a " solid " nose. The B-25H which followed (1,000 were built) utilised a less heavy 75 mm. cannon, together with fourteen other .50 guns and provision for a torpedo or 3,200 lb. of bombs, making this Mitchell one of the most heavily armed aircraft in the world—though by the summer of 1944 the heavy cannon was abandoned.

Chief version of the Mitchell was the B-25J, which was in production from 1943 to 1945, a total of 4,318 being completed. This model reverted to the bombing role, but apart from its transparent nose, with modified gunnery, was otherwise similar to the B-25H. Some B-25Js were subsequently modified in the field to have a " solid " eight-machine-gun nose for ground attack. Before VJ-day, a number of " combat-weary " B-25s had been converted for home use as AT-24 aircrew trainers.

North American P-51 Mustang

Country of origin: **U.S.A.**
Purpose: **Long range escort fighter and ground attack.**

Makers: **North American Aviation Inc.**
Other U.S. designations: **A-36, F-6.**
In operational use: **1942/45.**

Originally conceived in 1940 to British specifications, the Mustang's potential was not immediately appreciated by U.S. authorities. When it was, its development proceeded apace and in 1944 it was rated by the Truman Senate War Investigating Committee as "the most aerodynamically perfect pursuit plane in existence"; and whilst one might dispute the precise wording of this statement the Mustang was undoubtedly one of the finest and most versatile fighters of World War 2. The first flight took place in October 1940, and the R.A.F. eventually received 620 Mustang I and IA and 50 Mustang IIs. A U.S. order was placed for 150 P-51 Apaches, similar to the Mustang IA, and 310 P-51A, similar to the Mk. II, principally distinguished by armament variations and an improved Allison engine in some of the P-51As. In 1942 the U.S. responded to recommendations to mate the Mustang airframe with the Rolls-Royce Merlin

P-51H

engine: four were converted in Britain and two, as XP-51Bs, in the United States, using Packard-built Merlins. The ultimate result was 1,199 P-51B and 1,750 P-51C utilising similar powerplants; some 887 of these were subsequently supplied as Mustang IIIs to the R.A.F., where they were given bulged cockpit hoods. The P-51D was by far the most widespread version; it was also the first to introduce the blister canopy, later Ds adding a small compensatory dorsal fin. Total P-51D production was 7,956 aircraft, including 280 Mustang IV for the R.A.F. and ten converted to TP-51D tandem-seat trainers. Both subsequent production models of the P-51, the P-51H (555 built) and P-51K (1,337 built) were too late for operational service. A ground attack/dive bomber version, the A-36A, was produced early in the aircraft's career, 500 of this model being completed. Photographic conversions included 482 to F-6A/B/C/D/K from P-51/-51A/C/D/K respectively. The P-82 Twin Mustang—two P-51s " married " by a common centre-section and tailplane and carrying a pilot in each fuselage—was only produced in small numbers before the war ended, but subsequently ran to 250 aircraft and became a standard long-range escort type.

BRIEF TECHNICAL DETAILS
(P-51D):
Engine: One 1,490 h.p. Rolls-Royce/ Packard Merlin V-1650-7 inline.
Span: 37 ft. 0 in.
Length: 32 ft. 3 in.
Height: 13 ft. 8 in.
Weight Empty: 7,125 lb.
      Loaded: 11,600 lb. (max.)
No. in crew: One.
Max. Speed: 437 m.p.h. at 25,000 ft.
Service Ceiling: 41,900 ft.
Max. Range: 2,080 miles.
Armament: Four or six .50 machine guns; up to 2,000 lb. of bombs or ten 5-inch rocket projectiles.

Second prototype XP-82 Twin Mustang

Petlyakov Pe-2

Country of origin: **RUSSIA**
Purpose: **Bomber, ground attack and reconnaissance.**

Design bureau: **V.M. Petlyakov.**
In operational use: **1941/45.**

Considered by many to be one of the most outstanding Russian aircraft of the war years, the Pe-2 performed a wide range of duties with no small success and achieved quite a reputation for ruggedness and adaptability. Originally conceived as a light bomber, and designated PB-100, the Pe-2 served on all Russian fronts from 1941 onwards and, although partially replaced by the Tu-2 in the last year or so of the war, continued to give useful service for some time afterwards. A good range and a useful machine gun armament made it a suitable type for close support roles, and its performance was also sufficient to warrant its employment as a day and night fighter, as well as on reconnaissance missions; it was even employed on occasion as a dive bomber. A further development of the Pe-2 was the Pe-3, which was produced specifically for night fighting and reconnaissance. Powered by two 1,310 h.p. M-105PF engines, the Pe-3 featured a " solid " nose and a shorter cockpit enclosure with a dorsal turret to the rear, and was in service by mid-1943.

BRIEF TECHNICAL DETAILS:
Engines: Two 1,100 h.p. Klimov VK-105R inlines.
Span: 56 ft. 4 in.
Length: 41 ft. 4 in.
Weight Empty: 12,900 lb.
       Loaded: 18,730 lb.
No. in crew: Two
Max. Speed: 335 m.p.h. at 16,400 ft.
Service Ceiling: 29,520 ft.
Normal Range: 1,200 miles.
Armament: One 12.7 mm. Beresin and four 7.62 mm. ShKAS machine guns; up to 2,200 lb. of bombs.

The Pe-8 which brought Mr. Molotov to Britain in 1942/I.W.M.

Petlyakov Pe-8

Country of origin: **RUSSIA**   *Design bureau:* **A.N. Tupolev.**
Purpose: **Heavy bomber.**   *In operational use:* **1941/45.**

By and large, the Soviet authorities did not seriously support the concept of the heavy strategic bomber during World War 2, and the Pe-8 was the only such type to see widespread service in that time. It originated in 1936 from a Tupolev design bureau under the direction of Petlyakov, originally bearing the design bureau designation ANT-42 and the Red Air Force designation TB-7. In its initial form—it first appeared in 1940—the aircraft was powered by four 1,100 h.p. Mikulin M-105 inline engines, but in the first production version these were replaced by AM-35A radials. Later models included one which appeared in 1943, although not in any great numbers, with 1,500 h.p. M-40F diesel inlines, and the final operational version, in which a return was made to a radial powerplant, the 1,700 h.p. M-82. Production terminated in 1944. A number of Pe-8 aircraft were used during the war as engine testbeds, and several were diverted to transport duties, one bringing Mr. Molotov to Britain in the spring of 1942; in their bombing role the aircraft were principally employed against German or Balkan targets. An interesting design feature of the Pe-8 was the installation of hand-operated gun positions in the undersides of the inner engine nacelles.

BRIEF TECHNICAL DETAILS:

Engines: Four 1,450 h.p. Mikulin AM-35A radials.
Span: 131 ft. 3 in.
Length: 80 ft. 6 in.
Weight Loaded: 67,750 lb.
No. in crew: Eleven.
Max. Speed: 274 m.p.h. at 25,000 ft.
Service Ceiling: 33,000 ft.
Max. Range: 2,320 miles.
Armament: Two 20 mm. ShVAK cannon, two 12.7 mm. Beresin and two 7.62 mm. ShKAS machine guns and up to 8,800 lb. of bombs.

P.108B bearing Bruno Mussolini's signature on the fuselage/*Italian Air Ministry*

Piaggio P.108B

Country of origin: **ITALY**   *Makers:* **Societa Anonima Piaggio & C.**
Purpose: **Heavy bomber.**   *In operational use:* **1942/43.**

When Italy entered World War 2 her bomber force, although strong, was composed entirely of medium bombers; she did not have a long range heavy bomber in service until two years later. The design of this type, the Piaggio P.108, was begun in 1937 and the prototype made its maiden flight in 1939. The P.108 had many advanced design features, but undoubtedly the most interesting one was the installation of a remotely-controlled gun barbette in each of the outboard engine nacelles. Located on the upper part of the cowling, each of these barbettes mounted a pair of 12.7 mm. machine guns with a wide arc of fire, and was operated by a crew member in the fuselage. The first version to be built was the P.108A: only one example of this model was built and this was eventually acquired by the Luftwaffe. The first and only service version was the P.108B, generally similar except for the substitution of a glazed forward bombing position in place of the " solid " nose of the A, and this model entered service with the Regia Aeronautica in 1942. Although only 163 P.108Bs were completed, squadrons of these bombers were active around the Mediterranean area and made several raids on the fortress of Gibraltar; it was in one such attack that Mussolini's son Bruno was killed in a P.108B. The type also served on the Russian front.

BRIEF TECHNICAL DETAILS
Engines: Four 1,500 h.p. Piaggio P.XII RC 35 radials.
Span: 105 ft. 0 in.
Length: 75 ft. 2 in.
Height: 17 ft. 1 in.
Weight Empty: 38,104 lb.
            Loaded: 64,900 lb.
No. in crew: Seven.
Max. Speed: 270 m.p.h. at 14,000 ft.
Service Ceiling: 19,685 ft.
Normal Range: 1,550 miles.
Armament: Eight 12.7 mm. Breda-SAFAT machine guns. Up to 7,716 lb. of bombs or three 18-in. torpedos.

Republic P-47 Thunderbolt

Country of origin: **U.S.A.**
Purpose: **Fighter and fighter-bomber.**

Makers: **Republic Aviation Corporation.**
In operational use: **1943/45.**

When official U.S. requirements for this fighter were drawn up in June 1940, Republic already had on the drawing board an XP-47 design for a *lightweight* fighter; the Thunderbolt which ultimately bore the P-47 designation was the largest and heaviest single-engined, single-seat fighter then built, weighing in its final form as much as a Beaufighter. The true Thunderbolt prototype was the XP-47B, an entirely new design built around the new 2,000 h.p. Double Wasp engine; this made its maiden flight on 6th May, 1941. The first version to enter service (in November 1942) was the P-47B, powered by a production Double Wasp engine and featuring a sliding cockpit hood; 171 of these were built, making their operational debut in April 1943. The P-47C, of which 602 were built, was a slightly lengthened model with provision for a ventrally-mounted fuel tank. The P-47D was the most numerous, 12,602 being built in four batches by Republic, with variations including external provision for fuel tanks or 500 lb. or 1,000 lb. bombs, and water-injected engines boosting the maximum speed to 433 m.p.h. Curtiss-Wright built a further 354 P-47Ds as P-47Gs, and 340 early series Ds were supplied to the R.A.F. as the Thunderbolt I. A further 590 aircraft, late Ds and subsequent series, became the R.A.F.'s Thunderbolt II. One D was modified (as the XP-47K) with a cut-down rear fuselage and bubble canopy, and this modification—with an added dorsal fin to restore full stability—became standard on many P-47Ds. The next major version was the P-47M, 130 (plus three YP-47M) being completed with a " souped-up " 2,800 h.p. engine, which gave a sprint speed of 470 m.p.h.

Final production of the Thunderbolt was devoted to the P-47N, 1,816 being completed. Produced primarily for Pacific operation, this coupled the P-47M engine and fuselage with a strengthened and extended wing and had a gross weight of 21,200 lb., compared with the 12,086 lb. of the XP-47B. Experimental Thunderbolts included the high-altitude XP-47E, the laminar-flow XP-47F and the high-speed XP-47H (2,500 h.p. Chrysler) and XP-47J.

BRIEF TECHNICAL DETAILS (P-47D):

Engine: One 2,535 h.p. Pratt & Whitney R-2800-59 Double Wasp radial.
Span: 40 ft. 9 in.
Length: 36 ft. 1 in.
Height: 14 ft. 2 in.
Weight Empty: 10,700 lb.
Loaded: 17,500 lb. (max.).
No. in crew: One.
Max. Speed: 429 m.p.h. at 30,000 ft
Service Ceiling: 42,000 ft.
Normal Range: 590 miles.
Armament: Six or eight .50 machine guns; up to 2,500 lb. of bombs or ten R.Ps.

Late production P-47D

P-47N

S.M. 79-II/I.W.M.

Savoia-Marchetti S.M. 79 Sparviero (Hawk)

Country of origin: **ITALY**
Purpose: **Medium bomber.**

Makers: **Societa Italiana Aeroplani Idrovolanti Savoia-Marchetti.**
In operational use: **1940/45.**

Despite its ugly three-motor layout and ponderous " hunchback " appearance, the S.M.79 was in fact a highly efficient aeroplane in its class, and was rated by many authorities as the best land-based torpedo-bomber of the war. Appearing at the end of 1934 as a commercial transport development of the S.M.81 Pipistrello, the prototype S.M.79 set up two world records for closed-circuit flying a year later. Ordered for the Regia Aeronautica, the initial production model was the S.M.79-I powered by three 780 h.p. Alfa Romeo 126 radial engines. Maximum internal bomb load was 2,750 lb., and the armament a variety of 12.7 mm. and 7.7 mm. machine guns; with full bomb load the S.M.79-I had a range of 1,180 miles. That invaluable testing-ground of practically every major Axis warplane, the Spanish Civil War, saw numbers of S.M.79s in successful operation on the side of the Nationalists; meanwhile, as early as 1937, the Italian Air Ministry was sponsoring trials with the S.M.79 as a torpedo-carrying aircraft, and towards the end of 1939 the S.M.79-II entered production to fulfil this role. By June 1940, when Italy entered the war, S.M.79s of both versions formed well over half of the total bomber force of the Regia Aeronautica, and the type was widely used in and around the Mediterranean area for anti-shipping, reconnaissance and conventional bombing duties. The Sparviero continued in service, after Italy's surrender, with both sides; the new Italian force which continued in support of Germany also operated a " cleaned-up " model known as the S.M.79-III, most of which were converted S.M.79-IIs. One other variant worthy of mention was a twin-engined model with a streamlined " glasshouse " nose section and modified fin and rudder known as the S.M. 79B. Built for export, the S.M. 79B was sold to several Balkan and other countries, with varying powerplants of Italian or German origin.

> **BRIEF TECHNICAL DETAILS (S.M. 79-II):**
> Engines: Three 1,000 h.p. Piaggio P.XI RC 40 radials.
> Span: 69 ft. 6¾ in.
> Length: 53 ft. 1¾ in.
> Height: 13 ft. 5¼ in.
> Weight Empty: 16,755 lb.
>   Loaded: 24,912 lb.
> No. in crew: Four.
> Max. Speed: 270 m.p.h. at 12,000 ft.
> Service Ceiling: 22,966 ft.
> Normal Range: 1,243 miles.
> Armament: Three 12.7 mm. Breda-SAFAT and one 7.7 mm. Lewis machine guns. Up to 2,750 lb. of bombs or two torpedos.

148

S.M.81 with Alfa Romeo engines/H. J. Nowarra

Savoia-Marchetti S.M. 81 Pipistrello (Bat)

Country of origin: **ITALY**
Purpose: **Bomber and transport.**

Makers: **Societa Italiana Aeroplani Idrovolanti Savoia-Marchetti.**
In operational use: **1940/45.**

Already in service with the Regia Aeronautica when Italy invaded Abyssinia in 1935, the S.M.81 Pipistrello was also employed operationally in the Spanish Civil War a few years later. A direct development of the commercial S.M.73 airliner of the early 1930s, the S.M.81 was in service well before the S.M.79 Sparviero (see opposite), despite its higher designation number, about 100 of the type contributing to Italy's total bomber force on her entry into World War 2. Most of these were employed by the Italian East African Command. As the war progressed the Pipistrello, an ageing aeroplane, became transferred to the second-line duties of paratroop and general-purpose transport, in which roles it served for the remainder of the war. Although most of them were used in the Mediterranean and North African theatres—some taking part in the assault on Greece in October 1940—a small number were dispatched to the Russian front in July 1941 to support the Luftwaffe. After Italy's surrender a number of S.M.81s served with the Aviazione della Repubblica Sociale Italiana, and a few survived to serve as transports with the post-war Italian Air Force. The S.M.81B was a twin-engined bomber development (*cf.* also the S.M.79B), which was supplied to Rumania.

BRIEF TECHNICAL DETAILS:
Engines: Three 560 h.p. Piaggio P.IX RC 40 radials.
Span: 78 ft. 9 in.
Length: 60 ft.-0¼ in.
Height: 15 ft. 9 in.
Weight Empty: 14,300 lb.
Loaded: 22,220 lb.
No. in crew: Six.
Max. Speed: 196 m.p.h. at 13,120 ft.
Service Ceiling: 22,960 ft.
Max. Range: 1,242 miles.
Armament: Four or five 12.7 mm. machine guns.

149

Short Stirling

Country of origin: **GREAT BRITAIN**   *Specification:* **B.12/36.**
Purpose: **Heavy bomber.**   *In operational use:* **1940/45.**
Makers: **Short Bros. Ltd.**

Although to the Stirling goes the distinction of being the first four-engined Allied bomber to enter service during World War 2, it was a victim of the failure of the planning staff to foresee accurately the requirements of a few years ahead, and did not achieve the prominence of its later team-mates, the Halifax and Lancaster. Unlike these, however, the Stirling did start out as a four-engined design. Preceded in 1938 by the S.31, a half-scale trial model, the S.29 Stirling prototype (L 7600), powered by Hercules II motors, made its maiden flight during May 1939 but was destroyed on landing. The first production Stirling Mk. I, now with the more powerful Hercules XI, flew twelve months later and was entering service in August 1940, though only a handful of aircraft were delivered during that year. Production was gradually stepped up during 1941, the first "heavy" raid on enemy-occupied territory being made during February. Although the Stirling had a fairly good defensive armament and could absorb a considerable amount of punishment, the increasing opposition met over the continent led to its being diverted mainly to night operations by the beginning of 1942. During 1941 three Stirlings, designated Mk. II, were tested with American Wright Cyclone engines as a safeguard against a possible shortage of Hercules, but this proved unnecessary and the next major production version was the Mk. III, with uprated Hercules engines, improved performance and a new dorsal turret. Although large numbers of this version were produced, by 1943 the Stirling was becoming outdated as a bomber and in its next form, the Mk. IV, it became a transport and glider tug for the Horsa. The final version, also a transport, was the Mk. V, featuring a lengthened and "solid" nose. Production of the Stirling, including 756 Mk. I, 875 Mk. III, 577 Mk. IV and 160 Mk. V, reached a grand total of 2,375 aircraft.

BRIEF TECHNICAL DETAILS (Mk. I):
Engines: Four 1,590 h.p. Bristol Hercules XI radials.
Span: 99 ft. 1 in.
Length: 87 ft. 3 in.
Height: 22 ft. 9 in.
Weight Empty: 44,000 lb.
　　Loaded: 59,400 lb.
No. in crew: Seven or eight.
Max. Speed: 260 m.p.h. at 10,500 ft.
Service Ceiling: 20,500 ft.
Normal Range: 1,930 miles.
Armament: Eight .303 Browning machine guns. Up to 14,000 lb. of bombs.

Sunderland G.R. Mk. V/*I.W.M.*

Short Sunderland

Country of origin: **GREAT BRITAIN**
Purpose: **Maritime patrol and reconnaissance.**
Makers: **Short Bros. Ltd.**

Specification: **R.2/33.**
In operational use: **1939/45.**

Evolved as a monoplane replacement for the biplane flying boats of the early 'thirties, the S.25 Sunderland was basically a military development of the famous pre-war " C " class Empire boats. It retained the two-deck layout, with officers' wardroom, crew's quarters, sleeping quarters, galley and workshop, and the prototype (K 4774) first flew in October 1937. The Mk. I (Pegasus XXII engines) entered service in the following summer, and 75 of this version were built. On the outbreak of World War 2 three squadrons were equipped with the type; they did much valuable work on maritime patrol, but Sunderlands also performed a considerable amount of transport work, evacuating hundreds from Norway, Greece and Crete. The Sunderland played a notable part in the defeat of the U-boat, claiming its first in January 1940, and was able to give a good account of itself in the air. Its capacity for defence—armament increased considerably with successive versions—earned it the nickname of " Flying Porcupine ", and it included many Ju 88s in an impressive list of " kills ". Succeeding the Mk. I in production at the end of 1941 came the Mk. II, 58 of which were built. Later examples incorporated a two-gun dorsal turret, and this version also introduced the Pegasus XVIII as powerplant. The Mk. III, whose prototype flew in June 1942, was by far the most numerous (407 built) and introduced various refinements, including an improved planing hull. The Sunderland IV, 31 of which were completed, became the Seaford, the final production Sunderland (143 built) being the Mk. V. Total Sunderland production, which ended in October 1945, thus reached over 700 aircraft, of which 250 were completed by Blackburn Aircraft Ltd. In the early war years the Sunderland shortage was augmented by a few Empire boats from British Airways; these were returned when the situation eased, and in 1943 the procedure was reversed by the release of a batch of " demilitarised " Sunderlands to the civil operator.

> **BRIEF TECHNICAL DETAILS**
> **(Mk. V):**
> *Engines:* Four 1,200 h.p. Pratt & Whitney Twin Wasp R-1830 radials.
> *Span:* 112 ft. 9½ in.
> *Length:* 85 ft. 4 in.
> *Height:* 32 ft. 10¼ in.
> *Weight Empty:* 37,000 lb.
>   *Loaded:* 60,000 lb.
> *No. in crew:* Thirteen.
> *Max. Speed:* 213 m.p.h. at 5,000 ft.
> *Service Ceiling:* 17,900 ft.
> *Normal Range:* 2,980 miles.
> *Armament:* Two .50 and eight or twelve .303 machine guns; up to 2,000 lb. of bombs.

Si 204D/H. J. Nowarra

Siebel Si 204

Country of origin: **GERMANY**
Purpose: **Trainer, light transport and liaison.**

Makers: **Siebel Flugzeugwerke A.G.**
In operational use: **1941/45.**

Developed in 1940 from the pre-war Fh 104 Hallore medium-range transport, the prototype of the Si 204 flew for the first time in 1941 and was intended as a light communications aircraft. Apart from a few Si 204As (360 h.p. Argus As 410 engines), the main production of the Si 204 centred on the 204D, which was adapted to supersede the Fw 58 as an aircrew trainer. In this role the normal complement was five students in addition to the crew of two. In order to conserve the resources of the German aircraft industry for more essential military types, production of the Si 204D was delegated during the occupation to factories in Czechoslovakia and France. After the war the French SNCA du Centre continued to build it as a military aircraft under their own designation of N.C. 701, and in developed form as the N.C. 702 Martinet civil transport; the Czech Aero factory also turned out post-war military and civil versions in fairly substantial numbers.

BRIEF TECHNICAL DETAILS (Si 204D):

Engines: Two 575 h.p. Argus As 411 inlines.
Span: 69 ft. 9 in.
Length: 39 ft. 2¼ in.
Height: 13 ft. 11¼ in.
Weight Empty: 8,639 lb.
    Loaded: 11,902 lb.
Max. Speed: 219 m.p.h. at 9,840 ft.
Normal Range: 500 miles.
Service Ceiling: 24,600 ft.
Armament: Normally none.

Seafire Mk. III

Supermarine Seafire

Country of origin: **GREAT BRITAIN**
Purpose: **Carrier-borne fighter and reconnaissance.**

Makers: **Vickers-Armstrongs Ltd. (Supermarine Division).**
In operational use: **1942/45.**

The Royal Navy, lacking a fleet fighter of good performance, decided following the successful sea operation of the Hurricane to adopt the Spitfire for carrier service. Initial deck landing trials were undertaken late in 1941, aboard H.M.S. *Illustrious*, with a standard Spitfire VB fitted with an arrester hook and catapult gear, and an order ensued for the conversion of some 140 " hooked " Spitfire VBs under the new name Seafire IB. An additional 48 Mk. IB were built as such, and this version entered service in June 1942. No wing folding was employed on this or the Mk. IIC, a similar conversion of the Spitfire VC (except that the C and not the B wing was used). There were 372 Mk. IIC built. The Seafire III was by far the most important version (1,220 built), entering service in 1943 and being produced in photographic reconnaissance as well as fighter versions. The Mk. III was a considerable improvement over earlier Seafires, its capacity for wing folding greatly facilitating handling and storage, and was rated by some authorities as the best naval fighter anywhere in the world at the time. Parallel with the progress of the Spitfire, the Seafire was developed under Specification N.4/43 to take a Griffon powerplant, and this line began with the Griffon VI-powered Seafire XV which first flew in 1944 and eventually ran to 384 machines. The Mk. XV entered service in May 1945, but was still working up for Pacific operation when the war ended. Postwar development continued with the Mks. XVII, 45, 46 and 47, Seafires continuing in service to the Korean war. They began to be replaced from 1951, though the last F.A.A. squadron did not disband until 1954.

BRIEF TECHNICAL DETAILS (F. Mk. III):
Engine: One 1,470 h.p. Rolls-Royce Merlin 55 inline.
Span: 36 ft. 8 in.
Length: 30 ft. 0 in.
Height: 11 ft. 2 in.
Weight Empty: 5,400 lb.
Loaded: 7,100 lb.
No. in crew: One.
Max. Speed: 352 m.p.h. at 12,250 ft.
Service Ceiling: 33,800 ft.
Normal Range: 465 miles.
Armament: Two 20 mm. cannon and four .303 machine guns. One 500 lb. or two 250 lb. bombs optional.

153

Supermarine Spitfire

Country of origin: **GREAT BRITAIN**
Purpose: **Fighter, fighter-bomber and reconnaissance.**

Makers: **Vickers-Armstrongs Ltd.**
(Supermarine Division).
Specification: **F.37/34.**
In operational use: **1939/45.**

The recipient of more superlatives than any other aeroplane ever flown, Reginald Mitchell's classic Spitfire was built in greater numbers than any other British aircraft, appeared in some forty major versions and was the only British type in continuous production throughout World War 2. Evolved as a private venture from the unsuccessful Supermarine F.7/30, a Goshawk-powered machine with a cranked wing and fixed undercarriage, the new Spitfire was far ahead of the Air Ministry's F.5/34 Specification for an eight-gun monoplane fighter, and the later 1934 Specification was " written round " it. On 5th March 1936 at Eastleigh, Hampshire, Vickers' chief test pilot " Mutt " Summers took the Spitfire prototype (K 5054) on its maiden flight, the new Merlin C engine giving it a maximum speed not far short of 350 m.p.h. Before the Spitfire's career had ended, the excellence of the basic design, coupled with the remarkable development of the Merlin engine and its successor, the Griffon, had added more than 100 m.p.h. to this figure. Mitchell died before his progeny entered R.A.F. service, but not before he had seen, in 1937, two substantial contracts placed for the type. Deliveries of the Spitfire Mk. I began in 1938, and by the outbreak of war nine squadrons were equipped and orders stood at the then impressive total of 2,160 aircraft. While the Mk. Is were being delivered, an intensive development programme was already under way. In 1940 the Mk. II (1,175 h.p. Merlin XII) entered service; 920 examples of this version were followed by the P.R. IV (there was only one Mk. III) and the Mk. V fighter, one of the most widely used variants. The Spitfire utilised one of three basic wings: the A with eight .303 machine guns, the B with four 20 mm. cannon, and the " universal " C wing, first used on the Mk. VC. The first high altitude development was the long-span (40 ft. 2 in.) and pressurised Mk. VI. The Mk. VII, another high-altitude model, incorporated an extensively redesigned fuselage and a Merlin 60 powerplant which pushed the speed for the first time above 400 m.p.h. Only 140 of these were built, but the figure for the Mk. VIII rose to 1,658, including both high and low level fighter versions. Before the Mk. VIII entered service, a

Spitfire H.F. Mk. VII/Air-Britain

Spitfire L.F. Mk. XII/I.W.M.

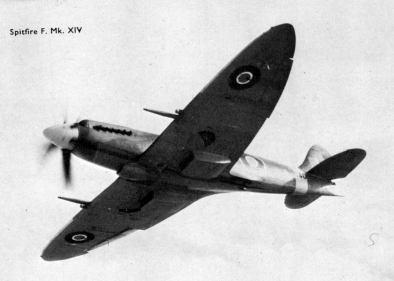

Spitfire F. Mk. XIV

" marriage of convenience " of the Merlin 60 engine and the Mk. VC airframe had produced, in 1942, the Spitfire IX. Combined production of the V and IX totalled 5,609 aircraft. Large numbers of Packard-built Merlin engines were supplied from the United States during the war; these were not, however interchangeable with the British Merlins, and thus gave rise to a new series of Mark numbers The first of these was the Mk. XVI, otherwise similar to the IX, of which there were 1,054. The introduction of the new Griffon engine marked yet another phase of Spitfire development, the first in this series being 100 Griffon II-powered Mk. XII. The Mk. XIV (1,055 built, including a batch of clipped-wing F.R. XIVE) was based on the standard Mk. VIII airframe, strengthened to take the Griffon 65 and having an enlarged vertical tail; final examples of the Mk. XIV were the first to introduce the cut-down rear fuselage and " teardrop " cockpit hood. To a Spitfire XIV (of 401 squadron) fell the distinction of destroying the first Me 262, and this was also the version chiefly successful against the V.1 flying bombs. Photographic Spitfires included the Mks. IV, VII, X, XI, XIII and XIX, the last of these being the fastest of all with a maximum speed of 460 m.p.h. Other versions too late to see war service included the Mks. XVIII, XX, 21, 22 and 24. The Spitfire, although it took second place to the Hurricane in the Battle of Britain, was a much more adaptable machine. Its flying qualities were legion, and it is doubtful if a warplane more popular with its pilots—and unpopular with its opponents!—has ever been conceived. During its 12-year career, more than 20,000 Spitfires of all versions were built.

BRIEF TECHNICAL DETAILS

(Mk. VB):
Engine: One 1,440 h.p. Rolls-Royce Merlin 45 inline.
Span: 36 ft. 10 in.
Length: 29 ft. 11 in.
Height: 11 ft. 5 in.
Weight Empty: 5,065 lb.
  Loaded: 6,650 lb.
No. in crew: One.
Max. Speed: 374 m.p.h. at 13,000 ft.
Service Ceiling: 37,000 ft.
Max. Range: 1,135 miles.
Armament: Two 20 mm. cannon and four .303 machine guns. One 500 lb. or two 250 lb. bombs optional.

(Mk. XIV):
Engine: One 2,050 h.p. Rolls-Royce Griffon 65 inline.
Span: 36 ft. 10 in.
Length: 32 ft. 8 in.
Height: 12 ft. 8¼ in.
Weight Empty: 6,600 lb.
  Loaded: 8,490 lb.
No. in crew: One.
Max. Speed: 448 m.p.h. at 26,000 ft.
Service Ceiling: 44,500 ft.
Max. Range: 850 miles.
Armament: Two 20 mm. cannon and four .303 machine guns. Up to 1,000 lb. of bombs.

Walrus Mk. I

Supermarine Walrus

Country of origin: **GREAT BRITAIN**
Purpose: **Reconnaissance and air/sea rescue.**
Makers: **Supermarine Aviation Works (Vickers) Ltd.**

Specification: **2/35 (first production).**
In operational use: **1939/45.**

Few people familiar with the appealing lines of Reginald Mitchell's beautiful Spitfire would believe him capable of designing such an aesthetic misfit as the Walrus amphibian. Yet in its way the lumbering " Shagbat ", as the Walrus was popularly known, was regarded with quite as much affection as its illustrious stablemate. Beginning life as the Seagull V, a private venture development of an earlier Supermarine amphibian, the prototype (K 4797) first flew on 21st June, 1933. It was immediately ordered by the Australian Government, and in August 1935 the first Air Ministry contract, for 12 Mk. I powered by Pegasus IIM.2, was placed. This was soon followed by a much larger repeat order, and eventually 287 Mk. I Walruses were completed. Entering Fleet Air Arm service in July 1936, this version became the first amphibian to be catapulted from a warship and served aboard R.N. battleships and cruisers as a fleet spotter, convoy patrol and anti-submarine aircraft. In addition to the Supermarine-built Mk. I, 453 Mk. II Walruses were built by Saunders-Roe. These machines, wooden-hulled and powered by a differ-

ent mark of Pegasus engine, served primarily with the R.A.F. Air/Sea Rescue service during the early part of the war. Throughout their career, which did not terminate until after VJ-day, Walruses were flown in practically every corner of the world, from East Africa to Iceland, Hong Kong to the West Indies. Apart from the innumerable lives saved by these aircraft, the spotting and other work performed by them throughout the Second World War was invaluable to the Allied cause.

BRIEF TECHNICAL DETAILS (Mk. II):

Engine: One 775 h.p. Bristol Pegasus VI radial.
Span: 45 ft. 10 in.
Length: 37 ft. 7 in.
Height: 15 ft. 3 in.
Weight Empty: 4,900 lb.
*   *Loaded:* 7,200 lb.
No. in crew: Four.
Max. Speed: 135 m.p.h. at 4,750 ft.
Service Ceiling: 18,500 ft.
Normal Range: 600 miles.
Armament: Two Vickers K machine guns.

SB-2/H. J. Nowarra

Tupolev SB-2

Country of origin: **RUSSIA** Design bureau: **A.N. Tupolev.**
Purpose: **Medium bomber.** In operational use: **1941/45.**

The SB-2, or ANT-40, was developed from Tupolev's earlier SB-1, both types seeing service in the Spanish Civil War of the latter 1930s and in Finland in 1939. The original SB-2 (830 h.p. M-34 inlines) entered production during 1936, and an aircraft of this type secured an official F.A.I. record in 1937 for carrying a 1,000 kg. (2,200 lb.) payload to an altitude of 40,177 ft. Production of this version was completed in 1941 and development continued with the much-improved SB-2*bis*, this model being principally employed by the Red Air Force during the war years. Although obsolete by 1945, the SB-2*bis* performed useful service, particularly during the earlier part of the Russo-German conflict, on round-the-clock raids against enemy positions, and was still one of Russia's standard medium bombers in 1943. Among other developed versions of the basic type may be numbered a dive-bomber project by Archang-elski, designated Ar-2 or SB-2RK. Despite the greater power of its 1,100 h.p. M-105R engines, this was not a successful venture and was ultimately abandoned. The SB-3 was an aircrew trainer version in which the pupil occupied an open cockpit position in the nose of the aircraft, ahead of the standard crew cabin. The PS-41 was a transport variant with a "solid" nose and the gun positions eliminated.

BRIEF TECHNICAL DETAILS
(SB-2bis):
Engines: Two 990 h.p. M-103 inlines.
Span: 70 ft. 6 in.
Length: 41 ft. 6 in.
Weight Empty: 9,436 lb.
  Loaded: 14,330 lb.
No. in crew: Three.
Max. Speed: 280 m.p.h. at 16,400 ft.
Service Ceiling: 27,890 ft.
Max. Range: 1,430 miles.
Armament: Four 7.62 mm. machine guns; up to 1320 lb. of bombs.

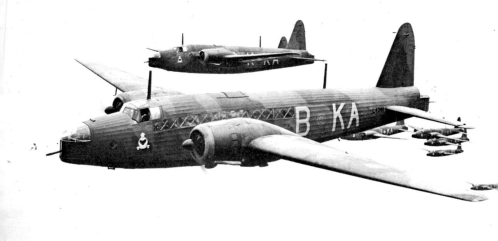

Vickers Wellington

Country of origin: **GREAT BRITAIN**
Purpose: **Medium bomber and recon.**
Makers: **Vickers-Armstrongs Ltd.**

Specification: **B.9/32.**
In operational use: **1939/45.**

One of the most outstanding aeroplanes of the war, the Wellington was note-worthy for the fantastic amount of punishment it could withstand, thanks largely to its revolutionary geodetic construction devised by Barnes Wallis of " dams " fame. The prototype (K 4049), powered by two 850 h.p. Bristol Pegasus X, first flew on 15th June, 1936, and a production order was placed the same year. The Mk. I, modified to accommodate twice the original bomb load and powered by two 1,000 h.p. Pegasus XVIII, entered service in October 1938, followed by the IA and IC (the IB was not produced). Wellingtons made the first raid of the war, against Wilhelmshaven, on 4th September, 1939; from December 1939 they switched to night operations and were the main night bombing type of the

Wellington Mk. IC

Wellington Mk. II

R.A.F. until the arrival of the " heavies ". They were also the first to drop the 4,000 lb. " blockbuster " bomb. Next in production were the Mk. II (Merlin X, 400 built), Mk. III (Hercules XI, 1,519 built) and Mk. IV (Pratt & Whitney Twin Wasp, 221 built). The Wellingtons V, VI and VII were for the most part experimental, the next big production version being the Mk. VIII for Coastal Command. As early as 1940, a few modified Mk. Is had successfully performed " de-gaussing " and minelaying duties; now the Mk. VIII, of which 394 were completed, emerged as a torpedo-bomber and general reconnaissance aircraft, carrying a Leigh Light in the bomb bay and external radar. From this were developed the G.R. XI, with an enclosed " chin " radome, and the pure-reconnaissance G.R. XII. The G.R. XIII and XIV were parallel versions with uprated Hercules engines. The principal production Wellington was the Mk. X, of which 3,804 were built from 1943 onwards. Transport conversions of the Mks. I, IA and IC, with turrets removed, the bomb bay sealed off and seats installed, became the C.I, C.XV and C.XVI. The Mk. IX was a " one-off " conversion of a IC as a troop transport. Night fighter training versions of the Mks. XI and XIII became the T.XVII and T.XVIII. Total Wellington production reached 11,461 aircraft, many serving as engine and armament test-beds.

BRIEF TECHNICAL DETAILS (Mk. X):
Engines: Two 1,585 h.p. Bristol Hercules VI radials.
Span: 86 ft. 2 in.   Length: 64 ft. 7 in.
Height: 17 ft. 6 in.
Weight Empty: 26,325 lb.
    Loaded: 31,500 lb.
No. in crew: Six.
Max. Speed: 255 m.p.h. at 14,500 ft.
Servic: Ceiling: 24,000 ft.
Norm il Range: 1,325 miles
Armament: Six .303 Browning machine guns; up to 6,000 lb. of bombs.

Wellington Mk. VIII

A-31 (Vultee V-72), built originally as an R.A.F. Vengeance Mk. II

Vultee A-35 Vengeance

Country of origin: **U.S.A.**
Purpose: **Dive bomber and target tug.**
Makers: **Vultee Aircraft Inc.**

Other U.S. designations: **A-31, TBV-I.**
In operational use: **1942/45.**

The Vengeance was originally produced to a British order placed in the summer of 1940 for an " answer " to the German Ju 87 dive bomber, and as such it was the R.A.F's first aircraft specifically designed for this role. It was another two years before the U.S.A.A.F. followed suit, by which time the reputation of the dive bomber as an operational type had declined to such an extent that the Vengeance's employment on these duties was limited. It continued to give useful service, however, on both sides of the Atlantic, in the important if less spectacular role of target tug. First flown in July, 1941, deliveries of the Vengeance to the R.A.F. began about a year later, and 32 of the initial batch were passed on to the Royal Australian Air Force. The R.A.F's operational use of the type was confined to the India-Burma theatre. The U.S.A.A.F. ordered for itself 300 aircraft equivalent to the British Vengeance II, designating them A-31A, but in the event only a few were retained for test purposes and the balance supplied to the R.A.F. as the Vengeance IA and III. The first fully-U.S. Vengeance was the A-35; 100 of these were completed, all but one of them later being converted to A-35As by the substitution of .50 guns for the original .303s. There followed a batch of 831 A-35Bs, a slightly improved version of which 562 were supplied to the R.A.F. as the Vengeance IV, but the bulk of these were employed almost entirely on target towing duties. Very little naval use was made of the Vengeance, though a small number gravitated to the U.S. Navy as the TBV-1 and the Royal Navy employed a few Vengeance IVs as target tugs. Production of the Vengeance terminated in May 1944 after the completion of just over 1,900 aircraft.

BRIEF TECHNICAL DETAILS:
(A-35A):
Engine: One 1,600 h.p. Wright R-2600-19 Cyclone radial.
Span: 48 ft. 0 in.
Length: 39 ft. 9 in.
Height: 15 ft. 4 in.
Weight Empty: 10,060 lb.
Loaded: 13,500 lb.
No. in crew: Two.
Max. Speed: 273 m.p.h. at 11,000 ft.
Service Ceiling: 21,500 ft.
Normal Range: 600 miles.
Armament: Five .50 machine guns; up to 2,000 lb. of bombs.

161

Lysander Mk. I, Finnish Air Force/*Eino Ritaranta*

Westland Lysander

Country of origin: **GREAT BRITAIN**
Purpose: **Army co-operation.**
Makers: **Westland Aircraft Ltd.**

Specification: **A.39/34.**
In operational use: **1939/44.**

Known to all with great affection as the " Lizzie ", the Lysander, with its lozenge-shaped high braced wings and inordinately large " spatted " under-carriage, was a familiar sight in European skies during the early years of World War 2.   Two prototypes were built to the original Air Ministry Specification and the first of these, K 6127, made its maiden flight in June 1936.   Three months later an initial production contract was placed for 144 machines, and the first Lysanders Mk. I entered R.A.F. service towards the end of 1938.   During the early war years the type was in widespread use in France and North Africa, though in 1941, as the Curtiss Tomahawk began to replace it for Army co-operation, production was phased out and ceased in January 1942.   Thereafter the Lysander gradually transferred to other duties.   Several Mks. I and II (905 h.p. Perseus XII in the latter) were converted for target towing, and many other Mk. II for air/sea rescue and glider towing.   A considerable number of Mk. IIIs (870 h.p. Mercury 20 or 30) were built as target tugs, and also worthy of mention is the modified Lysander III for the Special Air Service.   Fitted with a jettison-able auxiliary fuel tank under the belly, this version was used for dropping British intelligence agents into enemy-occupied territory.   The Lysander was also employed on occasion as a light bomber, carrying small bombs or supply containers on the stub-wings attached to its wheel spats.   Total production reached 1,593 aircraft, comprising 131 Mk. I, 433 Mk. II and 804 Mk. III built in Great Britain, and 225 by the National Steel Car Corporation in Canada.

BRIEF TECHNICAL DETAILS (Mk. I):
Engine: One 890 h.p. Bristol Mercury XII radial.
Span: 50 ft. 0 in.   *Length:* 30 ft. 6 in.
Height: 11 ft. 6 in.
Weight Empty: 4,065 lb.
Loaded: 5,920 lb.
No. in crew: Two.
Max. Speed: 229 m.p.h. at 10,000 ft.
Service Ceiling: 26,500 ft.
Normal Range: 500 miles.
Armament: Four .303 machine guns; up to six small bombs.

Yak-9D/*via Jean Alexander*

Yakovlev Yak-9

Country of origin: **RUSSIA**   *Design bureau:* **A.S. Yakovlev.**
Purpose: **Fighter.**   *In operational use:* **1942/45.**

By far the most widely produced of any Yakovlev fighter during the war years, the Yak-9 was very much a " pilot's aeroplane ": light, easy on the controls and with excellent manoeuvrability and performance at altitudes up to about 16,000 ft.   Several thousand Yak-9s were built, serving with Polish units and the famous French Normandie Squadron as well as with the Red Air Force.   The Yak-9 resulted from further refinements in design and construction of the Yak-7B, amongst them modifications to the wings (to accommodate additional fuel) and the relocation of the cockpit further aft.   The type first entered production during 1942, making its operational debut at the Battle of Stalingrad in October of that year.   In 1943 there appeared two further versions, the Yak-9D and Yak-9T.   The former was primarily intended for bomber escort duties, having a reduced armament and sufficient extra fuel to give a maximum range of 882 miles.   The Yak-9T appeared in two versions, data for the first batch of which is given below.   The second version was armed with a single 75 mm. cannon, with which it was employed with reasonable success on anti-shipping duties. Later variants, differing primarily in armament and equipment installations, included the Yak-9L and the Yak-9M. The Yak-9U, a considerably improved and cleaner-looking machine powered by the 1,650 h.p. M-107A engine, had entered production before the war ended and, with the Yak-9P (the final version) equipped Soviet and satellite fighter squadrons for many years afterwards.

BRIEF TECHNICAL DETAILS
(Yak-9T):
Engine: One 1,260 h.p. Klimov M-105 PF inline.
Span: 32 ft. 9¾ in.
Length: 28 ft. 0½ in.
Height: 8 ft. 0 in.
Weight Empty: 6,063 lb.
    Loaded: 7,055 lb.
No. in crew: One.
Max. Speed: 363 m.p.h. at 16,400 ft.
Service Ceiling: 36,090 ft.
Normal Range: 516 miles.
Armament: One 37 mm. Nudelman cannon and one 12.7 mm. Beresin machine gun.

163

Yokosuka D4Y Suisei *(Comet)*

Country of origin: **JAPAN**
Purpose: **Dive bomber and reconnaissance.**

Designers: **Yokosuka Naval Air Depot.**
In operational use: **1942/45.**

The Suisei (*Judy*) under the Allied code naming system) was that comparative rarity among 1939-45 warplanes: an aircraft which was produced in quantity in both inline- and radial-engined versions.   By and large, the former were deployed from aircraft carrier bases, and the latter from shore stations.   The initial production version was the D4Y1 Model 11, which was powered by a 1,185 h.p. Aichi Atsuta 21 inline engine, virtually a replica of the German DB601.   The Model 21 was generally similar, but in the D4Y2 (Model 22) the higher-powered Atsuta 32 (1,400 h.p.) was substituted, increasing the maximum speed to 360 m.p.h., and the fin and rudder were modified and increased in area.

The Suisei version which was eventually to appear in the greatest numbers, however, was the radial-engined Model 33 (D4Y3); all versions were, inevitably, called upon to participate in suicide raids towards the end of the war, and limited use was made of the type for night fighting.   The Suisei was evolved primarily as a replacement for the Aichi D3A1 *Val*, and it was the Aichi company which handled most of the total Suisei production (all versions) of 2,319 aircraft. This total also included 500 machines completed by the Hiro Arsenal.

**BRIEF TECHNICAL DETAILS
(D4Y3):**
Engine: One 1,560 h.p. Mitsubishi Kinsei 62 radial.
Span: 37 ft. 8¾ in.
Length: 33 ft. 4 in.
Height: 10 ft. 9½ in.
Weight Empty: 5,514 lb.
      Loaded: 8,270 lb.
No. in crew: Two.
Max. Speed: 350 m.p.h. at 19,360 ft.
Service Ceiling: 34,450 ft.
Max. Range: 944 miles.
Armament: One 7.9 mm. and two 7.7 mm. machine guns; up to 1,650 lb. of bombs.

Yokosuka MXY-7 Ohka
(Cherry Blossom)

Country of origin: **JAPAN**   *Designers:* **Yokosuka Naval Air Depot**
Purpose: **Piloted flying bomb.**   *In operational use:* **1944/45.**

Considering the purpose for which the Ohka was designed, popular opinion no doubt felt that the Allied code name (*Baka*, Japanese for " fool ") was more appropriate than that bestowed on it by its native country; but the suicide raids of the Japanese Army and Navy pilots during World War 2 were not considered by the Japanese to be any laughing matter. Indeed, when they began they were the exclusive right of a special Kamikaze (*Divine Wind*) Corps, to which it was a high honour to belong—although later they were made a compulsory duty for ordinary pilots, many of whom had to be forcibly strapped into their cockpits. The prototype MXY-7 was flown in the early autumn of 1944, a training glider version following shortly afterwards. In September 1944 production commenced of the Ohka Model 11, the only operational version, 755 of which were completed up to March 1945 before being superseded on the assembly lines by later models. These included the slightly smaller Ohka 22, fifty of which were built with a 110 h.p. engine driving a Campini-style compressor to give 441 lb. propulsive thrust; the Ohka 33 (intended for carriage by the G8N1 Renzan bomber and powered by a 1,047 lb. s.t. gas turbine) was abandoned in favour of the similarly-powered Ohka 43, designed for launching from catapults, which was to have entered production in October 1945. The Ohka 11 was carried by a "mother" plane, usually a G4M2e *Betty*, beneath whose open bomb bay it was shackled during flight. The launch generally took place at about 27,000 ft. and a speed of 200 m.p.h., from which the Ohka would glide at some 230 m.p.h. for about 50 miles towards its target before cutting in its rocket motors for the final 50-degree death dive.

BRIEF TECHNICAL DETAILS
(Model 11):
Engines: Three 588 lb. thrust Type 4 Mk. I Model 20 solid fuel rocket motors.
Span: 16 ft. 5 in.
Length: 19 ft. 8½ in.
Weight Empty: 970 lb.
    Loaded: 4,718 lb.
Crew: One.
Max. Speed: 570 m.p.h. in final dive.
Normal Range: approx. 55 miles.
Armament: 2,645 lb. of H.E. in nose warhead.

Yokosuka P1Y Ginga (Milky Way)

Country of origin: **JAPAN**
Purpose: **Bomber, night fighter and reconnaissance.**

Designers: **Yokosuka Naval Air Depot.**
In operational use: **1944/45.**

In function, if not in fame, the P1Y1 (*Frances*) was to the Japanese Navy what the Ju 88 was to the Luftwaffe or the Mosquito to the Royal Air Force. Although brought into being primarily as a bomber, it was capable of performing with almost equal success as a torpedo bomber, night fighter and reconnaissance aircraft. Design of the Ginga was begun in 1940 by the First Naval Air Technical Arsenal at the Yokosuka Naval Air Depot, but when the type was accepted for service as the P1Y1 in 1943 production was assigned to the Nakajima company, who eventually completed 1,002 of this version. As the war neared its end, Japan stood in greater need of defensive fighters than offensive bombers, and steps were taken to produce a night fighter version of the Ginga. The contract for this was awarded to Kawanishi, whose P1Y2-S Kyokko (*Aurora*) utilised the less troublesome 1,850 h.p. Kasei 25 as its powerplant, was fitted with rudimentary A.I. radar and carried an armament of three 20 mm. cannon. Only 97 P1Y2-S were completed, however, and these had not finished their pre-service trials before VJ day, although a few P1Y1-S conversions from Nakajima-built bombers saw limited operational service. The proposed Homare-powered P1Y3-S development did not get beyond the project stage.

BRIEF TECHNICAL DETAILS (P1Y1):
Engines: Two 1,820 h.p. Nakajima Homare 11 radials.
Span: 65 ft. 7½ in.
Length: 49 ft. 2½ in.
Height: 14 ft. 1¼ in.
Weight Empty: 14,748 lb.
  Loaded: 23,148 lb.
No. in crew: Three.
Max. Speed: 345 m.p.h. at 19,360 ft.
Service Ceiling: 33,530 ft.
Max. Range: 1,600 miles.
Armament: One 20 mm. cannon and one 13.2 mm. machine gun; up to 1,760 lb. of bombs or one 1,875 lb. torpedo internally.

Minor Types

Aeronca L-3 Grasshopper

Data apply to L-3B.
Purpose: Liaison and observation.
Engine: One 65 h.p. Continental O-170-3.

Span: 35 ft 0 in.
Max. Speed: 80 m.p.h.

In its initial form this aircraft was known as the YO-58 Defender, a two-seat trainer. Developed for the observation role, a total of 409, including the prototypes, were built under O-58 designations. With the establishment of the Grasshopper class of light aircraft, these received new designations in the L-3 series, and a further 1,030 aircraft were built from the outset as L-3B and -3C. In addition, 26 commercial Aeronca Model 65s were impressed for service as the L-3D to J. Most wartime versions were externally similar, differing only in equipment, but some commercial L-3s had Franklin or Lycoming engines.

B7A1/H. J. Nowarra

Aichi B7A Ryusei (*Shooting Star*)

Purpose: Torpedo bomber.
Engine: One 1,875 h.p. Nakajima Homare 11 radial.

Span: 47 ft. 3 in.
Max. Speed: 337 m.p.h. at 20,345 ft.

Code named *Grace* by the Allies, the two-seat Ryusei was first flown in May 1942 and entered production during April 1944. For a single-engined aircraft, it had the useful load of 2,205 lb. of bombs or one torpedo, and was armed with two 20 mm. cannon and one 12.7 mm. machine gun. Production of the Ryusei, delayed first by engine difficulties and later by earthquake, was slow; only just over 100 aircraft had been completed by the war's end, and comparatively few of these had reached J.N.A.F. squadrons. Some were, however, encountered in operations in home waters.

E13A1/H. J. Nowarra

Aichi E13A

Purpose: Reconnaissance.
Engine: One 1,080 h.p. Mitsubishi Kinsei 43 radial.

Span: 47 ft. 6¾ in.
Max. Speed: 234 m.p.h. at 7,150 ft.

It was an aeroplane of this type—later code named *Jake* by the Allies—that made the reconnaissance which preceded the Japanese air attack on Pearl Harbour, and the E13A1 remained in service until the end of the war.   Designed in 1938, it entered production in 1941, but only 132 machines had been completed by the parent firm before construction was delegated to the Kyushu company, who built a further 1,100 machines.   The *Jake* was a leading ship-borne reconnaissance type and was widely used in the Pacific war, participating in the Coral Sea, Midway and Solomons campaigns.

E16A1

Aichi E16A Zuiun   (*Auspicious Cloud*)

Purpose: Reconnaissance.
Engine: One 1,300 h.p. Mitsubishi Kinsei 54 radial.

Span: 41 ft. 11⅞ in.
Max. Speed: 279 m.p.h. at 18,305 ft.

The Zuiun (code name *Paul*) was produced by the Aichi concern as a later-generation successor to their E13A1 floatplane *Jake*.   It was intended primarily for the reconnaissance role, although more use was made of the type as a dive bomber, carrying a pair of 550 lb. bombs.   A three-seater, the Zuiun had an all-up weight of 8,598 lb., a range of 600 miles and an armament of two 20 mm., one 13.2 mm. and two 7.7 mm. guns; a total of 259 of these aircraft were built.

Airspeed Horsa

Purpose: Transport glider.
Span: 88 ft. 0 in.

Entering Army service in the late autumn of 1942, the A.S.51 Horsa was the first British glider to have a tricycle undercarriage. The main wheels of this were jettisoned after take-off, touchdown being made on the castoring nosewheel and a sprung central skid. With a capacity for 30 men or an equivalent freight load, the Horsa had an all-up weight of 15,500 lb. It was first used operationally in the invasion of Sicily in the summer of 1943, and subsequently with great success on D-day and at Arnhem. About 400 Horsas were at one time used by the U.S. forces as a kind of "reverse Lend-Lease". Total Horsa production was 3,655 machines.

Antonov A–7

Purpose: Transport glider.
Span: 62 ft. 3 in.
Length: 37 ft. 9 in.

The Red Air Force made little use of gliders during World War 2, but the A-7 won a design competition held in December 1940 for a " partisan transport glider ", and some 400 of this type were subsequently built. Usual tugs were Russian SB-2 or DB-3 bombers, although it is noteworthy that a number of Armstrong Whitworth Albemarle tugs were exported to Russia before D-day.

Arado Ar 96B

Purpose: Advanced trainer.
Engine: One 450 h.p. Argus As 410A inline.

Span: 36 ft. 0 in.
Max. Speed: 211 m.p.h. at 9,840 ft.

The two-seat Ar 96B was adopted in 1940 as a standard training aircraft for the Luftwaffe, and entered quantity production soon afterwards. Two versions were built, for primary and advanced training respectively, and differing only in equipment. Developed versions were the Ar 199 and Ar 296, the latter being produced post-war by the French company SIPA under the designation S.10.

Ar 232A/*Hanfried Schliephake*

Arado Ar 232

Purpose: Transport.
Engines: Two 2,000 h.p. BMW 801E radials (Ar 232A); four 690 h.p. Gnome-Rhone 14M radials (Ar 232B).

Span: 104 ft. 4 in. (Ar 232A); 109 ft. 10¾ in. (Ar 232B).
Max. Speed: 211 m.p.h. at 15,100 ft. (Ar 232B).

Apart from the differences in powerplant and wing span, the Ar 232A and Ar 232B were virtually the same design. The aircraft carried a crew of four and a useful load of some 10,000 lb., but were not used very widely; only 40 were built, and most of the work for which they were designed continued to be done by the Ju 52/3m, Me 323 and Go 242/244. An interesting feature was a fixed tricycle undercarriage which could be " broken " to allow the aircraft to lower itself on to 10 pairs of smaller wheels along the underside of the main fuselage pod, bringing it closer to the ground for loading and unloading. A later project, the Ar 432, was identical in appearance to the Ar 232B but was constructed of wood and metal instead of all metal.

Arado Ar 234 Blitz   *(Lightning)*

Data apply to Ar 234B-2.
Purpose: Bomber.
Engines: Two 1,980 lb.s.t. Junkers Jumo 004B turbojets.

Span: 46 ft. 3½ in.
Max. Speed: 461 m.p.h. at 19,685 ft.

With an operational ceiling of 36,000 feet and a range of more than 950 miles with a 2,200 lb. bomb load, the Ar 234—the world's first jet bomber—ought to have been a valuable addition to the Luftwaffe strength.   Such was not the case, however, and it was used operationally on only a small scale.   The first series version was the reconnaissance Ar 234B-1, which flew in December 1943 and entered production the following June; this was reported over the Western Front later in 1944.   The Ar 234B-2, a bomber, entered production at about the same time and appeared in action at the beginning of 1945.   In the early months of 1944 the first flight took place of the Ar 234C: this had four BMW 003 turbojets, mounted in pairs, and was altogether a much more efficient aircraft, with a top speed of 546 m.p.h.   Like many otherwise good designs, however, it arrived too late to make any effective contribution to the German war effort.

Arado Ar 240

Data apply to Ar 240C-0.
Purpose: Heavy Interceptor
Engines: Two 1,750 h.p. DB603A inlines

Span: 54 ft. 5½ in.
Max. Speed: 454 m.p.h. at 36,700 ft.

Originally intended to perform high altitude reconnaissance, fighting and dive bombing duties, the Ar 240 was conceived in 1938 and the first prototype flew in June 1940, powered by 1,175 h.p. DB601A inline engines. However, its whole development was hamstrung by changes in official priorities and general indecision as to its most suitable role, and only fifteen of the type were completed.   The developed Ar 440 was generally similar to the Ar 240C except for a powerplant of DB 603G inline engines, but again official interest waned and only four prototypes were completed.

171

Armstrong Whitworth Albemarle

Purpose: Special transport and glider tug.
Engines: Two 1,590 h.p. Bristol Hercules XI radials.

Span: 77 ft. 0 in.
Max. Speed: 265 m.p.h. at 10,500 ft.

Taken over by Armstrong Whitworth from the Taurus-powered Bristol 155 designed to Spec. B.18/38 for a medium bomber (which explains some similarity to the Beaufort — page 36) the Albemarle finally served only as a special transport and glider tug. The first British military aircraft with a tricycle undercarriage, it entered service in January 1943, seeing action in the Sicily, Normandy and Arnhem landings. Six hundred Albemarles were built, serving in the approximate ratio of two transports to one glider tug. Principal service versions were the Mks. I, II, V and VI.

Avro Manchester

Purpose: Heavy bomber.
Engines Two 1,760 h.p. Rolls-Royce Vulture inlines.

Span: 90 ft. 1 in.
Max. Speed: 265 m.p.h. at 17,000 ft.

Designed to A.M. Spec. P.13/36 for a twin-engined medium bomber built around two of the new Rolls-Royce Vulture engines, the Manchester had a good performance, including a range of 1,200 miles with a maximum bomb load of 10,350 lb. The prototype (L 7246) flew on 25th July, 1939, and the 200 production Manchesters were operational from November 1940 to June 1942. The first prototype and the Mk. IA had twin fins and rudders, the second prototype and the Mk. I a third central fin. The brief and unfortunate service life of the Manchester was the fault not of the basic design—which was developed into the successful Lancaster—but of the under-developed and unreliable Vulture engines which powered it.

Avro York

Purpose: Transport.
Engines: Four 1,280 h.p. Rolls-Royce Merlin XX inlines.
Span: 102 ft. 0 in.
Max. Speed: 298 m.p.h. at 21,000 ft.

Based on the Lancaster wing and powerplant, with a completely new fuselage and tail assembly, the York was designed to A.M. Spec. C.1/42 and made its maiden flight in the same year. With the wartime dependence upon the United States for the supply of transport aircraft, the York had a low production priority, and until 1945, when the first fully-equipped transport squadron was formed, the few aircraft delivered were employed as V.I.P. transports and flying conference rooms. The bulk of the 257 Yorks built were delivered after the end of the war, and the type played a prominent part in the Berlin Airlift of 1949.

Beechcraft AT-10 Wichita

Purpose: Trainer.
Engines: Two 295 h.p. Lycoming R-680-9 radials.
Span: 44 ft. 0 in.
Max. Speed: 190 m.p.h.

The Beechcraft Wichita appeared at approximately the same time as the Cessna Bobcat (page 184), which it resembled in both appearance and function. Of plywood construction, the Wichita was an aircrew "transition" trainer used quite widely during the early part of the war. A total of 2,371 were completed for the U.S.A.A.F., 1,771 of them by Beech and 600 by the Globe Aircraft Corporation, before production ceased in 1944. One machine was experimentally fitted with the "butterfly" tail later introduced on the Bonanza lightplane.

Beechcraft UC-43 Traveler

Purpose: Light transport.
Engine: One 450 h.p. Pratt & Whitney R-985-AN-I Wasp Junior radial.

Span: 32 ft. 0 in.
Max. Speed: 195 m.p.h. at 5,000 ft.

The Beechcraft Traveler was an adaptation of the five-seat civil Model 17, many variants of which were employed by the U.S. forces during World War 2. Three Model D-17-S were evaluated by the U.S.A.A.F. as YC-43s, and orders for 207 UC-43s and 63 GB-1s were executed for the Air Force and Navy respectively. In addition, 118 commercial Model 17s were impressed for war service with designations ranging from UC-43A to K. Thirty UC-43s and 75 GB-2s from U.S. contracts were supplied to the Royal Navy under Lend-Lease: these were known as the Traveller I and used for light transport and communication duties.

SNB-2 Navigator/*U.S. Department of Defense*

Beechcraft UC-45 Expediter

Data apply to UC-45F.
Purpose: Light transport.
Engines: Two 450 h.p. Pratt & Whitney R-985-AN-I Wasp Junior radials.

Span: 47 ft. 8 in.
Max. Speed: 206 m.p.h. at sea level.

Several developed versions of Beechcraft's 1936 Model 18 feederliner saw service with Allied air forces during the war on a variety of duties. Transport and general purpose versions were produced in quantity for the U.S.A.A.F. (UC-45), U.S. Navy (JRB), R.A.F. and Royal Navy (Expediter I and II), and some JRBs had a domed extension to the cabin or observation duties. More specialised developments included the AT-7 Navigator (navigation trainer), of which 1,112 were built, and the AT-11 Kansas (1,582 built), a bombing and gunnery trainer; both were also employed by the U.S. Navy as the SNB. A few AT-7As could be converted to float or ski landing gear.

Bell P-59 Airacomet

Purpose: Jet fighter trainer
Engines: Two 2,000 lb.s.t. General Electric J31-GE-3 turbojets.

Span: 45 ft. 6 in.
Max. Speed: 413 m.p.h. at 30,000 ft.

The first aircraft in the United States to be built for jet propulsion, the Airacomet was Bell's answer to a September 1941 requirement for a fighter built around two Whittle-type turbojets. The first of three XP-59A (this designation was undoubtedly a security cover, since the original XP-59 was a quite different project with a pusner radial motor) first flew on 1st October, 1942; these were followed by 13 YP-59A evaluation aircraft, two of which went to the U.S. Navy as XF2L-1. First production aircraft, designated P-59A, began delivery in the autumn of 1944, being classified by this time as fighter trainers for the P-80; 20 P-59As were built, followed by 30 P-59Bs with slightly longer fuselage.

Bell P-63 Kingcobra

Data apply to RP-63C.
Purpose: Aerial gunnery target.
Engine: One 1,510 h.p. Allison V-1710-117 inline.

Span: 38 ft. 4 in.
Max. Speed: 410 m.p.h. at 25,000 ft.

Based on a modified Airacobra (XP-39E), two XP-63 prototypes and one XP-63A were built, the first of these flying on 7th December, 1942. Intended to succeed the P-39 as a fignter and fighter-bomber, the P-63 was never used as such by the U.S.A.A.F. Of the 3,303 production total, the P-63A (1,725 built) and P-63C (1,227 built) versions were mostly supplied under Lend-Lease to the Soviet and Free French air forces, with whom they gave excellent service. U.S.A.A.F. use was confined to the RP-63A (100 built), RP-63C (200 built) and RP-63G (32 built), which were employed as aerial gunnery targets. The Packard-powered XP-63B project was cancelled, and other versions included one P-63D (redesign and engine change), 13 P-63E (similar to the D with additional equipment modifications), and two P-63F (based on the E with modified fin and further change of powerplant).

I.W.M.

Beriev Be–2

Purpose: General. utility
Engine: One 680 h.p. M-17 inline.

Span: 43 ft. 11½ in.
Max. Speed: 136 m.p.h.

The Be-2 or MBR-2 was one of the few indigenous flying boat designs to serve with the Russian forces during the Second World War, another being the twin-engined MDR-6 (page 185). Produced inifially for short-range coastal reconnaissance work, it first appeared in 1931, but despite its age rendered useful service both during and after the war on a variety of coastal duties. Some were employed by Aeroflot as transport aircraft. Production exceeded 1,500 machines, including a large number of the MBR-2*bis*, which was a much-improved version powered by an 860 h.p. M-34 engine.

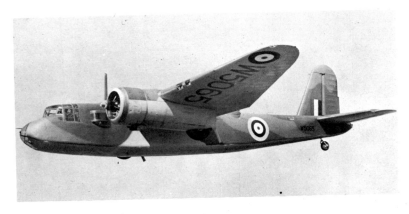

Blackburn Botha

Purpose: Reconnaissance and torpedo-bomber
Engines: Two 880 h.p. Bristol Perseus X or 930 h.p. Perseus XA radials.

Span: 59 ft. 0 in.
Max. Speed: 249 m.p.h. at 5,500 ft.

Selected, with the Beaufort and Lerwick (pages 36 and 231), for the Coastal Command re-equipment programme in the autumn of 1939, the Botha was seriously under-powered and had only a brief and scarcely a successful career. Designed to A.M. Spec. M.15/35, it entered service just after the beginning of the war but was withdrawn from operational employment some 18 months later. Remaining Bothas continued in service until 1944 as navigation and gunnery trainers.

Blackburn Roc

Purpose: Fighter.
Engine: One 905 h.p. Bristol Perseus XII radial.
Span: 46 ft. 0 in.
Max. Speed: 196 m.p.h. at 6,500 ft.

The first fleet fighter to carry a power-operated turret, the Roc, like its R.A.F. counterpart the Defiant, had a short life in its intended role and was quickly relegated to training and target-towing duties. Designed to Spec. O.30/35, the first Roc flew on 23rd December 1938 and the type entered Fleet Air Arm service in February 1940. Boulton Paul, who designed the 4-gun turret, also completed the 136 Rocs that were built.

Blackburn Skua

Purpose Fighter and dive bomber.
Engine: One 830 h.p. Bristol Perseus XII radial.
Span: 46 ft. 2 in.
Max. Speed: 225 m.p.h. at 6,500 ft.

To the Skua goes the distinction of claiming the first German aircraft (a Do 18) destroyed by the Fleet Air Arm in World War 2. Like the Roc, which it much resembled, it was something of a pioneer, being the Fleet Air Arm's first operational monoplane. Designed to A.M. Spec. O.27/34, the Skua entered service in November 1938 and three squadrons were equipped by the outbreak of war. In 1941 they were replaced as front line aircraft, but continued to serve for a number of years as target tugs and trainers. Two Mercury-powered prototypes and 190 production aircraft were completed.

Blohm und Voss Bv 222 Wiking *(Viking)*

Data apply to Bv 222C-0.
Purpose: Transport.
Engines: Six 1,000 h.p. Junkers Jumo 207C inlines.

Span: 150 ft. 11 in.
Max. Speed: 242 m.p.h. at 16,400 ft.

Designed before the war for transatlantic flying boat services with Deutsche Luft Hansa, the first prototype of the Bv 222 first flew on 7th September, 1940. Six more prototypes and seven production machines (Bv 222C) were completed, adapted for military service as freight and personnel transports. The first war reports of them came from the Mediterranean area in the autumn of 1942, and they were often seen in that locality during the North African campaign. The Bv 222 had a maximum range of 3,790 miles and was a prodigious load-carrier, having a crew of 11 and accommodation for up to 110 fully-equipped troops, a maximum weight over 100,000 lb. and an endurance of about 28 hours. A projected development, the Bv 238, was even larger, having a wing span of 197 feet and an all-up weight of over 175,000 lb., but only one was completed.

One of the TWA C-75s/U.S.A.F.

Boeing C-75 Stratoliner

Purpose: Long-range transport.
Engines: Four 1,100 h.p. Wright GR-1820-G102A Cyclone radials.

Span: 107 ft. 3 in.
Max. Speed: 241 m.p.h. at 6,000 ft.

The Boeing 307 Stratoliner was designed in 1936 as a pressurised, 33-passenger airliner, and a production line was established by Boeing in 1937 for ten of these aircraft. The first machine (which would ultimately have gone to Pan American Airways) flew on 31st December, 1938, but was destroyed in a crash three months later. Three Stratoliners eventually went to P.A.A., by whose pilots they were flown on military transport missions during the war; they were returned to the airline in 1944. Five of the remaining six aircraft (the other was purchased by Mr. Howard Hughes) went to T.W.A., being taken over later by the U.S.A.A.F. Air Transport Command and designated C-75 These also were " demobilised " in 1944.

Boeing-Stearman Kaydet

PT-13

Data apply to PT-17.
Purpose: Primary trainer.
Engine: One 220 h.p. Continental R-670-5 radial.

Span: 32 ft. 2 in.
Max. Speed: 124 m.p.h.

This original Stearman design was taken over by Boeing after the start of World War 2, and with the greater resources of the bigger company behind it, was produced on a wide scale as one of the war's standard basic trainers. Over 10,000 were built for both the U.S.A.A.F. and the U.S. Navy, with PT-13, -17, -18 and -27 and N2S designations respectively; these were generally similar except in the choice of powerplant. Many aircraft of this type were supplied to countries outside the United States, including Peru, Venezuela, Great Britain and China.

Boulton Paul Defiant

Defiant Mk. Is/I.W.M.

Data apply to Mk. II.
Purpose: Night fighter and target tug.
Engine: One 1,280 h.p. Rolls-Royce Merlin XX inline.

Span: 39 ft. 4 in.
Max. Speed: 313 m.p.h. at 19,000 ft.

When it appeared on 11th August 1937, the Defiant represented a new fighter concept: it was the first in the world to dispense with a fixed forward-firing armament, using instead a power-operated turret behind the cockpit. The concept was, however, short-lived. Designed to Spec. F.9/35, the Defiant entered service early in 1940, and after a brief period of glory was diverted to night fighting in August 1941. Although some measure of success was achieved in this role, it was nowhere near comparable with other contemporary fighters and by the Spring of 1942 was being relegated to target towing duties. The Mk. III was actually built for this purpose, and most of the Mk. IIs and a few Mk. Is were eventually converted. A number of these also served overseas with the Fleet Air Arm. A total of 1,060 Defiants were built up to February 1943.

179

Italian Air Ministry

Breda Ba 65

Purpose: Ground attack and reconnaissance.
Engine: One 1,000 h.p. Fiat A.80 RC 41 or Piaggio P.XI RC 40 radial.

Span: 40 ft. 6 in.
Max. Speed (single-seat version): 255 m.p.h. at 14,100 ft.

A pre-war design, the Ba 65 saw service with the Regia Aeronautica as a close-support aircraft in the Italian invasion of Abyssinia.   A small number remained in service when Italy entered the war; most of these were employed on reconnaissance or light bombing duties in North Africa, though a few were reported in action in the Balkans.   The Ba 65 could accommodate an observer in addition to the pilot.

R.A.F. Buffalo Mk. I

Brewster F2A

Data apply to F2A-3
Purpose: Carrier-based fighter.
Engine: One 1,200 h.p. Wright R-1820-40 Cyclone radial.

Span: 35 ft. 0 in.
Max. Speed: 321 m.p.h. at 16,500 ft.

This barrel-like little aeroplane was the U.S. Navy's first monoplane fighter, and entered service in 1939.   It was basically a sound design, but was the victim of official vacillation concerning various aspects of its construction and equipment and became one of the few U.S. failures of the war.   It was however used quite successfully against the Russians by the Finnish Air Force, who employed a batch of 44 F2A-2s.   The prototype XF2A-1 flew in January 1938, somewhat under-powered with only an 850 h.p. Cyclone engine.   Principal U.S. version was the F2A-3, 108 of which were ordered in January 1941.   Export models were ordered by Belgium (40) and Great Britain (170), the latter naming the aircraft Buffalo.   The occupation prevented delivery of most of the Belgian order, but 38 of these were eventually acquired by Britain.   A handful were sent with an F.A.A. squadron to Crete in 1941, but most British Buffalos were assigned to the R.A.F., who allocated them as landplanes for duty in the Far East.   Buffalo losses in this theatre were heavy, as were those among the 50 or so F2As which operated during 1942 with the Royal Netherlands Indies Army Air Corps.

Brewster SB2A Buccaneer

Purpose: Dive bomber and reconnaissance.
Engine: One 1,700 h.p. Wright R-2600-8
Double Cyclone radial.

Span: 47 ft. 0 in..
Max. Speed: 274 m.p.h. at 12,000 ft.

More widely known under its R.A.F. name of Bermuda, the SB2A-1 carrier-based dive bomber was among the less successful American aircraft of World War 2. First flown in 1941, the type went into production the following year for the U.S. Navy, Great Britain and the Netherland East Indies. It fell very short of expectations, however, and only a small number became operational with the Navy; an Army contract was cancelled before any had been delivered. Of the 750 aircraft completed, 450 machines were allocated to the R.A.F., but these too were found unsatisfactory and were relegated to training or target towing.

Bristol Bombay

Purpose: Bomber-transport.
Engines: Two 1,010 h.p. Bristol Pegasus XXII
radials.

Span: 95 ft. 9 in.
Max. Speed: 192 m.p.h. at 6,500 ft

Designed to meet a 1931 Specification (C.26/31), the Bombay did not fly until 1935 and was not delivered to the R.A.F. until March 1939, by which time it was virtually obsolete. Nevertheless the 50 or so aircraft completed gave useful service as transports in the Mediterranean and Middle East theatres, and some were even used on night bombing raids in North Africa.

Bristol Buckingham

Purpose: Light bomber and transport.
Engines: Two 2,520 h.p. Bristol Centaurus VII
or XI radials.

Span: 71 ft. 10 in.
Max. Speed: 336 m.p.h. at 12,000 ft.

Arising out of a 1941 idea for a day bomber version of the Beaufighter, the Buckingham did not perform its intended role because by the time it was available in quantity the Mosquito, which had a better performance, was already a conspicuous success. Production, which was to have run to 400 Buckinghams, was cut back to 119 aircraft, of which the first 65 were eventually modified as transports and the final 54 built as such from the outset. As a high-speed courier and transport, the Buckingham carried a crew of three and four passengers. Range was 2,360 miles.

Buckmaster prototype

Bristol Buckmaster

Purpose: Advanced trainer.
Engines: Two 2,520 h.p. Bristol Centaurus VII
radials.

Span: 71 ft. 10 in.
Max. Speed: 352 m.p.h. at 12,000 ft.

One of the fastest, as well as most powerful, trainers of its time, the Buckmaster was conceived in 1943 following the reduction in the Buckingham production programme and the ordering of prototypes for the Brigand ground attack aircraft. In addition to the 119 Buckinghams actually completed, components for another 110 were available, and by the installation of dual controls, elimination of the dorsal-turret and ventral " gondola " the Buckmaster emerged. The first was delivered to the R.A.F. in 1945, the type remaining in service until 1955.

182

Auster Mk. V

British Taylorcraft Auster

Data apply to Mk. IV.
Purpose: Artillery observation and communications.

Engine: One 130 h.p. Lycoming O-290-3.
Span: 36 ft. 0 in.
Max. Speed: 130 m.p.h. at sea level.

From fourteen licence-built examples of the American Taylorcraft Plus C taken over at the outbreak of the war, the number had grown by 1945 to over 1,600 Austers built by Taylorcraft Aeroplanes (England) Ltd. They pioneered the now-familiar A.O.P. (Air Observation Post) role, and served in every European, Mediterranean and North African theatre of the war. Most numerous version was the Mk. V (780 built), preceded by the Mks. I (100 built), II (2), III (467) and IV (255), the Mks. I and III being powered by the Cirrus Minor and Gipsy Major respectively.

Italian Air Ministry

Cant Z.501 Gabbiano *(Gull)*

Purpose: Maritime patrol.
Engine: One 900 h.p. Isotta-Fraschini "Asso" XI R2 C 15 inline

Span: 73 ft. 10 in.
Max. Speed: 171 m.p.h. at 8,200 ft.

When Italy entered the war in 1940 the Regia Aeronautica possessed 15 squadrons of Z.501s, totalling some 200 aircraft. They were used for maritime reconnaissance or light bombing throughout the war, a few continuing after the Italian surrender with the Co-Belligerent Air Force.

Caproni Ca 310 to 314

Data apply to Ca 313.
Purpose: Reconnaissance and light bomber.
Engines: Two 650 h.p. Isotta-Fraschini "Delta" RC 35 radials.

Span: 53 ft. 2 in.
Max. Speed: 279 m.p.h. at 15,090 ft.

Stemming from the pre-war Ca 309 Ghibli (Desert wind) "police" aircraft, a series of twin-engined Caproni designs appeared before and during the war, though none was used very widely in the war itself. Briefly, the Ca 310 Libeccio (South-west wind) reconnaissance aircraft resembled the Ca 309 except for higher-powered engines: the Ca 311 and 311M (reconnaissance/light bomber) featured modified and extensively glazed nose sections; the Ca 312 and 312M corresponded broadly to these two except in powerplant; the Ca 312*bis* was a twin-float version; the Ca 313 and 314 were further-improved versions with additional engine changes. Export versions of the Ca 311 and Ca 313 were delivered to Russia and Sweden respectively. Under development when Italy surrendered was a further version, the Ca 331, based on the Ca 311.

Cessna AT-17 and UC-78 Bobcat

Data apply to AT-17.
Purpose: Advanced trainer.
Engines: Two 225 h.p. Jacobs R-755-9 radials.

Span: 41 ft. 11 in.
Max. Speed: 175 m.p.h. at sea level.

Based on the pre-war T-50 commercial cabin monoplane, this aircraft was first produced for military service as the Lycoming-powered AT-8 for the U.S.A.A.F. and as the Jacobs-powered Crane for the R.C.A.F. With the Jacobs engine standardised, the type was later re-designated AT-17, and this version was built in quantity for U.S. use. Considerable numbers were produced as standard trainers for the Commonwealth Joint Air Training Plan, although the Crane had originally been ordered only as a stop-gap. During 1942/43 the Bobcat was adapted as a light, four-five seat personnel transport under the designation UC-78 (Navy JRC-1); well over 3,000 examples of this transport version were completed.

Chetverikov MDR-6

V. Nemecek

Purpose: Patrol and reconnaissance.
Engines: Two 1,100 h.p. M-63 radials.
Span: 64 ft. 11½ in.
Max. Speed: 224 m.p.h. at 16,400 ft.

This medium-sized flying boat was developed in 1936/39 for reconnaissance duties, but was not produced in great numbers. It was mostly used during the war for coastal patrol and mine-spotting, and on escort duty for convoys into Murmansk. The normal crew complement was four or five men, and a defensive armament of two 7.62 mm. guns was usually carried. Later versions included the MDR-6A (1941) and MDR-6B (1944), which were powered by Klimov VK-105 in-line engines and had retractable wingtip floats.

PB2Y-5

Consolidated PB2Y Coronado

Data apply to PB2Y-3.
Purpose: Long range patrol bomber or transport.
Engines: Four 1,200 h.p. Pratt & Whitney R-1830-88 Twin Wasp radials.
Span: 115 ft. 0 in.
Max. Speed: 224 m.p.h. at 19,500 ft.

Winner of a 1935 U.S. Navy design competition for a four-engined patrol bomber, the XPB2Y-1 Coronado made its maiden flight in December 1937 and was handed over to the Navy for evaluation in the following August. The first operational version, the PB2Y-2, entered service in 1941, during which year the PB2Y-3 began to follow it on the production lines. A passenger/cargo adaptation of the latter was the PB2Y-3R, with R-1830-92 engines, a crew of five (instead of the bomber's ten) and accommodation for up to 44 passengers or a 16,000 lb. cargo load. Some PB2Y-3 bombers were converted, with the -92 engines to PB2Y-5 models. The PB2Y-5H was a "hospital ship" variant with provision for 25 stretcher cases. Ten Coronados operated with R.A.F. Transport Command during 1944 on various transatlantic routes.

185

Consolidated PB4Y-2 Privateer

Purpose: Maritime patrol bomber.
Engines: Four 1,350 h.p. Pratt & Whitney R-1830-94 Twin Wasp radials.

Span: 110 ft. 0 in.
Max. Speed: 247 m.p.h. at 14,000 ft.

The original contract for the Privateer was placed in May 1943, the first of three prototypes flying on 20th September the same year. It was developed, quite independently of the single-finned Liberator, from the PB4Y-1, and was used exclusively in the Pacific theatre, although comparatively few of the 740 eventually built were operational before VJ-day. A transport version was designated RY-3, 46 of these going to the U.S. Navy and 27 to the R.A.F. early in 1945 as the Liberator IX. Churchill's LB-30 Commando transport was eventually modified to RY-3 standard, apart from retaining its original engines.

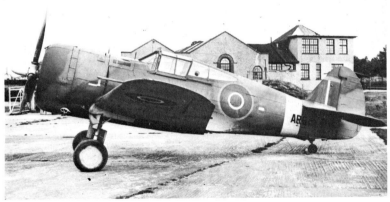

R.A.F. Mohawk IV/*I.W.M.*

Curtiss P-36 Mohawk

Data apply to P-36A.
Purpose: Fighter.
Engine: One 1,050 h.p. Pratt & Whitney R-1830-13 Twin Wasp radial.

Span: 37 ft. 4 in.
Max. Speed: 300 m.p.h. at 10,000 ft.

Serving with the U.S.A.A.F. mainly in its P-36A form, of which 177 examples were completed, the Mohawk was first delivered in 1938. Total home production reached 210 machines, the only other major variant being the P-26C (31 built) with revised wing armament. As the Hawk 75, the P-36 was the subject of several pre-war export orders, and many diverted from France served with the R.A.F. as the Mohawk III. These were later joined by a number of Mohawk IV specifically ordered by Great Britain, and served in the Middle East and India.

186

Curtiss SBC Cleveland

Data apply to SBC-4.

Purpose: Dive bomber.
Engine: One 950 h.p. Wright R-1820-34 Cyclone radial.

Span: 34 ft. 0 in.
Max..Speed: 237 m.p.h. at 15,200 ft.

Developed from the first Curtiss Helldiver, the F8C of 1928, the SBC-3, of which 83 were built, was to be found aboard several U.S. carriers during the early years of the war. Armed with twin machine guns and with provision for one 1,100 lb. bomb or an auxiliary fuel tank under the belly, the SBC-4 entered U.S.N. service in 1939. Of a total of 50 ordered by France, five found their way to Great Britain to become the R.A.F's Cleveland I.

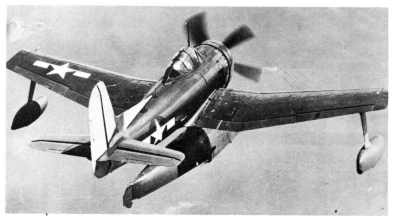

Curtiss SC-1 Seahawk

Purpose: Shipborne scout.
Engine: One 1,350 h.p. Wright R-1820-62 Cyclone radial.

Span: 41 ft. 0 in.
Max. Speed (floatplane): 313 m.p.h. at 28,600 ft.

The design of the Seahawk was initiated in June 1942 as a replacement for the SO3C Seamew. A contract was awarded in August of that year for seven aircraft, and the first of two XSC-1s made its maiden flight on 16th February, 1944; by the end of April 1944 all seven had been completed, though the type did not see its first action until June 1945, just before the invasion of Borneo. Some 566 landplane and floatplane versions of the single-seat SC-1 were completed, and after the war were followed by nine examples of the two-seat SC-2.

187

Curtiss SO3C Seamew

Purpose: Observation.
Engine: One 520 h.p. Ranger V-770-6 inline

Span: 38 ft. 0 in.
Max. Speed (floatplane): 190 m.p.h. at 7,500 ft.

The Seagull, as this type was originally known, was not one of the United States' most successful aircraft, but some 800 examples were built by the parent company and by Ryan as the SOR-1. The XSO3C-1 first flew in 1940, and the Seamew remained in U.S. service until it was withdrawn early in 1944; both landplane and floatplane versions were used. A hundred SO3C-2s were delivered to the Royal Navy, whose name Seamew was subsequently adopted by the U.S. Navy. The Fleet Air Arm Seamews were used only on training duties, including a further thirty " Queen Seamews " converted as radio-controlled target drones.

Royal Navy Flamingo

de Havilland Flamingo

Purpose: Transport.
Engines: Two 930 h.p. Bristol Perseus XVI radials.

Span: 70 ft. 0 in.
Max. Speed: 239 m.p.h. at 6,500 ft.

Produced as a civil airliner for Jersey Airways, the D.H.95 Flamingo first flew in 1938 and entered airline service in the following year. When the war broke out, those so far completed were handed over to the Royal Air Force, and the remainder of the total of 16 were completed under military specifications. They were used by the King's Flight of the R.A.F. at Benson, Oxfordshire along with one true military example, to which was given the name Hertfordshire.

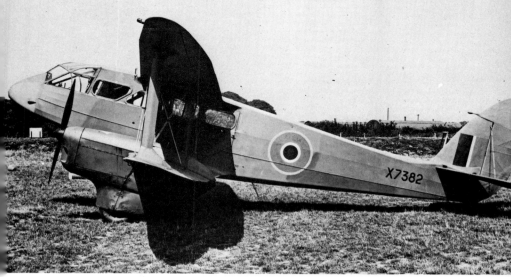

de Havilland Dominie

Purpose: Trainer and communications.
Engines: Two 200 h.p. de Havilland Gipsy Six
inlines.

Span: 48 ft. 0 in.
Max. Speed: 157 m.p.h. at 1,000 ft.

    A military version of the famous Dragon Rapide of the middle and late 'thirties, several Dominies were already in R.A.F. service before World War 2, although the name was not bestowed until after the outbreak. The navigation and radio trainer version was the Mk. I, the communications version the Mk. II. Wartime Dominie production was 475, in addition to which a number of Rapides were impressed for military service. The type was also used by the Fleet Air Arm, and after the war several Dominies were converted back to Rapide standard.

Tiger Moth Mk. II

de Havilland Tiger Moth

Purpose: Basic trainer.
Engine: One 130 h.p. de Havilland Gipsy
Major inline.

Span: 29 ft. 4 in.
Max. Speed: 109 m.p.h. at 1,000 ft.

    Entering service with the R.A.F. in February 1932, the Tiger Moth was still in widespread use more than fifteen years later, and is surely one of the most famous and well-loved aeroplanes ever built. More than 1,000 of them were in R.A.F. service by September 1939, and wartime production rose to 4,005 in the United Kingdom, most of them built by Morris Motors; many also served with the Royal Navy. Under the Commonwealth Air Training Plan nearly 3,000 more, were built in Canada, Australia and New Zealand, and some Canadian-built Tiger Moths were employed by the U.S.A.A.F. under the designation PT-24. The Mk. II, which was the chief production version, differed mainly in powerplant, the Mk. I having a 120 h.p. Gipsy III engine. The Queen Bee was a radio-controlled target version of which 420 were built.

189

DFS 230B-1/*I.W.M.*

DFS 230

Purpose: Transport glider
Span: 68 ft. 5½ in

Carrying a pilot and up to eight fully-armed troops, the DFS 230A was first reported in action in Belgium in May 1940. Towed variously by He 111, Hs 126, Ju 52/3m, Ju 87 and Bf 110 aircraft, it had a maximum all-up weight of 4,600 lb. including a disposable load of 2,800 lb. A jettisonable wheel undercarriage was fitted for take-off, the landing being made by means of skids under the forepart of the fuselage. The DFS 230B and C were externally similar, the latter having small forward-firing rockets underneath for braking purposes.

Do 18D-1/*H. J. Nowarra*

Dornier Do 18

Data apply to Do 18G.
Purpose: Reconnaissance.
Engines: Two 700 h.p. Junkers Jumo 205D
inlines.

Span: 77 ft. 9 in.
Max. Speed: 161 m.p.h. at 5,800 ft.

A reconnaissance aircraft with the typically long and lean lines of pre-war Dornier flying boats, the Do 18 was a 1937 design for a transatlantic mail carrier for Deutsche Luft Hansa, and was developed from the famous " Wal ". The civil version was the Do 18E, from which was developed the first military series, the Do 18D. The chief production series, the Do 18G, was used fairly widely during the early war years on reconnaissance and air-sea rescue duties; 71 of this type were built. Other less-used models included the unarmed Do 18H trainer and the Do 18N, another A.S.R. version.

Dornier Do 24

Data apply to Do 24T.
Purpose: Reconnaissance and transport.
Engines: Three 1,000 h.p. Bramo 323R radials.
Span: 83 ft. 7 in.
Max. Speed: 190 m.p.h. at 6,560 ft.

The Dutch Air Force was the first service to employ the Do 24, the type being built in Holland by Aviolanda; these aircraft, from the third prototype onwards, were powered by 760 h.p. Wright Cyclone American engines. In 1940 the invading German forces re-converted a number of them to their own use, under the revised designation Do 24N, for air/sea rescue duties. In 1941 German production of the transport and reconnaissance Do 24T was resumed, and production of this sub-type was also undertaken by Aviolanda, De Schelde, S.N.C.A.N. and Weserflug. The 146 Do 24s completed included some delivered to Sweden; the type was also licence-built in Spain.

Douglas A-26 Invader

A-26B

Data apply to A-26B.
Purpose: Light bomber and ground attack.
Engines: Two 2,000 h.p. Pratt & Whitney R-2800-27 or -79 Double Wasp radials.
Span: 70 ft. 0 in.
Max. Speed: 373 m.p.h. at 10,000 ft.

A development of Douglas's already successful A-20 design (page 56), the A-26 Invader exceeded all its weight and performance requirements and would have been produced in even greater numbers had the war not ended when it did. The first flight of the XA-26, on 10th July, 1942, was followed by those of the XA-26A night fighter project and the XA-26B with a 75 mm. nose cannon. First major production version was the A-26B, featuring a " solid " nose with six .50 machine guns in addition to those in dorsal and ventral turrets; 1,355 of this version were completed. The A-26C " lead ship " of which 1,091 were built, had a transparent " bombardier " nose, and with the B was the only operational model. A few A-26s were converted as JD-1 target tugs for the U.S. Navy.

191

Douglas B-18 Bolo

Data apply to B-18A.
Purpose: Medium bomber.
Engines: Two 1,000 h.p. Wright R-1820-53 Cyclone radials.

Span: 89 ft. 6 in.
Max. Speed: 215 m.p.h. at 10,000 ft.

Based on the DC-3 commercial transport, the B-18 design won a U.S.A.A.C. competition in 1936 and was ordered into production The initial deliveries of 133 B-18s (930 h.p. Wright R-1820-45) were followed by 217 B-18As of which the first 44 were completed to A standard after originally being ordered as B-18s.   The B-18A featured a redesigned and longer nose section, improving the bomb-aimer's position, and incorporated a power-operated dorsal turret; 122 B-18As were converted in 1939/40 to B-18Bs by the addition of maritime reconnaissance radio equipment and, in some cases, a tailcone extension containing submarine detection gear.   The B-18 was never used as a bomber during World War 2, most of its assignments consisting of coastal patrol or paratroop training.   Twenty B-18As were used by the R.C.A.F. as the Digby I, also for maritime duties.

Douglas TBD-1 Devastator

Purpose: Torpedo bomber
Engine: One 900 h.p. Pratt & Whitney R 1830-64 Twin Wasp radial.

Span: 50 ft. 0 in.
Max. Speed: 206 m.p.h. at 8,000 ft.

The Douglas Devastator was flown in prototype form in 1935, and 129 aircraft of this type were subsequently completed, the first of these entering service in 1937.   Although their defensive armament of one .50 and one .30 gun afforded inadequate protection, and losses were heavy, the Devastators formed a very important part of the carrier torpedo bomber force of the U.S. Navy during the early stages of the Pacific war and inflicted great damage upon Japanese shipping. One 21-in. torpedo or one 1 000 lb. bomb could be carried semi-internally.

192

XAT-21/U.S.A.F.

Fairchild AT-21 Gunner

Purpose: Gunnery trainer.
Engines: Two 520 h.p. Ranger V-770-11 or -15 inlines.

Span: 52 ft. 8 in.
Max. Speed: 225 m.p.h. at 12,000 ft.

Ordered into production in 1942, 175 Gunners were built, 106 by the parent company, 39 by Bellanca and 30 by McDonnell. The aircraft was a five-seater, based on Fairchild's earlier designs of the XAT-13 and XAT-14 bombing trainers with internal equipment altered to provide for aerial gunnery training.

PT-19A

Fairchild PT-19, -23 and -26

Data apply to PT-19A.
Purpose: Basic trainer
Engine: One 200 h.p. Ranger L-440-3 inline.

Span: 36 ft. 0 in.
Max. Speed: 132 m.p.h.

Despite three separate designations, the differences between the aircraft of this series lay mainly in variations of internal equipment, except for the employment of the 320 h.p. Continental engine in the PT-23. Production lasted from February 1940 to May 1944; during that time nearly 8,000 of these aircraft were turned out by the Aeronca, Howard, St. Louis and Fleet (Canada) companies in addition to the parent firm, who themselves built almost 5,000. The PT-23 and PT-26 Cornell were adopted by the Canadian Government as primary trainers for the Commonwealth Joint Air Training Plan, and 1,150 of these models were completed by the Fleet company in Canada. Normally the aircraft were seen with open cockpits, but sliding hoods were fitted to some PT-23A and to the PT-26. Some PT-23s were modified to accommodate two stretchers.

Fairchild UC-61 Forwarder

Data apply to UC-61A.

Purpose: Light transport and communications.
Engine: One 165 h.p. Warner R-500-1 Super
    Scarab radial.

Span: 36 ft. 4 in
Max. Speed: 130 m.p.h.

Adapted from Fairchild's commercial four-seat Model 24, the Forwarder was originally produced in its light military transport form for the Royal Air Force, as the Argus I. It was later adopted by the U.S.A.A.F. as the UC-61 and the UC-61A, the latter equating to the R.A.F. Argus II. Early in 1944 the UC-61K (Argus III) went into production, having a 200 h.p. Ranger L-440-7 inline motor in place of the Warner radial. Main production centred on these three versions—163 UC-61 and 512 UC-61A (plus several hundred for the R.A.F.) and 306 UC-61K being completed. Sub-types of the Forwarder from B to J, which numbered only 14 in all, were secondhand civil machines purchased for military use. Nine Model 24R-40, with the Ranger engine, were also impressed for service under the designation UC-86, and a number of Forwarders were employed by the U.S. Navy as the GK-1.

Battle Mk. I

Fairey Battle

Purpose: Light bomber.
Engine: One 1,030 h.p. Rolls-Royce Merlin I,
    II, III or IV inline.

Span: 54 ft. 0 in.
Max. Speed: 241 m.p.h. at 13,000 ft.

Although it represented quite an advance over the Hawker biplanes which it replaced, the Battle was obsolescent in 1939 and remained in first-line service for only another year afterwards. Designed to Spec. P.27/32, the prototype Battle (K 4303) flew in March 1936 and the first production aircraft entered service a year later. A Battle gunner claimed the first German aircraft shot down during the war, and the R.A.F's first two V.Cs. of the war were won by Battle pilots, but the type was underpowered and under-armed and was soon transferred to training and target towing duties. A total of 2,419 Battles were built, over half of them by Austin Motors Ltd.

194

Fairey Seafox

Purpose: Reconnaissance.
Engine: One 395 h.p. Napier Rapier VI inline.

Span: 40 ft. 0 in.
Max. Speed: 124 m.p.h. at 5,860 ft.

Catapult seaplanes were used very little by the Royal Navy in World War 2, but the Fairey Seafox will be remembered as the " spotter " from H.M.S. *Exeter* which carried out daily reconnaissances throughout the Battle of the River Plate in December 1939. Designed to A.M. Spec. 11/32, the Seafox entered Fleet Air Arm service in April 1937 and at the outbreak of war equipped several British cruisers. One unusual feature of the Seafox, brought about by the requirements of catapult operation, was that the observer's cockpit was enclosed, whereas that of the pilot was open. Total production was 64 aircraft.

G.12 LGA/Italian Air Ministry

Fiat G.12

Purpose: Troop and freight transport.
Engines: Three 770 h.p. Fiat A.74 RC 42 radials.

Span: 94 ft. 2½ in.
Max. Speed: 242 m.p.h.

The Fiat G.12T was one of a number of trimotor transport aircraft employed by the Italian air arms during the Second World War. Stemming from the G.12C of 1937, the G.12T entered service in 1941 and small numbers continued to serve after the armistice with both the Co-Belligerent Air Force and the Aviazione della RSI. Later versions which served with the post-war Italian Air Force included the G.12LA and the G.12LP.

Fiat G.55 Centauro

Purpose: Fighter.
Engine: One 1,475 h.p. licence-built DB 605A
inline.

Span: 38 ft. 9 in.
Max. Speed: 385 m.p.h. at 22,966 ft.

Adopted in 1942 to succeed the G.50, the Centauro was one of the best fighter aircraft to be produced in Italy during the Second World War. However, it was not placed in production until 1943, with the result that very few had been delivered to the Regia Aeronautica before Italy surrendered in June of that year. Production continued after this, however, and most of the 100-odd machines of this type which were completed saw their service with the Italian air arm that continued in support of Germany.

Fiat R.S. 14

Purpose: Torpedo-bomber and reconnaissance.
Engines: Two 840 h.p. Fiat A.74 RC 38
radials.

Span: 64 ft. 0½ in.
Max. Speed: 254 m.p.h. at 13,120 ft.

Italy's last operational floatplane torpedo-bomber, the Fiat R.S. 14 began life as a land-based bomber under the designation A.S.14. It was adapted first for coastal patrol and ultimately to the torpedo-bombing role, but due largely to the success of the Cant Z.506B and S.M. 79 in the latter function it did not enter service in very large numbers.

Fleet Finch, restored post-war/*Neil A. Macdougall*

Fleet Finch and Fort

Data apply to Finch II.
Purpose: Basic trainer.
Engine: One 125 h.p. Kinner B-5 radial.

Span: 28 ft. 0 in.
Max. Speed: 113 m.p.h.

The Model 16 Finch I was a development of the Consolidated Fleet primary trainer, manufacture of which was begun in Canada by Fleet Aircraft in 1930, the Canadian company eventually taking over the entire world rights in the aircraft. Between 1939 and 1941 a total of 606 Finch I and Model 16B Finch II were built for R.C.A.F. use under the Commonwealth Joint Air Training Plan. The Model 60 Fort was an advanced trainer, also used in the C.J.A.T.P. and produced to R.C.A.F. requirements. The Fort was built in two versions, the Model 60-L with 250 h.p. Jacobs engine and the 60-K with a 330 h.p. Jacobs. Span was 36 ft. 0 in. and maximum speed 191 m.p.h. Production of the Fort ceased, after 101 had been built, in favour of the Fairchild Cornell.

Ta 152H-0/*H. J. Nowarra*

Focke-Wulf Ta 152

Data apply to Ta 152C-1.
Purpose: Fighter-bomber.
Engine: One 2,300 h.p. (with boost) Daimler-Benz DB 603LA inline in annular cowling.

Span: 36 ft. 1 in.
Max. Speed: 463 m.p.h. at 34,000 ft.

The Ta 152 (prefix letters were taken from the name of its designer, Kurt Tank) was a logical—and promising—development of the successful "long-nosed" Fw 190D. With its excellent performance, a service ceiling of over 40,000 ft. and an armament of four 20 mm. and one 30 mm. cannon, the Ta 152 would have been a most useful addition to Luftwaffe strength had it been available earlier; as it was, only a handful of squadrons were equipped (with the Ta 152C) at the time of the capitulation.

197

Air-Britain

FZG-76

Purpose: Short range pilotless aircraft with explosive warhead.
Engine: One 600 lb.s.t. Argus As 014 pulse-jet

Span: 17 ft. 8¼ in.
Typical Speed: 360 m.p.h. at 2,500 ft.

Known alternatively as the Vergeltungswaffe (*Revenge Weapon*) 1, or more simply V.1, the FZG-76 was an ingenious device by any standard of the day, and was first used operationally against Britain in mid-June 1944. Although handicapped by hasty development, it was by no means the simple device that many thought it to be, and revealed itself as a potent, if sometimes unreliable, weapon. Piloted versions were test-flown before Service use, one such pilot being the famous German woman flier Hanna Reitsch. The FZG-76 was powered by a simple " stovepipe " jet propulsion engine and the first prototype missile was built by the Fieselerwerke G.m.b.H. under the designation Fi 103. The production version, which differed considerably, carried about 1,870 lb. of H.E. in the nose warhead and some 150 gallons of fuel which was expended at the rate of 1 gallon per mile. Total weight was 4,750 lb.; internal equipment included magnetic compass, autopilot, range-setting and flight controls.

General Aircraft Hamilcar

Purpose: Troop and tank transport glider.
Span: 110 ft. 0 in.
Max. Towing Speed: 150 m.p.h.

Designed to A.M. Spec. X.27/40, the Hamilcar was used with great success in the Normandy landings of 1944 and was the first Allied glider capable of transporting a 7-ton tank. Possible loads included a Tetrarch Mk. IV or U.S. Locust tank, two Bren carriers or scout cars, or a mobile Bofors gun. After a half-scale trial model had been made, the full-size prototype flew on 27th March, 1942, and 390 Hamilcar Is were built—all but the first 22 by various woodworking firms in the U.K. The designation Hamilcar X covered 22 Mk. I gliders converted in response to Spec. X.4/44 for a power-assisted version. With two 965 h.p. Bristol Mercury 31 radials installed, the Hamilcar X had a loaded weight of 47,000 lb. (compared with the glider's 36,000 lb.), a maximum speed of 145 m.p.h. and a range of 1,530 miles. Usual tug for the glider version was the Halifax III.

General Aircraft Hotspur II

I.W.M.

Purpose: Training glider.
Span: 45 ft. 10¾ in.

The G.A.L. 48 Hotspur I, designed to A.M. Spec. 10/40, had a pointed-tip wing with a span of 61 ft. 10 in.   This version did not achieve series production, and on the principal version, the Mk. II, some eight feet were taken off each wingtip to improve performance and handling characteristics.   Originally intended as an operational troop carrier, the Hotspur relinquished this role to the Horsa and was primarily employed for operational training with the Airborne Division. Usual tugs were Hawker Hectors or Audaxes.   Experimentally, one G.A.L. 48B Twin Hotspur was completed, consisting of two standard fuselages and outer wing sections joined by a new " centre section " and a common tailplane.

Go 242A-0/*H. J. Nowarra*

Gotha Go 242 and Go 244

Data apply to Go 244.
Purpose: Troop and freight transport.
Engines: Two 750 h.p. Gnome-Rhone 14M radials.

Span: 80 ft. 4½ in.
Max. Speed: 180 m.p.h. at 10,000 ft.

The Gothaer Waggonfabrik A.G. were principally occupied during the Second World War with series production of aircraft designed by other companies; of their own designs, the only ones to achieve production status were the Go 242 and Go 244.   The Go 242A-1 (cargo) and A-2 (troop) gliders had skid landing gear, the 242B a fixed tricycle undercarriage, and the Go 244 was basically a powered version of the Go 242B.   The gliders, usually towed by the Ju 52/3m or the " Siamese twin " He 111Z, were used in moderate numbers from 1942, but the Go 244s, after a brief appearance in the Western Desert, became relegated to training duties.

199

Grumman J2F Duck

Data apply to J2F-5.
Purpose: Utility transport.
Engine: One 900 h.p. Wright R-1820-54 Cyclone radial.

Span: 39 ft. 0 in.
Max. Speed: 190 m.p.h.

Extensive series of this little two-seat Grumman amphibian were built for the United States Navy and Coast Guard from 1935 onwards, the final version being the Columbia-built J2F-6 which remained in service for some years after the war.

Grumman J4F Widgeon

Data apply to J4F-I.
Purpose: General.
Engines: Two 200 h.p. Ranger L-440C-5 inlines.

Span: 40 ft. 0 in.
Max. Speed: 153 m.p.h.

This four/five-seat general purpose amphibian first appeared as a civil type in 1940, under the maker's model number G-44. In 1941 a militarised version entered service with the U.S. Coast Guard as the J4F-1 for coastal patrol duties. The J4F-2 for the U.S. Navy appeared in 1942, and small numbers were supplied to the U.S.A.A.F. (OA-14), Great Britain and Canada. Those of the Royal Navy, originally named Gosling, were employed mainly on communications duties in the West Indies, and those of the R.C.A.F. were given similar employment in Canada.

R.A.F. Goose

Grumman JRF

Data apply to JRF-5.

Purpose: General purpose amphibian.
Engines: Two 450 h.p. Pratt & Whitney R-985-AN-6 Wasp Junior radials.

Span: 49 ft. 0 in.
Max. Speed: 201 m.p.h. at 5,000 ft.

Adapted for military use from Grumman's eight-seat Model G-21 commercial amphibian of 1937, this aircraft entered service with the United States Navy as the JRF-1 and with the U.S. Coast Guard as the JRF-2. Developed versions of these were, respectively, the JRF-4 and JRF-3. During their career, the JRFs (275 of which were completed for the U.S. Navy and Coast Guard) served as light transports, target tugs, navigation trainers, photographic reconnaissance and air-sea rescue aircraft. The U.S.A.A.F. received 31 OA-9 and five OA-13, both generally similar to the JRF series; a number of JRF-5 were supplied to the R.C.A.F., and both JRF-5 and -6 to the R.A.F., who named the type Goose.

U.S.A.F.

G.S.T.

Purpose: Reconnaissance and rescue.
Engines: Two 1,000 h.p. Shvetsov ASh-62IR radials.

Span: 104 ft. 0 in.
Max. Speed: 190 m.p.h. at 10,500 ft.

The G.S.T. (initials of the Russian State Aircraft Factory, which was responsible for its production) was a licence-built version of the Consolidated PBY Catalina flying-boat which rendered such useful service to the American and British forces during the war. As with the Li-2, Russian-built engines were substituted for the American Twin Wasps, but performance remained approximately the same. Armament of the G.S.T. consisted of three 12.7 mm. or 7.62 mm. machine guns. In addition to the Soviet-built machines, 138 American-built PBN-1s were supplied to Russia in 1943/44 under Lend-Lease.

201

Handley Page Harrow

Purpose: Transport.
Engines: Two 925 h.p. Bristol Pegasus XX radials.

Span: 88 ft. 5 in
Max. Speed: 200 m.p.h. at 10,000 ft.

The Handley Page Harrow was originally designed, to A.M. Spec. 29/35, as a transport, and 100 were ordered during that year. In 1936, under the R.A.F. expansion scheme, it was decided to adapt the type as a bomber, and it entered service in this capacity in April 1937. By the outbreak of World War 2 all Harrow squadrons had re-equipped with Wellingtons, and the Harrow was restored to its original purpose for war service—though a few performed minelaying duties in 1940/41. In the transport role, the Harrow (sometimes also called the Sparrow) could accommodate 20 troops or an equivalent freight load. The first 38 aircraft were Mk. I (830 h.p. Pegasus X) and the remainder, to which the above data apply, Mk. II.

Handley Page Hereford

Purpose: Medium bomber and bombing trainer.
Engines: Two 955 h.p. Napier Dagger VIII inlines.

Span: 69 ft. 2 in.
Max. Speed: 265 m.p.h. at 15,500 ft.

The Hereford was practically identical to the Hampden (page 89) except for its powerplant, which conferred a slightly better performance. However, teething troubles with the Dagger engines restricted Hereford production to the 100 machines originally ordered, which were built at Belfast by Short Bros. & Harland to Spec. 44/36. These were virtually non-operational as bombers, and those that were not converted to Hampden standard served from 1940 onwards as bombing crew trainers.

Hawker Audax and Hardy

Audax/Air Ministry

Data apply to Audax.

Purpose: Army co-operation.
Engine: One 530 h.p. Rolls-Royce Kestrel IB inline.

Span: 37 ft. 3 in.
Max. Speed: 170 m.p.h. at 2,380 ft.

Although the Audax first entered R.A.F. service in 1931, and was out of production two years before the outbreak of World War 2, the type served during the first year or two of the war in the Middle East theatre. For most of this time it was pursuing its designed function of Army co-operation, though in the final stages of its war service its more usual role was that of trainer or glider tug at stations in the United Kingdom. A development of the Hawker Hart, the Audax was built to A.M. Spec. 7/31. Another Hart variant was the Hardy, similar to the Audax but with a higher-powered Kestrel engine and adaptable for a wider range of duties. By late 1941 it too had been superseded by more modern types.

Hawker Hector

Air Ministry

Purpose: Army co-operation.
Engine: One 805 h.p. Napier Dagger III inline.

Span: 36 ft. 11¼ in.
Max. Speed: 187 m.p.h. at 6,560 ft.

The Hector entered service with the Royal Air Force in February 1937 as a successor to the Hawker Audax. Like its predecessor, it remained useful during the early war years and finally faded out after a spell on glider towing duties at home stations. Production of the Hector ran to 178 aircraft and was undertaken by Westland Aircraft Ltd. at Yeovil.

203

Henley Mk. II/*I.W.M.*

Hawker Henley

Purpose: Target tug.
Engine: One 1,030 h.p. Rolls-Royce Merlin II inline.

Span: 47 ft. 10½ in.
Max. Speed (with drogue): 272 m.p.h. at 17,500 ft.

Designed to the same Specification (P.4/34, for a fast monoplane light bomber) that eventually produced the Fairey Fulmar (page 65), the Hawker Henley was obviously inspired by its stablemate the Hurricane, and actually used similar outer wings and tailplane to the latter. Due to a change of policy the Henley was not after all required for the light bomber role, and the production contract was reduced in May 1937 from 350 to 200 aircraft. These were completed (by the Gloster Aircraft Co.) for the less glamorous but very necessary job of high-speed target tug, under the designation T.T. Mk. III, serving until replaced from 1942 onwards by the Defiant and Martinet.

He 162A-2/*Air-Britain*

Heinkel He 162 Salamander

Purpose: Fighter.
Engine: One 1,760 lb.s.t. BMW 003E-1 turbojet.

Span: 23 ft. 7¾ in.
Max. Speed: 522 m.p.h. at 19,700 ft.

Rushed prematurely into service as a last-ditch weapon during the closing stages of the European war, the single-seat He 162 progressed from drawing board to first flight in *ten weeks.* Although it was an ingenious design, with quite a pleasing appearance, such rapid evolution could not be expected to meet with resounding success, and the He 162 was a perfect little terror to fly. Made of lightweight non-strategic materials, the Volksjager (*People's Fighter*), as it was alternatively known, began to be delivered to Luftwaffe units in February 1945. Total production of the He 162A amounted to only 116 machines by VE-day. Very few were encountered operationally, but even if they had been it is unlikely that they would have affected the situation seriously.

Heinkel He 219 Uhu *(Owl)*

He 219A-5/R1/*Hanfried Schliephake*

Data apply to He 219A-7.
Purpose: Night fighter.
Engines: Two 1,900 h.p. Daimler-Benz DB 603G inlines (in annular cowlings).

Span: 60 ft. 8½ in.
Max. Speed: 416 m.p.h. at 22,965 ft.

The He 219 was designed as a high altitude interceptor in 1940, but it was in response to an RLM requirement in 1942 for a specialised night fighter that it achieved recognition. The first prototype flew on 15th November, 1942. Early trials were successful and full-scale production commenced in August 1943 with the He 219A-1, although only 268 of the various models were produced. The He 219 had a good performance and was strongly armed, with six 30 mm. and two 20 mm. cannon, but it was yet another victim of personal and political dissension behind the scenes which kept it out of full operation until it was too late to make any effective contribution.

Hs 123A-1/*Archiv Schliephake*

Henschel Hs 123

Data apply to Hs 123A-1.
Purpose: Ground attack.
Engine: One 870 h.p. BMW 132D radial.

Span: 34 ft. 5 in.
Max. Speed: 214 m.p.h. at 4,000 ft.

Designed in 1934, first flown in 1935, serving in the Spanish Civil War in 1937, obsolescent in 1939 yet still operational in 1945: such was the history of the Hs 123. Conceived originally as a dive-bomber, it was subsequently employed for ground attack, supply-dropping and glider-towing duties. It was in the close support role that the Hs 123A was most widely used during the war, its service for the most part being on the Russian front. Although prototypes were completed and tested for Hs 123B and C versions, neither of these actually entered production.

Henschel Hs 126

Data apply to Hs 126B.

Purpose: Reconnaissance.
Engine: One 870 h.p. BMW 132D radial.

Span: 47 ft. 7 in.
Max. Speed: 221 m.p.h. at 9,850 ft.

Originally designed in 1937 as a reconnaissance and artillery observation aircraft, the Hs 126 was ordered in considerable numbers by the RLM, and during the early years of the war was widely used in these roles. From 1942 onwards, however, it began to give way to the Fw 189 and was transferred to such secondary duties as training and glider towing, on which it remained for the rest of the war. Some 600 Hs 126s of all types were built, and the type was encountered on all fronts. Principal service version was the Hs 126B.

Henschel Hs 129

Data apply to Hs 129B.

Purpose: Anti-tank and close support.
Engines: Two 750 h.p. Gnome-Rhone 14M radials.

Span: 44 ft. 6 in.
Max. Speed: 253 m.p.h. at 12,467 ft.

The Hs 129 was designed to take over from the Ju 87D the specialised function of tank " busting". The first prototype (two 465 h.p. Argus As 410A) flew in 1939, followed by the pre-production Hs 129A-0 and the Gnome-Rhone-powered initial production series, the Hs 129B. Used primarily on the Russian front, one of the principal variants was the Hs 129B-1/R2, armed with one 30 mm. and two 20 mm. cannon, two 7.9 mm. machine guns and two 110 lb. bombs. In place of the 30 mm. gun, the B-2/R4 had an enormous ventral gondola housing a 75 mm. anti-tank cannon. Production of the Hs 129 terminated in 1944 after more than 800 aircraft had been completed.

206

Junkers Ju 86

Data apply to Ju 86P.

Purpose: Reconnaissance and bomber.
Engines: Two 1,000 h.p. Junkers Jumo 207 inlines.

Span: 83 ft. 11¾ in.
Max. Speed: 242 m.p h. at 39,000 ft.

The Ju 86 was originally intended as a bomber, the Ju 86D and E (BMW 132 engines) being produced for this role. Performance, however, did not come up to requirements and the type was adapted, first as a transport and trainer (Ju 86G) and later for reconnaissance (Ju 86P). The latter featured a pressurised cabin, a change of powerplant (to a pair of Jumo 207 inlines) and a wing extended from 74 ft. to 84 ft. The Ju 86R, with a wing extended to 104 ft. 11¼ in. and higher-powered Jumo 207B-3 engines, offered a better performance including a ceiling of some 45,000 ft. which took it beyond the reach of nearly all Allied interceptors. Ju 86 reconnaissance aircraft were successful in informing the German High Command of Russian troop movements in 1941, but few were encountered over the United Kingdom.

Junkers Ju 252 and Ju 352 Herkules

Data apply to Ju 352A.

Purpose: Transport.
Engines: Three 1,200 h.p. Bramo 323R-2 radials.

Span: 112 ft. 2¼ in.
Max. Speed: 205 m.p.h. at 7,900 ft.

The Junkers Ju 252 (powered by three 1,410 h.p. Jumo 211Js) was designed in response to a call in 1939 for a successor to the obsolescent Ju 52/3m, and prototypes were under construction when the war broke out. Although a successful enough design, it was an all-metal aeroplane and would have made unnecessarily heavy demands on strategic materials. The production order was thus cut to fifteen machines and subsequent interest centred upon the Ju 352 Herkules, a basically similar (though rather more angular) aircraft making use of lower-priority materials. The first Ju 352 flew in October 1943, six more prototypes and 43 production Ju 352A-1s being completed inside a year. Neither the Ju 252 nor the 352, however, could match the record of the ageing Ju 52/3m they were supposed to replace, and which soldiered on alongside them right to the end of the war.

Junkers Ju 388

Data apply to Ju 388L-1.
Purpose: Reconnaissance.
Engines: Two 1,810 h.p. BMW 801TJ radials.

Span: 72 ft. 2 in.
Max. Speed: 383 m.p.h. at 40,300 ft.

A progressive development of the Ju 188, which it outwardly resembled, the Ju 388 was intended as a multi-role aircraft. As things turned out, however, only one version—the Ju 388L reconnaissance model—was produced in time to see service with the Luftwaffe before the war ended. This version had a good top speed and a maximum range of over 2,000 miles, and was armed with three 13 mm. MG 131 machine guns for defence. Other versions on the verge of production were the Ju 388J Stortebeker, a night fighter, and the Ju 388K bomber.

H6K5

Kawanishi H6K

Data apply to H6K4.
Purpose: Maritime patrol and transport.
Engines: Four 1,070 h.p. Mitsubishi Kinsei 46 radials.

Span: 131 ft. 2¾ in.
Max. Speed: 211 m.p.h. at 13,120 ft.

Stemming from a pre-war flying boat of which the H6K2 was the principal service model, this ageing machine remained in production during the early war years as the H6K4, and 174 examples were completed. It was employed primarily on long-range sea patrol, for which it carried a crew of nine; as a transport (H6K4-L); and, occasionally, as a torpedo bomber. The Allied code name *Mavis* was applied to this type, which could carry a maximum bomb load of 3,527 lb. and had the impressive range of 3,107 miles. The H6K was out of production by the middle war years and was superseded in service by the much-improved H8K *Emily*.

Kawanishi H8K

Purpose: Maritime bomber and reconnaissance.
Engines: Four 1,850 h.p. Mitsubishi Kasei 22 radials.

Span: 124 ft. 7½ in.
Max. Speed: 283 m.p.h. at 15,485 ft.

Entering production in 1941 as the H8K1 to replace the obsolescent H6K, at a time when Japan stood in dire need of such a good long range patrol aircraft, the *Emily* was, nevertheless, not to serve in very large numbers with the J.N.A.F. The refined H8K2 appeared in 1943, including a batch of 36 H8K2-L transports known to the Japanese as Seiku (*Clear Sky*), and total production reached 167 machines. The *Emily* was an original design, having a 4,000-mile range, a crew of ten and an all-up weight of 54,013 lb. A defensive armament of five 20 mm. cannon and four 7.7 mm. machine guns was carried, in addition to a maximum bomb load of 4,410 lb.

Kawanishi N1K1 Kyofu (*Mighty Wind*)

Purpose: Fighter.
Engine: One 1,460 h.p. Mitsubishi Kasei 15 radial.

Span: 39 ft. 4½ in.
Max. Speed: 302 m.p.h. at 18,680 ft.

A first-class design with an excellent performance, the N1K1 (code name *Rex*) made its appearance in August 1942. Three months later, however, the first steps were taken to convert the basic design to one for a landplane fighter—the N1K1-J Shiden described on page 106—and in consequence only 97 Kyofus were completed as such. Armed with two 20 mm. cannon and two 7.7 mm. machine guns, these aircraft nevertheless gave extensive service, being employed towards the close of the war in the defence of the Japanese mainland.

209

Kawasaki Ki.48

Data apply to Ki.48-IIa.
Purpose: Light bomber.
Engines: Two 1,130 h.p. Nakajima Ha.115 radials.

Span: 57 ft. 3¾ in.
Max. Speed: 314 m.p.h. at 18,372 ft.

Although it remained in production from July 1940 until October 1944, during which time approximately 2,000 examples were built, the Ki.48 (*Lily*) was not an outstanding success. It saw service on most fronts in the Pacific war, but its manoeuvrability and general performance did not measure up to expectation. Test-flown during the autumn of 1939, about 550 Ki.48-I had been completed by 1942, powered by Ha.25 engines. This model was followed by the Ki.48-IIa and a dive-bomber version, the Ki.48-IIb, some of the latter featuring a small dorsal extension to the fin. A number of Ki.48s were modified for experimental duties, one becoming a testbed for a ramjet engine, and others guided missile carriers. A " lead ship " project with much-augmented armament, which never came to fruition, was designed Ki.81.

Kawasaki Ki.56

Purpose: Transport.
Engines: Two 990 h.p. Mitsubishi Ha. 25 radials

Span: 64.ft. 5½ in.
Max. Speed: 249 m.p.h. at 11,155 ft.

The Lockheed Super Electra was one of a number of American transport aircraft used before the war by Japan Airways, and at the beginning of hostilities the type was adopted by the J.A.A.F. During 1940/41, fifty-six of these aircraft were manufactured for the Army by Kawasaki; they then handed over production to the Tachikawa company, who built a further 688 in the ensuing three years. In 1938, Kawasaki had also begun work on modifying the American design to Japanese standards, and 119 examples of this modified machine were completed as the Ki. 56 (*Thalia*).

Kawasaki Ki.100

Data apply to Ki.100-Ia.
Purpose: Fighter and fighter-bomber.
Engine: One 1,500 h.p. Mitsubishi Ha. 112-II Type 4 radial.

Span: 39 ft. 4¼ in.
Max. Speed: 367 m.p.h. at 32,800 ft.

The Ki.100, result of a " marriage of convenience " during the final year of the Japanese war, emerged as one of the best fighter aircraft ever put up by the Army Air Force. To utilise some 270 Ki.61 *Tony* airframes vainly awaiting delivery of their Ha.140 inline engines, it was decided to install, as a matter of expediency, the readily-available Ha.112-II radial, and the first Ki. 61 so converted was flown on 1st February 1945. By the end of May, 256 such conversions had been made, the " new " aircraft being designated Ki. 100-Ia. Such was their success that a refinement with a rear-view cockpit canopy, the Ki.100-Ib, was placed in immediate production; 99 of this version were completed, as were several prototypes of the Ki.100-II. The latter, with a super-charged engine to improve altitude performance, was to have entered production in September 1945. Although mainly employed as a home defence fighter, the Ki.100 also had provision for carrying two 550 lb. bombs externally.

Kawasaki Ki.102

Data apply to Ki. 102b.
Purpose: Attack fighter.
Engines: Two 1,500 h.p. Mitsubishi Ha.112-II radials.

Span: 50 ft. 1 in.
Max. Speed: 360 m.p.h. at 19,685 ft.

Although only a small quantity were completed and placed in service before the Japanese surrender, the Ki.102 heavy assault fighter—code name *Randy*—quickly showed itself to be a useful addition to the J.A.A.F. ranks. The first of three prototypes was completed in March 1944, these being followed by twenty Ki.102b with an impressive armament of one 57 mm. and two 20 mm. cannon, one 12.7 mm. machine gun and provision for 1,100 lb. of bombs. Maximum range was 1,243 miles and ceiling just over 36,000 ft. Six Ki.102b were later modified, with 1,370 h.p. Ha.112-IIru supercharged engines, as prototypes for the Ki.102a high altitude inter-ceptor, but teething troubles restricted production of this version to fifteen aircraft. Only two Ki.102c, a radar carrying night-fighter, with slightly greater dimensions and two additional cannons were completed.

211

Kyushu QIWI Tokai (*Eastern Sea*)

Purpose: Anti-submarine and patrol.
Engines: Two 610 h.p. Hitachi Tempu 31 radials.

Span: 52 ft. 5⅞ in.
Max. Speed: 200 m.p.h. at 4,396 ft.

The Tokai (code name *Lorna*) was a modest design, 153 machines being built during the war by the Kyushu company (formerly Watanabe). A crew of three was normally carried, and some Tokais were equipped with crude forms of radar and submarine detection gear. The aircraft's performance included a ceiling of 14,730 ft. and a 914-mile range ; it had an all-up weight of 10,582 lb., and an armament of one 20 mm. cannon and one 7.7 mm. machine gun. Up to 1,100 lb. of bombs could also be carried.

James Gilbert

Lisunov Li–2

Purpose: Transport.
Engines: Two 1,000 h.p. Shvetsov ASh-62IR radials.

Span: 95 ft. 0 in.
Max. Speed: 225 m.p.h.

The Li-2, originally known by the functional designation PS-84, was the Douglas DC-3 transport built, with certain modifications, under licence in the Soviet Union and employing Russian-designed engines. Surplus Li-2s were disposed of after the war to re-equip the airlines of satellite countries.

Lockheed C-69 Constellation

Purpose: Troop transport.
Engines: Four 2,200 h.p. Wright R-3350-35 Cyclone radials.

Span: 123 ft. 0 in.
Max. Speed: 329 m.p.h. at 16,000 ft.

Begun in 1939 as a commercial airliner designed for T.W.A., the Constellation was taken over as a military project on America's entry into the war, and the first flight of the aircraft, on 9th January, 1943, was made by a military C-69.   Only 20 Constellations were delivered before the end of World War 2, consisting of nineteen 65-seat C-69 and one 43-seat C-69C.   Other orders, which included the 100-seat C-69A, 94-seat C-69B and 57-seat C-69D, were cancelled after VJ day and production turned over to civil Constellations for the airlines.

Lockheed PV-2 Harpoon

Purpose: Maritime patrol bomber.
Engines: Two 2,000 h.p. Pratt & Whitney R-2800-31 Double Wasp radials.

Span: 75 ft. 0 in.
Max. Speed: 282 m.p.h. at 13,700 ft.

The Harpoon was a progressive development of the PV-1 Ventura (page 114), featuring redesigned wings of greater span, a new tail assembly and greater range and bomb load.   If could be heavily armed with up to ten .50-in. machine guns and also had provision for R.P. batteries; 4,000 lb. of bombs or mines, or one 1,800 lb. torpedo, could be carried internally, and the Harpoon's range was more than 2,000 miles.   The U.S.N. received in all some 535 Harpoons, which were employed quite extensively during the closing stages of the war.

213

Macchi C.205V Veltro *(Greyhound)*

Purpose: Fighter and fighter-bomber.
Engine: One 1,475 h.p. licence-built DB 605A inline.

Span: 34 ft. 8½ in.
Max. Speed: 399 m.p.h. at 23,620 ft.

The Veltro was basically the airframe of the Macchi C.202 Folgore fighter (see page 116) re-engined with the more powerful DB 605A engine from Germany. It was highly manoeuvrable and a delightful aeroplane to fly, but unfortunately for Italy it did not come into service until mid-1943 and thus saw little active service. Armed with two 20 mm. wing cannon and two 12.7 mm. nose machine guns, the Veltro could carry two bombs of up to 330 lb. each in the fighter-bomber role.

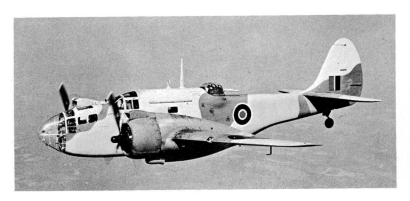

Martin A-30 Baltimore

Data apply to A-30A (Baltimore V).
Purpose: Medium bomber.
Engines: Two 1,700 h.p. Wright R-2600-29 Double-Row Cyclone radials.

Span: 61 ft. 4 in.
Max. Speed: 320 m.p.h. at 11,600 ft.

Never operational with the U.S. forces, the Baltimore was designed in 1940 to R.A.F. requirements for a medium bomber to succeed the A-22 Maryland (see page 268). The first A-30 flew on 14th June, 1941, and the entire production of 1,575 aircraft was delivered to Britain. Baltimores were used, from 1942 onwards, on bombing and reconnaissance missions by the R.A.F. and Allied air forces under R.A.F. command, exclusively in the Mediterranean theatre. Different mark numbers from I to V principally reflected variations in the armament fitted.

Martin PBM Mariner

Data apply to PBM-3C.
Purpose: Patrol bomber and transport.
Engines: Two 1,700 h.p. Wright Cyclone
R-2600-12 radials.

Span: 118 ft. 0 in.
Max. Speed: 198 m.p.h. at 13,000 ft.

Ordered in 1937 by the U.S. Navy, a quarter-scale model preceded the XPBM-1 Mariner which first flew in 1939. Subsequent production of the Mariner, which continued until 1947, centred upon the PBM-1, PBM-3 and PBM-5, including the PBM-5A amphibian. Principal wartime versions were the PBM-1 and -3, which were used mainly for U.S. coastal patrol; a few were similarly employed by R.A.F. Coastal Command. The PBM-3R was an adapted version of 1942, with strengthened floor and loading facilities for 20 passengers or up to 9,000 lb of freight.

Italian Air Ministry

Meridionali Ro 37

Purpose: Reconnaissance and general duties.
Engine: One 550 h.p. Fiat A.30 inline.

Span: 36 ft. 4 in.
Max. Speed: 184 m.p.h. at 9,840 ft.

One of Italy's Spanish War veterans, the Ro 37 (whose designation derives from the Romeo company by whom it was designed) was already obsolete when Italy entered the war. Built originally for reconnaissance, it was too slow to evade Allied interceptors and became relegated to second-line duties such as communications, training and Army co-operation.

Messerschmitt Bf 108 Taifun (Typhoon)

Data apply to Bf 108B.
Purpose: Communications and light transport.
Engine: One 240 h p Argus As 10C inline.

Span: 34 ft. 5 in.
Max. Speed: 196 m.p.h. at 8,000 ft.

A four-seat cabin monoplane designed in 1933, the Bf 108 has had a long life and examples are still to be seen flying today. Before the war it enjoyed considerable success as a sporting aircraft, and on the outbreak of war proved an ideal vehicle for communications duties and as a personal transport. Wartime production was delegated in 1942 to the S.N.C.A. du Nord factory in Occupied France, and the same company continued production of a further 285 after VE day as the Nord 1000, 1001 and 1002 Pingouin, powered by French engines.

MiG-3/I.W.M.

Mikoyan/Gurevich MiG-1 and MiG-3

Data apply to MiG-3.
Purpose: Fighter and fighter-bomber.
Engine: One 1,350 h.p. Mikulin AM-35A inline.

Span: 33 ft. 9½ in.
Max. Speed: 407 m.p.h. at 22,965 ft.

The now famous Mikoyan/Gurevich partnership began in 1940 with the design of the I-61 (MiG-1) which made its maiden flight in March of that year, powered by a 1,200 h.p. AM-35 engine. This open-cockpit single-seater was not an especially successful design, although over 2,000 were built before being supplanted in 1941 by the improved MiG-3, which earned its designers a Stalin Prize. Even the MiG-3 however, despite its excellent top speed, had several shortcomings, and although it too was produced in considerable numbers these had largely been relegated to reconnaissance duties by the end of 1943.

216

Magister Mk. I/I.W.M.

Miles Magister

Purpose: Basic trainer.
Engine: One 130 h.p. de Havilland Gipsy Major I inline.

Span: 33 ft. 10 in.
Max. Speed: 132 m.p.h. at 1,000 ft.

The Magister was the R.A.F.'s first monoplane trainer, and was also one of its most famous. Produced in response to A.M. Spec. T.40/36, the " Maggie " entered service in October 1937 and remained in full-scale use throughout World War II. Over 1,200 Magisters were built, many of them being returned to civil flying after the war under the title Hawk Trainer Mk. III.

Martinet Mk. I

Miles Martinet

Purpose: Target tug.
Engine: One 870 h.p. Bristol Mercury XX or XXX radial.

Span: 39 ft. 0 in.
Max. Speed: 237 m.p.h. at 15,000 ft.

In contrast to such diverse types as the Henley, Defiant and Battle, which were converted from other functions for gunnery target towing, the Miles Martinet was designed as a target tug from the outset. Very similar to the Master III trainer, on which it was based, the Martinet superseded the former in production in 1942 and was in extensive use during the remainder of the war, a total of 1,724 being completed. The type continued in service for several years after the end of World War 2.

217

Miles Master

Data apply to Mk. II.
Purpose: Advanced trainer.
Engine: One 870 h.p. Bristol Mercury XX radial.

Span: 39 ft. 0 in.
Max. Speed: 243 m.p.h. at 10,000 ft.

The prototype Master, a development of F. G. Miles' earlier and promising Kestrel trainer, first flew in 1938 and early production machines were delivered to the R.A.F. in the Spring of the following year.   The Mks. I and IA, of which 900 were built, were powered by the 715 h.p. Rolls-Royce Kestrel XXX inline engine, but subsequent versions featured a radial powerplant.   The first and most numerous of these was the Mk. II, production of which reached a total of 1,799; the final version (602 built) was the Master III, powered by the 825 h.p. Pratt & Whitney Wasp Junior and having a " clipped " wing of 35 ft. 7 in. span.

Miles Mentor

Purpose: Trainer and communications.
Engine: One 200 h.p. de Havilland Gipsy Six inline.

Span: 34 ft. 9½ in.
Max. Speed: 156 m.p.h.

The M.16 Mentor entered Royal Air Force service during 1938, and altogether 45 of these aircraft were delivered for radio training and light communications duties.   Many of these were still in service in 1944 after five years of intensive war service.

Miles Messenger

Purpose: A.O.P. and communications.
Engine: One 140 h.p. de Havilland Gipsy Major ID inline.

Span: 36 ft. 2 in.
Max. Speed: 115 m.p.h.

Produced at the request of the War Office for a light and nimble two-seat Air Observation Post, the M.38 Messenger was a development of the twin-finned M.28 which served in small numbers as an R.A.F. communications aircraft. The Messenger prototype made its first flight on 12th September, 1942, and was built in small numbers to A.M. Spec. 17/43. With its docile handling qualities and an all-up weight of about one ton, it was an obvious " club " aeroplane, and several M.48s (a developed version) are still to be found on the British Civil Register.

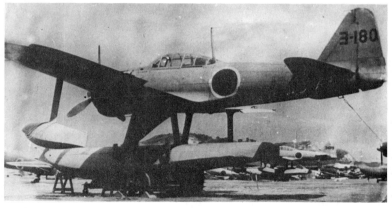

Mitsubishi A6M2 – N

Purpose: Fighter and reconnaissance.
Engine: One 925 h.p. Nakajima Sakae 12 radial.

Span: 39 ft. 4½ in.
Max. Speed: 270 m.p.h. at 14,110 ft.

Code named *Rufe* by the Allies, the A6M2-N, as its J.N.A.F. designation implies, was a floatplane adaptation of the A6M2 Zero fighter. This project was allocated to the Nakajima company, who began work in February 1941 and between April 1942 and September 1943 completed 327 of these aircraft. Although encountered in the Aleutian Islands and at Guadalcanal, the A6M2-N's principal employment was on reconnaissance and home defence missions rather than the ground support role for which it was originally intended.

Mitsubishi F1M2

Purpose: Reconnaissance.
Engine: One 780 h.p. Mitsubishi Zuisei 13 radial.

Span: 36 ft. 1 in.
Max. Speed: 229 m.p.h. at 9,840 ft.

Known to the Allies as *Pete*, 524 aircraft of this type were completed by the parent company and the Sasebo Naval Arsenal, all except four being of the F1M2 version. A two-seater, the modestly-powered F1M2 was fairly extensively used throughout the Pacific zone from shore bases and seaplane tenders. It was capable of carrying a pair of 132 lb. bombs and, despite its light armament of only three 7.7 mm. machine guns, was also employed occasionally as a fighter.

J2M3 captured by U.S. forces/*Musée de l'Air*

Mitsubishi J2M Raiden (*Thunderbolt*)

Purpose: Fighter.
Engine: One 1,820 h.p. Mitsubishi Kasei 23a radial.

Span: 35 ft. 5½ in.
Max. Speed: 371 m.p.h. at 19,360 ft.

This single-seat fighter—code name *Jack* —was another fundamentally good design that never quite made the grade. The work of Horikoshi, designer of the Zero, it was beset by structural failures, engine troubles and production difficulties, and instead of the three or four thousand aircraft originally planned only five hundred or so finally materialised. Three J2M1 prototypes (1,460 h.p. Kasei 13), the first of which flew on 20th March 1942, were followed by 155 J2M2 (Kasei 23), whose standard armament was two 20 mm. cannon and two 7.7 machine guns. The latter were replaced in the J2M3 by two further 20 mm. cannon. Only two J2M4s were completed, these being high-altitude examples with an engine turbo-supercharger and a six-cannon armament. In May 1944 the first J2M5 (1,820 h.p. Kasei 26, two 20 mm. cannon and 381 m.p.h. top speed) was flown, and some 30-40 of this version were eventually built. The J2M6 and J2M7 were modifications of earlier series, the former being the J2M3 with a " blister " cockpit hood and the latter a Kasei 26-engined version of the J2M2.

K3M3 bearing green surrender crosses on white background/*H. J. Nowarra*

Mitsubishi K3M

Purpose: Radio and navigation trainer.
Engine: One 580 h.p. Nakajima Kotobuki II-Kai-I radial.

Span: 51 ft. 9¼ in.
Max. Speed: 146 m.p.h.

This machine first appeared as the K3M1 in 1931/32 with a 300 h.p. Hispano-Suiza engine, and was an adaptation of the Fokker "Universal" for training purposes. The principal J.N.A.F. service version was the K3M2 (300 h.p. Amakaze 11 radial), of which 317 were built by Mitsubishi. A close rival, however, was the Watanabe-built K3M3 which entered production in 1939 and ran to 301 machines. Several of the latter, as the K3M3-L, were employed on transport duties. The K3M3, known by the code name *Pine* during the war, was a three/five-seater with a normal loaded weight of 4,850 lb. Provision was made for two 132 lb. bombs for " guerilla " raids and a single 7.7 mm. gun was carried for defence.

H. J. Nowarra

Mitsubishi Ki.51

Purpose: Reconnaissance and dive bomber.
Engine: One 950 h.p. Mitsubishi Ha. 26-II radial.

Span: 39 ft. 8¼ in.
Max. Speed: 263 m.p.h at 9,840 ft.

A development of the Ki.30, the Ki.51 *Sonia* entered production in 1939 and was produced in two basic versions: the Ki.51a for reconnaissance and the Ki.51b dive bomber, the latter carrying 440 lb. of bombs. The Ki.51, production of which totalled 1,472 machines, was a highly manoeuvrable aeroplane and proved to be very adept at eluding interceptor fighters. An armament of three 7.7 mm. machine guns was normally carried.

Mitsubishi Ki.57

Data apply to Ki.57-II.
Purpose: Transport.
Engines: Two 1,050 h.p. Mitsubishi Ha. 102 radials.

Span: 74 ft. 1¾ in.
Max. Speed: 292 m.p.h. at 19,030 ft.

Evolved from the MC-20 civil transport and bearing close resemblance to its stablemate, the Ki.21 *Sally* bomber, the Ki.57 (code name *Topsy*) was a standard J.A.A.F. transport type of World War 2. Built in two versions, the Ha.5-powered Ki.57-I, and the Ki.57-II, approximately 500 *Topsys* were completed by Mitsubishi; normal accommodation included a crew of four and eleven passengers.

B5N2/*H. J. Nowarra*

Nakajima B5N

Purpose: Torpedo bomber.
Engine: One 1,000 h.p. Nakajima Sakae 11 radial.

Span: 50 ft. 11 in.
Max. Speed: 235 m.p.h. at 11, 810 ft.

The Nakajima *Kate* was conceived in 1936 and the prototype (770 h.p. Hikari) first flew in January 1937. The B5N1 first became operational as a light bomber in China, but most aircraft of this version were converted to B5N1-K trainers as they were replaced during 1939/40 by the B5N2. Over 1,200 of both versions were built, and the force which attacked Pearl Harbour included forty B5N1 torpedo bombers from the aircraft carrier *Soryu*. Although somewhat vulnerable to fighter attack, the B5N also performed useful service in the later war years on anti-submarine duties.

Nakajima E8N1

Purpose: Reconnaissance.
Engine: One 580 h.p. Nakajima Kotobuki II-KAI radial.

Span: 33 ft. 0¾ in.
Max. Speed: 184 m.p.h.

Yet another of the seemingly endless assortment of Japanese reconnaissance floatplanes, the E8N1 (*Dave*) was primarily occupied as a "spotter" aircraft launched from warship catapults. Designed in 1933, 550 were built by the parent company and Kawanishi and saw quite extensive service during the early war years. The E8N1 was a two-seater, with a loaded weight of 4,519 lb. and an armament of two 7.7 mm. guns and 132 lb. of bombs.

Nakajima Ki.44 Shoki

Data apply to Ki.44-IIb.
Purpose: Fighter and fighter-bomber.
Engine: One 1,520 h.p. Nakajima Ha. 109 Type 2 radial.

Span: 31 ft. 0 in.
Max. Speed: 376 m.p.h. at 17,060 ft.

Although produced in fairly substantial numbers (1,223 of all versions) the Shoki, or *Tojo*, was not initially popular with J.A.A.F. pilots, who, accustomed to light and manoeuvrable fighters, did not care much for its heavy handling characteristics. Once its virtues—high speed and climb— were realised, it became more popular, although losses were still inclined to be heavy. In the latter war years the type was largely employed on interception duties in defence of the Japanese mainland. The first of the ten Shoki prototypes flew in August 1940, and production versions included the Ki.44-Ia (40 built entering service in the second half of 1942) the Ki.44-Ib and -Ic. -IIb and -IIc.

H. J. Nowarra

Nakajima Ki.49 Donryu *(Dragon Swallower)*

Purpose: Medium bomber.
Engines: Two 1,450 h.p. Nakajima Ha.109 Type 2 radials.

Span: 67 ft. 0 in.
Max. Speed: 306 m.p.h. at 17,060 ft.

Initially overshadowed by the Ki.21, and later by the much superior Ki.67, the *Helen*, as the Ki.49 was named by the Allies, did not appear in very great numbers, although it was by no means a poor design.   Comparatively few examples of the Ki.49-I were built, most of the 754 production aircraft consisting of the Ki.49-II type, to which the above data apply.   The Ki.49 first entered service in February 1942, and many were later used for transport and anti-submarine duties. Normal loaded weight was 22,376 lb., including a 2,200 lb. bomb load, and maximum range was 1,490 miles.   Heavily-armed fighter versions, which did not achieve production status, were the Ki.58 and Ki.80.

Nippon Ku.8

Purpose: Troop and cargo glider.
Span: 75 ft. 0 in.

Chief among the very small number of glider types used by Japan during the war was the Ku.8, originally code-named *Goose*. (This was subsequently amended to *Gander* to avoid confusion with the Grumman amphibian used by the R.A.F.). Carrying a crew of two and 15-20 armed troops, the Ku.8 jettisoned its main undercarriage after take-off, landing on the fixed under-fuselage skids; the tailwheel was also fixed.   Small vehicles or artillery pieces, when carried, were loaded from the front, the whole nose section hinging to starboard for the purpose. Troop entry was via the outward-opening door in the fuselage side. The "Ku" prefix in the official designation was taken from "Kakku", the Japanese verb "to glide". Usual tug for the *Gander* was the Mitsubishi Ki.21.

224

UC-64A/U.S.A.F.

Noorduyn C-64 Norseman

Purpose: Light transport and communications
Engine: One 600 h.p. Pratt & Whitney R-1340-AN-1 Wasp radial.

Span: 51 ft. 6 in.
Max. Speed: 162 m.p.h. at 5,000 ft.

First designed in 1935 for use in Canada, the Norseman was ordered as a light transport for the U.S.A.A.F. towards the end of 1942, production centring mainly on the C-64A version, following a small batch of generally similar YC-64. The C-64A, of which 746 were built, carried a crew of two and provided accommodation for eight passengers or an equivalent freight load; the data above apply to this version. The C-64A was also used by the R.C.A.F. (as the Norseman IV and VI) for wireless operator and navigation training, and three C-64A were transferred to the U.S. Navy with the designation JA-1. Six C-64B, with provision for six passengers only, were produced in floatplane form for the Engineer Corps.

Northrop A-17

R.A.F Nomad Mk. I/I.W.M.

Data apply to A-17A.
Purpose: Light attack bomber.
Engine: One 825 h.p. Pratt & Whitney R-1535-13 Wasp Junior radial.

Span: 47 ft. 9 in.
Max. Speed: 220 m.p.h. at 2,500 ft.

The A-17 attack aircraft was developed, via the YA-13 (later XA-16), from the Northrop Gamma mailplane of pre-war days. During 1935-36, 110 A-17s were built for the U.S.A.A.F., followed by 129 A-17As with improved power and a retractable undercarriage. Two of the latter were subsequently adapted as three-seat A-17AS command transports. Great Britain and France received 61 and 32 of the A-17A model respectively, the former being awarded the name Nomad. In the event these fell short of R.A.F. requirements and all but one were transferred to the South African Air Force.

YP-61/U.S.A.F.

Northrop P-61 Black Widow

Data apply to P-61B.
Purpose: Night fighter.
Engines Two 2,250 h.p. Pratt & Whitney
R-2800-65 Double Wasp radials.

Span: 66 ft. 0 in.
Max. Speed: 366 m.p.h. at 20,000 ft.

The Black Widow was noteworthy during the war on two counts: it was the first U.S. aircraft designed and built specifically for night fighting; and after years of close security its existence was "announced" to the world in a strip cartoon in a public newspaper after it had performed in a military display during January 1944. The first of two XP-61s flew on 21st May, 1942; by the summer of 1944 the type was in service, and by the end of that year was operating over Europe from bases in France. The P-61 was radar-equipped and carried a usual armament of four 20 mm. cannon and four .50 machine guns. The principal models in service before VJ day were the P-61-1/5, P-61A, B and C. These were generally similar except in powerplant model and in the absence of dorsal turret on the P-61A and B and some P-61-1s. A photographic version was designated F-15.

I.W.M.

Percival Petrel

Purpose: Communications and light transport.
Engines: Two 205 h.p. de Havilland Gipsy Six
II inlines.

Span: 46 ft. 8 in.
Max. Speed: 195 m.p.h. at 1,000 ft.

The Percival Q.6 light transport first appeared in 1937 and until the summer of 1939 was the fastest aircraft on British internal air routes. In 1938 seven of the Mk. V version were completed for the Royal Air Force to Spec. 25/38. These aircraft were given the service name Petrel, and served alongside the civil Q.6s throughout World War 2, several returning afterwards to the Civil Register. Versions with both fixed and retractable undercarriages were flown.

Percival Proctor

Data apply to Mk. IV.
Purpose: Radio trainer and communications.
Engine: One 210 h.p. de Havilland Gipsy Queen II inline.

Span: 39 ft. 6 in.
Max. Speed: 160 m.p.h. at sea level.

Preceded by 15 " militarised " Vega Gulls, the first prototype of the true military Proctor (P 5998) flew on 8th October, 1939. The R.A.F. received 147 Mk. I and the Fleet Air Arm 100 Mk. IA. Apart from the absence of dual controls, the Mk. II was generally similar, 50 going to the R.A.F. and 150 to the Royal Navy. The Mk. III was exclusively for R.A.F. use, 437 being built by F. Hills and Sons of Manchester, and the final version was the longer, four-seat Proctor IV (originally named Preceptor). Most of the 258 Mk. IVs were also Hills-built. Large numbers of ex-service Proctors came on to the civil market after the war, but the type also remained in diminishing use by the R.A.F. until 1955.

Piper L-4 Grasshopper

Data apply to L-4B.
Purpose: Light liaison and observation.
Engine: One 65 h.p. Continental O-170-3.

Span: 35 ft. 3 in.
Max. Speed: 89 m.p.h. at sea level.

One of the most widely used of the " L " class, the Piper Grasshopper was employed in the European and Pacific theatres on an assortment of missions including mail, food and equipment transportation, smoke-bombing, and the laying of field telephone cables. Total production was well over 5,500 of which the principal versions were the L-4A (most of these were originally designated O-59A), L-4B, L-4H and L-4J. A three-seat training glider, the Piper TG-8, was evolved from the L-4 during 1942-43; 253 of these were completed for the U.S.A.A.F.

I-153 in Finnish Air Force markings/*Eino Ritaranta*

Polikarpov I–15

Data apply to I-153.
Purpose: Fighter and fighter-bomber.   *Span:* 32 ft 9¾ in.
Engine: One 1,000 h.p. M-62 radial.   *Max. Speed:* 267 m.p.h at 16,400 ft.

Originating in 1932, the I-15 (700 h.p. M-25) first flew in October 1933 and a modified machine of this type, flown by Vladimir Kokkinaki, established a World Altitude Record of 47,818 ft. in November 1935.   Both the I-15 and the developed I-15*bis* (750 h.p. M-25B) were widely used in the Spanish Civil War and the Russo-Finnish campaigns, and although obsolete by World War 2 a small number served briefly during the opening stages.   Alongside them fought the I-153, a modified version developed by Shcherbakov which had a retractable undercarriage, but these too had mostly disappeared by the end of 1941.

Polikarpov I–16

Purpose: Fighter and fighter-bomber.   *Span:* 29 ft 6¼ in.
Engine: One 1,000 h.p. Shvetsov M-62 radial.   *Max. Speed:* 326 m.p.h. at sea level.

Designed at about the same time as the I-15, the I-16 was a much more radical conception for its time, and although obsolete by the beginning of World War 2 continued to render valuable service until more modern machines replaced it in 1943.   A fast and rugged little aeroplane, it attracted much foreign interest before the war and was widely employed by the Russians in Spain and Finland.   Normal armament was two 20 mm. ShVAK and two 7.62 mm. ShKAS guns, plus provision for small bombs or six rocket projectiles underwing.

228

Aeroplane Photo Supply

Polikarpov Po–2

Purpose: General duties.
Engine: One 110 h.p. Shvetsov M-11 radial.

Span: 37 ft. 6 in.
Max. Speed: 93 m.p.h.

Few aircraft can so have justified the description "maid-of-all-work" as this Russian lightplane which first appeared in 1928. It was then known as the U-2, and intended as a basic trainer. Subsequent civil and military duties covered almost every aspect of flying, including aerial taxi, ambulance, crop spraying, agent dropping, glider tug, communications, supply, reconnaissance, rocket projectile carrying, and even night bombing. Versions existed with two and three open cockpit seats, and ski landing gear could be fitted. Early ambulances carried their stretcher cases on the inboard sections of the lower mainplanes, though on later models they were transferred to a covered rear cockpit.

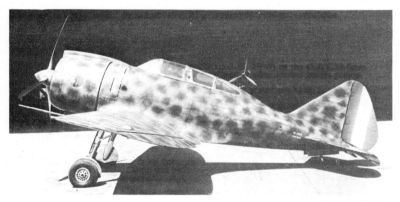

Italian Air Ministry

Reggiane Re 2000 Falco I *(Falcon)*

Data apply to Series I.
Purpose: Fighter.
Engine: One 1,000 h.p. Piaggio P.XI RC 40
radial

Span: 36 ft. 1 in.
Max. Speed: 336 m.p.h. at 18,040 ft

The Re 2000, which first appeared in 1938, was an attractive-looking little aeroplane bearing a close resemblance to the American Seversky P-35 fighter. Designed to meet the same requirement as the Macchi C.200 Saetta (see page 115), it was eventually produced for export after the latter had been adopted for the Regia Aeronautica, although the Italian Navy did subsequently operate a small number of the improved Re 2000 Series II and III.

229

Reggiane Re 2001 Falco II and Re 2005 Sagittario (Archer)

Data apply to Re 2001.
Purpose: Fighter and fighter-bomber.
Engine: One 1,150 h.p. Daimler-Benz DB 601A inline.

Span: 36 ft. 0½ in.
Max. Speed: 350 m.p.h. at 17,876 ft.

Developed in 1941, the single-seat Re 2001 was one of several useful Italian designs to follow the importation of liquid-cooled aero-engines from Germany, and was basically the Re 2000 adapted to take the new powerplant. The Falco's performance, particularly its manoeuvrability, were good, but Marshal Badoglio's surrender came when only 252 had been completed and these did not see widespread service. The Re 2005 was a strengthened and slightly smaller development of the 2001. Equipped with the 1,475 h.p. DB 605A (the radiator being transferred from the wing to beneath the fuselage), the Re 2005 differed further in having an outward-retracting under-carriage. Only 48 aircraft had been completed at the surrender, these being operated subsequently by the German-directed Fascist Air Force.

Republic P-43 Lancer

Purpose: Fighter and reconnaissance.
Engine: One 1,200 h.p. Pratt & Whitney R-1830-35 Twin Wasp radial.

Span: 36 ft. 0 in.
Max. Speed: 351 m.p.h. at 20,000 ft.

Bearing obvious family resemblance to the Seversky P-35 and the XP-41, to which its design owed much, and to the later P-47 Thunderbolt (page 146), the Lancer's career began with the first deliveries of a batch of thirteen YP-43 to the U.S.A.A.F. in September 1940. No modifications were found necessary on the production batch of 54 P-43s which followed, the first significant change being the installation of the improved R-1830-49 engine, which offered a better performance, in the P-43A; 80 of this version were completed. The 125 P-43A-1 which followed utilised the R-1830-57. Subsequently, 150 P-43A and A-1 aircraft were modified as P-43Bs by the installation of reconnaissance cameras, and a number of this version were supplied to the R.A.A.F. The Chinese Air Force received 108 P-43A and A-1 fighters under Lend-Lease.

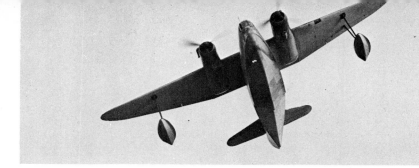

Saro Lerwick

Purpose: Maritime patrol.
Engines: Two 1,375 h.p. Bristol Hercules II
  radials.

Span: 80 ft. 10 in.
Max. Speed: 216 m.p.h. at 4,000 ft.

The Lerwick, designed to A.M. Spec. R.1/36, was one of the aircraft chosen shortly before the war for the re-equipment of Coastal Command. It first appeared in 1938, the last of 21 aircraft was delivered in May 1941, yet in 1942 the type was declared obsolete. The reason for this has remained unexplained, officially, ever since—though the brief two-year life of the Lerwick was not apparently over-successful. It ended its service days on training duties, being replaced in its operational role by the American Catalina.

Saro London

Purpose: Maritime patrol.
Engines: Two 920 h.p. Bristol Pegasus X
  radials.

Span: 80 ft. 0 in.
Max. Speed: 155 m.p.h. at 6,560 ft.

The prototype London (K 3560) made its maiden flight in 1934 (designed to A.M. Spec. R.24/31), and the first Mk. Is (Pegasus III) were delivered to Coastal Command in 1936. After ten Mk. Is, production continued with the Mk. II, of which a further 38 were built. Londons were still in front-line service when World War 2 began; they remained with the R.A.F. until replaced by Catalinas in 1941, serving thereafter with the Royal Canadian Air Force.

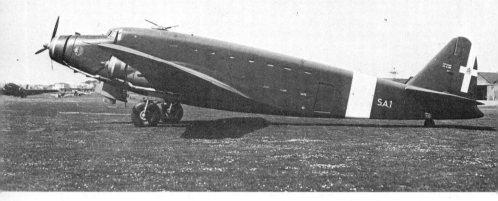

Savoia-Marchetti S.M. 82 Canguro *(Kangaroo)*

Data apply to S.M.82T.
Purpose: Heavy transport.
Engines: Three 850 h.p. Alfa Romeo 128 RC 18 radials.

Span: 97 ft. 5 in.
Max. Speed: 211 m.p.h. at 8,200 ft.

Italy's largest transport, the Canguro was developed from the earlier S.M. 75 Marsupiale and was one of the better-looking trimotor designs turned out by the Axis powers. Payloads were widely varied, ranging from fuel supplies to armed troops (of whom 40 could be accommodated) and dismantled single-seat fighters. A number of S.M. 82s were used under Luftwaffe direction following the Italian surrender in 1943.

Savoia-Marchetti S.M. 84

Purpose: Torpedo-bomber.
Engines: Three 1,000 h.p. Piaggio P.XI RC 40 radials.

Span: 69 ft. 6½ in.
Max. Speed: 292 m.p.h. at 16,400 ft.

A development of the S.M. 79 Sparviero (see page 148), the S.M. 84 was structurally and visually similar save for the cantilever twin-finned tail unit and minor changes in armament. It was not produced in very great numbers.

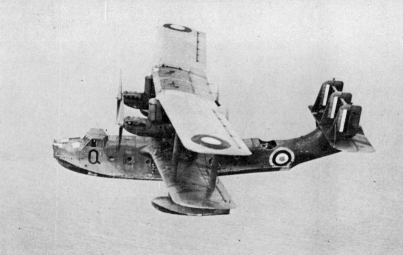

Short Singapore III

Purpose: Maritime reconnaissance.
Engines: Two 560 h.p. Rolls-Royce Kestrel III
MS (tractor) and two 560 h.p. Kestrel II MS
(pusher).

Span: 90 ft. 0 in.
Max. Speed: 145 m.p.h. at 2,000 ft.

The original Singapore, the Mk. I, first appeared in 1926, and the example used by Sir Alan Cobham on his round-Africa flight became world-famous. The Mk. II of 1930 was not produced in quantity, but in March 1935 a development of this, the Mk. III, went into production and 37 were built for the R.A.F. A few remained in limited service for a while after the outbreak of war.

R-4B

Sikorsky R-4

Data apply to R-4B.
Purpose: Observation and rescue.
Engine: One 200 h.p. Warner R-550-3 Super
Scarab radial.

Rotor diameter: 38 ft. 0 in.
Max. Speed: 82 m.p.h.

In 1939, Igor Sikorsky demonstrated his VS-300, the world's first fully practical and successful helicopter. From it he subsequently developed the VS-316 which, under its military title XR-4, first flew on 13th January, 1942. During 1943 extensive tests were carried out with this and the three YR-4As, and with the completion of 27 YR-4Bs and 100 R-4Bs the type became the first production helicopter in the world. It was employed during the war by both the Army and, as the HNS-1, by the U.S. Navy, and formed the basis of the R-5 and R-6 designs which were attaining maturity when the war ended.

Stinson AT-19 and UC-81

Royal Navy Reliant Mk. I

Data apply to AT-19.
Purpose: Navigation trainer.
Engine: One 280 h.p. Lycoming R-680-1 radial.

Span: 41 ft. 11 in.
Max. Speed: 135 m.p.h.

For light transport and communications work, some 47 five-seat commercial Model SR-9 and SR-10 aircraft, with various powerplants, were acquired during the war from their civil owners and utilised under a series of UC-81 designations ranging up to UC-81N. Wartime production covered 500 similar aircraft, equipped for navigation training duties, which were given the U.S. A.A.F. designation AT-19 and supplied under Lend-Lease to the Fleet Air Arm as the Reliant.

Stinson L-5

L-5/U.S.A.F.

Data apply to L-5E.
Purpose: Liaison and light transport.
Engine: One 185 h.p. Lycoming O-435-1.

Span: 34 ft. 0 in.
Max. Speed: 118 m.p.h.

Based upon the pre-war Voyager cabin monoplane, the two-seat L-5 was first flown in 1941 and was originally designated O-62. Altogether more than 3,500 examples were built, including the L-5B (ambulance or cargo carrier), L-5C (aerial camera), L-5E, L-5G (improved E with engine change) and some 306 L-5s built for the U.S. Navy as the OY-1. A substantial number of L-5s were supplied under Lend-Lease to the R.A.F. with which, as the Sentinel, they were widely used on the Burma front for communications, spotting and ambulance duties.

Supermarine Sea Otter

Sea Otter A.S.R. Mk. II/Air Ministry

Purpose: Air/sea rescue.
Engine: One 855 h.p. Bristol Mercury XXX
radial.

Span: 46 ft. 0 in.
Max. Speed: 150 m.p.h. at 5,000 ft.

The last biplane to be designed by Supermarine, and the last to serve with the Royal Air Force, the Sea Otter was a successor to the famous Walrus (page 157). It was designed to A.M. Spec. S.7/38, incorporating aerodynamic improvements and a more powerful engine, which gave it a performance superior to that of its predecessor. Production of the 290 aircraft built was undertaken by Saunders-Roe Ltd. between 1943 and 1946, the first entering service at the end of 1944. The type operated in home waters and in the Far East during the remaining war years, and continued in service for some years afterwards.

Supermarine Stranraer

Stranraer prototype

Purpose: Maritime patrol.
Engines: Two 920 h.p. Bristol Pegasus X
radials.

Span: 85 ft. 0 in.
Max. Speed: 165 m.p.h. at 6,000 ft.

A small number of Stranraer flying boats remained with two R.A.F. squadrons in September 1939, and continued to give useful service for a few months until replaced by later types. Designed by R. J. Mitchell, the prototype appeared in 1935 and the Stranraer joined Coastal Command the following year. Forty were built by Canadian-Vickers for the R.C.A.F. between 1938 and 1941

Tachikawa Ki.54

Ki-54b/H. J. Nowarra

Purpose: Advanced trainer and transport.   *Span:* 58 ft. 0⅞ in.
Engines: Two 450 h.p. Hitachi Ha.13A radials.   *Max. Speed:* 228 m.p.h. at 6,560 ft.

This twin-motor aircraft first made its appearance in 1940, and was code-named *Hickory* by the Allies. Its performance, considering the modest powerplant, was markedly better than that of many of its predecessors, and versions equipped for navigation, bombing and gunnery training soon made their appearance. Towards the end of the war some Ki.54s were modified as 5/9-seat transports, and some were also employed on suicide missions. Total production of the type was approximately 1,200.

U.S.A.F.

Taylorcraft L-2 Grasshopper

Data apply to L-2B.
Purpose: Light liaison and observation.   *Span:* 35 ft. 5 in.
Engine: One 65 h.p. Continental O-170-3.   *Max. Speed:* 90 m.p.h.

The L-2 was a member of an extensive range of aircraft operated by the U.S.A.A.F. under the generic name " Grasshopper ", and large numbers were supplied for Army use during the war years. Developed out of the pre-war Taylorcraft Tandem Trainer, from which they differed principally in having much increased window area, those built expressly for service use were designated L-2, -2A, -2B and -2M. Commercial models purchased for military use were designated from L-2C to -2L, bringing the total employed to nearly 2,000.

236

TB-3 with AM-34 engines/*H. J. Nowarra*

Tupolev ANT-6 (TB-3)

Purpose: Transport.
Engines: Four 830 h.p. AM-34 inlines.

Span: 132 ft. 10½ in.
Max. Speed: 155 m.p.h.

Appearing originally in 1930 as a bomber, this venerable machine remained in production for the next six years and many of them, under the designation G-2, served during the war as 30-seat paratroop transports. A few were even employed in their original role in the early stages of hostilities, carrying up to 6,600 lb. of bombs.

via Jean Alexander

Tupolev Tu–2

Purpose: Bomber and ground attack.
Engines: Two 1,850 h.p. Shvetsov ASh-82FNV radials.

Span: 61 ft. 10½ in.
Max. Speed: 357 m.p.h. at 12,000 ft.

One of the best Russian designs to emerge during the war years, the Tu-2 to a large extent replaced, during 1944/45, the Petlyakov Pe-2. Carrying a crew of four, the Tu-2 was armed with two 23 mm. cannon and five 12.7 mm. Beresin machine guns and could accommodate up to 5,000 lb. of bombs. Service ceiling was over 36,000 ft. and all-up weight 28,224 lb.

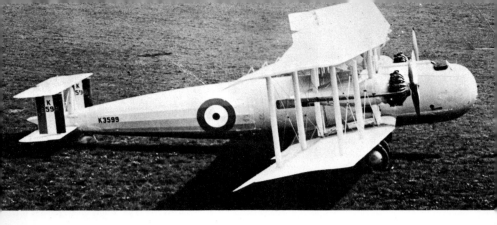

Vickers Valentia

Purpose: Troop transport.
Engines: Two 650 h.p. Bristol Pegasus II radials.

Span: 87 ft. 4 in.
Max. Speed 130 m.p.h. at 5,000 ft.

Developed from the Victoria—many early Valentias actually being converted Victoria Mk. Vs—the Valentia was very active as a transport aircraft in the Middle East during the mid-'thirties. Entering service in 1934, it remained in R.A.F. service, albeit in decreasing numbers, until as late as 1943.

Warwick A.S.R. Mk. I

Vickers Warwick

Data apply to A.S.R. Mk. I.
Purpose: Air/sea rescue.
Engines: Two 1,850 h.p. Pratt & Whitney Double Wasp R-2800 radials.

Span: 96 ft. 8¼ in.
Max. Speed: 224 m.p.h.

Originally intended as a Wellington replacement (to Spec. B.1/35), the Warwick did not finally enter production until 1942, by which time it was no longer required as a bomber. The air/sea rescue Mk. I (399 built) entered service in 1943, followed by 130 Centaurus-powered Mk. IIs, which were similarly employed. Fourteen Mk. Is were converted as B.O.A.C. transports, transferring to Transport Command in 1944, and were followed by 100 Mk. III transport versions. Final version was the Centaurus-powered Mk. V (210 built), which was not in service until after the war.

Vickers Wellesley

Purpose: Bomber.
Engine: One 925 h.p. Bristol Pegasus XX radial.

Span: 74 ft. 7 in.
Max. Speed: 228 m.p.h. at 19,680 ft.

Surely one of the largest-span single-engined aircraft ever produced in quantity, the Wellesley was the first aeroplane to employ Barnes Wallis' geodetic method of construction. Initiated as a private venture, the type went into production in 1937 to A.M. Spec. 22/35, and by May of the following year 176 Wellesleys had been completed. Superseded by the outbreak of war by later types, the Wellesley nevertheless served in the Middle East as a bomber during 1940, and on reconnaissance duties until 1941.

Vought-Sikorsky OS2U

Data apply to OS2U-3.
Purpose: Reconnaissance
Engine: One 450 h.p. Pratt & Whitney R-985 -SB3 Wasp Junior radial

Span: 35 ft. 11 in.
Max. Speed (floatplane): 171 m.p.h. at 5,000 ft.

The OS2U was designed to replace the earlier Seagull scout, and was produced in both wheeled and floatplane versions. The XOS2U-1 flew in 1939, the OS2U-1 production model entering U.S. Navy service the following year as that service's first catapult monoplane. The two-seat OS2U was a versatile little machine, which during its career was employed on dive-bombing (with two 100 lb. or eight 30 lb. bombs), coastal patrol and rescue duties in addition to its original function. Most of its service was given in the Pacific theatre. Generally similar to the OS2U-1 were the OS2U-2 and -3 floatplanes, a total of 1,525 of all three versions being built by Vought-Sikorsky during the war. In addition the Naval Aircraft Factory completed 300 of a landplane version of the OS2U-3 as the OS2N-1, and a further 100 OS2U-3s were supplied in 1942 to the Royal Navy as the Kingfisher I.

Vought-Sikorsky SB2U Vindicator

Data apply to SB2U-3.
Purpose: Scout and dive-bomber.
Engine: One 750 h.p. Pratt & Whitney R-1535-02 Wasp radial.

Span: 42 ft. 0 in.
Max. Speed: 243 m.p.h. at 9,500 ft.

Designed in 1935 and first flown in its XSB2U-1 form on 5th January, 1936, the Vindicator was Vought-Sikorsky's first monoplane venture. The SB2U-1 entered service with the U.S. Navy in 1937, and the Marine Corps' SB2U-2 and -3, which followed, were generally similar. During 1938 a number of these aircraft were ordered by the French Government, but most were destroyed or captured by the Nazis during the early stages of the war. The last 50 aircraft of the order were taken over in 1941 by Great Britain and re-titled Chesapeake I by the Royal Navy. They were not, however, a great success and were quickly relegated to training duties.

BT-13

Vultee BT-13 and BT-15 Valiant

Data apply to BT-13A.
Purpose: Basic trainer.
Engine: One 450 h.p. Pratt & Whitney R-985-AN-1 Wasp Junior radial.

Span: 42 ft. 2 in.
Max. Speed: 156 m.p.h. at sea level.

Vultee's first really successful aircraft following a row of rather disappointing earlier designs, the Valiant was a standard primary trainer of the war years: some remained in service until as late as 1950, ten years after the first production aircraft were delivered. Altogether more than 11,000 Valiants were built, of which all but about 2,000 went to the U.S.A.A.F. The U.S. Navy version was designated SNV-1.

240

Vultee-Stinson L-1 Vigilant

Data apply to L-1A.
Purpose: Light liaison and observation.   *Span:* 50 ft. 11 in.
Engine: One 295 h.p. Lycoming R-680-9 radial.   *Max. Speed:* 122 m.p.h.

Designed and built originally by Stinson as the O-49, the Vigilant was taken over by Consolidated-Vultee and eventually received the first designation in the newly-established " liaison " category.   The main service versions were the L-1 (142 built, formerly O-49) and the larger and somewhat improved L-1A (182 built, formerly O-49A).   Three O-49/L-1 aircraft were converted for ambulance work as the L-1B, and a further 25 L-1As were adapted, as L-1C/D/E/F, for similar duties and for glider pickup training.   About 100 Vigilants were used by the R.A.F. for liaison and artillery spotting.

Waco CG-4A

Purpose: Transport and assault glider
Span: 83 ft. 8 in.
Max. Towing Speed: 150 m.p.h.

A consortium of sixteen manufacturing plants throughout the U.S.A. between them built 13,909 CG-4As during tne war years—easily the biggest production run of any glider of the period. With an all-up weight of 9,000 lb., the CG-4A (known in the R.A.F. as the Hadrian) could accommodate 15 fully-equipped troops, two of whom would act as pilot and co-pilot, or an equivalent freight load.   It was the standard U.S. glider for most of the war, and figured prominently in the Allied landings in Sicily and Normandy; usual tugs were the C-46 and C-47.   A developed version, the CG-15A, did not achieve the same prominence, although Waco turned out 427 of the later machine.

241

Waco CG-13A

Purpose: Troop and cargo glider.
Span: 85 ft. 6¾ in.
Max. Towing Speed: 190 m.p.h.

Basically a scaled-up version of the same company's CG-4A design, the CG-13A featured an upwards-hinging nose through which 30 troops (42 in the final model) or some four tons of freight could be loaded. Apart from the two XCG-13s built by Waco, production of the five YCG-13/13A and 132 CG-13As completed was undertaken by Northwestern Aeronautical Corporation and the Ford Motor Co. The Douglas C-54 was the usual tug, though C-46s and C-47s were also employed on occasion.

Whirlwind Mk. I

Westland Whirlwind

Purpose: Long-range fighter and fighter-bomber.
Engines: Two 885 h.p. Rolls-Royce Peregrine I inlines.

Span: 45 ft. 0 in.
Max. Speed: 360 m.p.h. at 15,000 ft.

Designed to A.M. Spec. F.37/35 and first flown (L 6844) on 11th October 1938, the Whirlwind did not enter Royal Air Force service until June 1940. It was unfortunate in being designed for a powerplant which suffered many teething troubles and which consequently was not produced in large numbers. As a long range escort and, with modifications, as a fighter-bomber, the Whirlwind had reasonable success, but the 112 machines built never achieved great heights and by 1943 they had been virtually superseded by other aircraft.

Yakovlev Yak–1 and Yak–7

Yak-1s/I.W.M.

Data apply to Yak-1.
Purpose: Fighter and fighter-bomber.
Engine: One 1,100 h.p. Klimov M-105PA inline.

Span: 32 ft. 9¾ in
Max. Speed: 364 m.p.h. at 16,400 ft.

As the I-26, the Yak-1 prototype first flew in mid-1940, two years after design work had begun, and secured for Alexander Yakovlev the Order of Lenin and a number of more material honours. Entering production in the late spring of 1941, the Yak-1 was in service by early 1942, successive versions incorporating progressive improvements in armament. Later modifications included cutting down the rear fuselage and installing a new cockpit enclosure with all-round visibility; initially known as the Yak-1M, this model was later re-engined with the 1,260 h.p. M-105PF and re-designated Yak-7B. Two-seat trainer versions of the Yak-1 and Yak-7B were, respectively, the Yak-1U and Yak-7U.

via Jean Alexander

Yakovlev Yak–3

Purpose: Fighter and ground attack.
Engine: One 1,222 h.p. Klimov M-105PF inline.

Span: 30 ft. 2¼ in.
Max. Speed: 403 m.p.h. at 16,400 ft.

Developed alongside the Yak-9 (page 163), the Yak-3 followed its stablemate into service in 1944, despite the fact that it bore an earlier design number. Slightly smaller than the Yak-9, the Yak-3 had an excellent performance below 16,000 ft. and thanks to this low-level ability it was quite widely used both as an escort fighter for ground-strafing Il-2s and Pe-2s and as a close support aircraft in its own right. Armament consisted of a single 20 mm. ShVAK cannon and two 12.7 mm. Beresin guns.

243

Yokosuka E14Y1

Purpose: Reconnaissance.　　　　　　　　*Span:* 35 ft. 11½ in.
Engine: One 360 h.p. Hitachi Tempu 12 radial.　*Max. Speed:* 104 m.p.h. at 2,800 ft.

Allotted the Pacific code name *Glen*, the E14Y1 was designed by the Yokosuka Naval Air Arsenal as a small reconnaissance type with a modest performance, which could be carried as a " spotter " aircraft by ocean-going submarines. It first appeared in 1940, and was reported off the coasts of the United States and Australia during later stages of the war. The E14Y1 weighed only 3,197 lb. loaded; a single 7.7 mm. gun, operated by the second crew member, was carried for defence. Production of the type, which was not extensive, was handled by the Kyushu company.

244

Aircraft of the Secondary Powers

Ministère des Armées "Air"

Amiot 143M

Purpose: Bomber and reconnaissance.
Engines: Two 870 h.p. Gnome-Rhone 14K radials.
Span: 80 ft. 6¼ in.
Length: 59 ft. 8½ in.

Weight Empty: 18,982 lb.
Weight Loaded: 20,723 lb.
Max. Speed: 189 m.p.h. at 13,120 ft.
Service Ceiling: 26,240 ft.
Normal Range: 746 miles.

The Amiot 143M, first delivered to the Armée de l'Air in 1935, was intended for use as a multi-seat fighter, day or night bomber and long range reconnaissance aircraft; in the bombing role, it could carry an offensive load of 3,960 lb. It was already obsolescent by the time it entered service, and obsolete by the outbreak of World War 2. A small number, however, were used, together with the Farman 222, on reconnaissance and leaflet dropping flights over Germany and Czechoslovakia, being the only French aircraft in service with adequate range for the purpose. After the fall of France, a small number were employed as transports by the Vichy Air Force. incorporating such refinements as a retractable undercarriage,.

Avia Av-135

Purpose: Fighter.
Engine: One 890 h.p. Avia-built Hispano-Suiza 12Y inline.
Span: 35 ft. 7 in.
Length: 27 ft. 10¾ in.
Weight Empty: 4,241 lb.

Weight Loaded: 5,428 lb.
Max. Speed: 332 m.p.h.
Normal Range: 342 miles.
Service Ceiling: 27,890 ft.
Armament: One 20 mm. cannon and two 7.9 mm. machine guns.

The Av-135 was a derivative of the Av-35 fighter produced for the Czechoslovak government in 1938. When the Germans overran the country they sanctioned continued development of the Av-135, and a batch of twelve was eventually produced and delivered in 1941 for the use of the Bulgarian Air Force.

Avia B-534

Purpose: Fighter
Engine: One 850 h.p. Avia-built Hispano-Suiza 12 inline.
Span: 30 ft. 10 in.
Length: 26 ft. 10¾ in.

Weight Empty: 3,218 lb.
Weight Loaded: 4,365 lb.
Max. Speed: 245 m.p.h. at 14,435 ft.
Max. Ceiling: 34,875 ft.
Armament: Four 7.7 mm. machine guns.

Evolved from the B-34 of 1932, the prototype of the B-534 single-seat fighter made its first flight in 1933 and was put into production for the Czech Air Force shortly afterwards, early models having open cockpits. Following the invasion of Czechoslovakia, large numbers of B-534s were acquired by the Luftwaffe and put into use as trainers and glider tugs, although a few were employed in their original role on the Russian front.

Bloch 150 and derivatives

Data apply to MB-152.
Purpose: Fighter.
Engine: One 1,080 h.p. Gnome-Rhone 14N-25 radial.
Span: 34 ft. 7 in.
Length: 29 ft. 10¼ in.
Weight Empty: 4,453 lb.

Weight Loaded: 5,908 lb. (max.).
Max. Speed: 320 m.p.h. at 13,120 ft.
Service Ceiling: 32,800 ft.
Normal Range: 373 miles.
Armament: Four 7.5 mm. machine guns or two 7.5 mm. guns and two 20 mm. cannon.

Marcel Bloch's MB-150 fighter design made its first flight in October 1937, and in May 1938 a developed version, tne MB-151, went into production for the Armée de l'Air; 85 of this type were completed. The Bloch was a first-class little fighter, and the MB-151 was quickly followed by nearly 700 examples of the MB-152, later aircraft in this series having the more powerful 1,100

245

Bloch 155

h.p. Gnome-Rhone 14N-49 as powerplant. In 1940, a batch of nine MB-151s was supplied to Greece, and both 151s and 152s also found their way eventually to the Rumanian Air Force, as well as continuing to serve with the Vichy Air Force after France had collapsed. A further development from the 152, a modified example of which served as its prototype, was the MB-155; this was first flown early in 1940, and was also powered by the Gnome-Rhone 14N-49. About 30 MB-155s were built, most of these serving with the Vichy Air Force or, subsequently, with the Luftwaffe. Completion of the prototype MB-157 (1,700 h.p. Gnome-Rhone 14R-4) was authorised by the German authorities, and this aircraft flew in March 1942, achieving a top speed of over 440 m.p.h.; it was not, however, put into production.

Breguet 690 and derivatives

Data apply to Br. 691.
Purpose: Light bomber dive bomber, fighter and reconnaissance.
Engines: Two 680 h.p. Hispano-Suiza 14AB radials.
Span: 50 ft. 6 in.
Length: 33 ft. 5½ in.
Weight Empty: 8,157 lb.
Weight Loaded: 11,684 lb.
Max. Speed: 286 m.p.h. at 13,120 ft.

Normal Range: 746 miles.
Armament: (B.2) One 20 mm. cannon and one 7.5 mm. machine gun, plus eight 110 lb. bombs;
(AB.2) One 20 mm. cannon and two 7.5 mm. machine guns, plus eight 110 lb. bombs;
(A.3) Three 7.5 mm. machine guns;
(C.3) Two 20 mm. cannon and one 7.5 mm. machine gun.

In 1938 the Breguet 690, powered by two 680 h.p. Hispano-Suiza 14AB radial engines, appeared as a multi-purpose type for the French Air Force. The first production model was the Br. 691, which differed primarily in having a more streamlined configuration and a higher all-up weight; this was produced in four versions, as a light bomber (Br. 691-B.2), dive bomber (AB.2), reconnaissance (A.3) and fighter (C.3). All but the Br. 691-AB.2 saw some operational service in the early stages of the war, the AB.2s being replaced for the dive bomber role by the Br.693 in April 1940. Other developments included the Br. 692, a test machine for the proposed Br. 700 fighter; the Br. 694, of which only the prototype was completed—this was the designation of the model accepted by Belgium for licence production; and the Br. 695, a proposed version using Pratt & Whitney Hornet engines.

Caudron 714

Purpose: Fighter.
Engine: One 450 h.p. Renault Rol inline.
Span: 29 ft. 5 in.
Length: 27 ft. 11¾ in.
Weight Empty: 3,086 lb.

Weight Loaded: 3,858 lb.
Max. Speed: 303 m.p.h. at 13,120 ft.
Service Ceiling: 29,855 ft.
Normal Range: 559 miles.
Armament: Four 7.5 mm. machine guns.

The C.714 design for a lightweight fighter first appeared in the summer of 1938, stemming from the experimental C.710 of 1936 and the C.713 of 1937. The C.714 entered production in mid-1939, and up to February 1940 ninety of the initial order for 100 machines were completed. Fifty of these were diverted to the Finnish Air Force, although in the event only a handful of them ever arrived. The remainder were delivered to Armée de l'Air squadrons, including one manned by Polish pilots. Two progressive developments, in collaboration with the Renault engine company, were designated C.R.760 and 770. Two prototypes of the former and one of the latter were completed, but after a few flights were destroyed to prevent their capture by the advancing German forces.

Caudron Goeland

Purpose: Transport and trainer.
Engines: Two 220 h.p. Renault Bengali Six inlines.
Span: 57 ft. 8⅞ in.
Length: 44 ft. 9¼ in.

Weight Empty: 6,005 lb.
Weight Loaded: 8,410 lb.
Max. Speed: 208 m.p.h.
Service Ceiling: 18,370 ft.
Max. Range: 1,056 miles.

The Caudron Goeland enjoyed a long and varied career, and some examples are still to be seen flying on the Continent today. It first appeared in 1934, and before the war was produced in several versions, chief among which was the military C.445 light transport and crew trainer for the Armée de l'Air. A variant, with modified additional windows, was used for ambulance

Ministère des Armées "Air"

duties. Upon the occupation of France, 55 Goelands were captured by the Luftwaffe, and production of the type was allowed to continue to equip the Vichy Air Force, the Luftwaffe and Lufthansa. A bomber trainer version was fitted with a glazed nose.

Commonwealth CA-12 Boomerang

Purpose: Fighter and fighter-bomber.
Engine: One 1,200 h.p. Pratt & Whitney R-1830-S3C4G Twin Wasp radial.
Span: 36 ft, 3 in.
Length: 25 ft. 6 in.
Weight Empty: 5,450 lb.
Weight Loaded: 7,000 lb.

Max. Speed: 296 m.p.h. at 7,600 ft.
Service Ceiling: 29,000 ft.
Max. Range: 930 miles.
Armament: Two 20 mm. cannon and four .303 in. machine guns; one 500 lb. bomb optional.

This single-seat fighter/fighter-bomber was designed and produced for emergency use by the Royal Australian Air Force, utilising many components of the Wirraway trainer. The prototype flew on 29th May, 1942, and the Boomerang was in service some 12 months later. A total of 250 was built, and they were employed in south-west Pacific theatres on such duties as ground strafing, army co-operation, pathfinding and reconnaissance. Production ceased in 1944.

Commonwealth CA-6 Wackett

Purpose: Trainer.
Engine: One 175 h.p. Warner Super Scarab radial.
Span: 37 ft. 0 in.
Length: 26 ft. 0 in.

Weight Empty: 1,906 lb.
Weight Loaded: 2,592 lb.
Max. Speed: 110 m.p.h. at sea level.
Service Ceiling: 16,000 ft.

Named after the R.A.A.F. officer who designed it, Wg. Cdr. L. J. Wackett, CA-6 was the production model's designation. The prototype, the CA-2, first flew on 19th October 1939, and was powered first by a Gipsy Major II and later by a 200 h.p. Gipsy Six inline. The CA-6 was in production from May 1941 to April 1942, a total of 200 being built during this time for various training duties with the R.A.A.F., mostly of an interim nature between the Tiger Moth basic and the Wirraway advanced trainers.

Commonwealth Wirraway

Purpose: Miscellaneous duties.
Engine: One 600 h.p. Australian-built Pratt & Whitney S1H1-G Wasp radial.
Span: 43 ft. 0 in.

Weight Empty: 3,980 lb.
Weight Loaded: 6,353 lb.
Max. Speed: approx. 200 m.p.h.

The Wirraway was the version of the North American NA-33 chosen for licence production in Australia, and the Australian prototype made its first flight on 27th March 1939; first deliveries were made to the R.A.A.F. in July of that year, the type being employed on general duties. Production was not phased out until 1946, by which time 755 Wirraways had been delivered. They were originally intended to be used as trainers, and it was their diversion to more active duties that was in part responsible for the emergence of the Wackett trainer to participate in the Empire Air Training Scheme.

DAR-10F

Purpose: Light and dive bomber.
Engine: One 950 h.p. Fiat A.74R radial.

Max. Speed: 295 m.p.h.

The original DAR-10 was designed in 1939 by the Darjavna Aeroplanna Rabotilnitza (Bulgarian State Aircraft Factory) as a multi-purpose aircraft, powered by a single radial engine and having a fixed undercarriage. The DAR-10F, which was only produced in small numbers, was a modified two-seat version for light bombing and dive bombing, carrying one 550 lb. and four 110 lb. bombs.

247

Dewoitine 520

Purpose: Fighter.
Engine: One 910 h.p. Hispano-Suiza 12Y-45 inline.
Span: 33 ft. 5½ in.
Length: 28 ft. 8¼ in.
Weight Empty: 4,608 lb.

Weight Loaded: 6,129 lb. (max.).
Max. Speed: 329 m.p.h. at 19,685 feet.
Service Ceiling: 36,090 ft.
Normal Range: 620 miles.
Armament: One 20 mm. cannon and four 7.5 mm. machine guns.

Undoubtedly France's best and most successful fighter in the period before the fall of France, the D.520 was designed to a 1937 specification, and the first of three prototypes flew for the first time on 2nd October, 1938, powered by an 890 h.p. Hispano-Suiza 12Y-21 engine. The D.520 commenced production early in 1939, first deliveries being made later that year. After France's capitulation the German authorities allowed production of the D.520 to continue, and for some time many equipped squadrons of the Vichy Air Force; at the end of 1942, numbers of the fighter were seized by the Germans, who put them to use as fighter-trainers for the Luftwaffe and presented others to the Regia Aeronautica for a similar purpose. Others were employed operationally by the air forces of Rumania and Bulgaria. Towards the end of 1944, many surviving D.520s were reclaimed by the Free French forces, and were used to harry the German retreat from France. The occupation of France curtailed or cancelled a number of projected developments of the D.520. These included the D.520T, with a 1,200 h.p. Hispano-Suiza 12Z-89; the D.520Z, with a 1,600 h.p. Hispano-Suiza 12Z; the D.521, with a 1,030 h.p. Rolls-Royce Merlin III; and the HD-780, a twin-float seaplane development with a 1,050 h.p. Hispano-Suiza 12Y-51. Total production of the D.520 amounted to just over 600 machines. Some of the reclaimed aircraft were modified after the war into D.520DC two-seat trainers.

Farman 222.1 Ministère des Armées "Air"

Farman 222

A number of these obsolete French bombers were used in the very early stages of the war on reconnaissance and leaflet raids over Germany and Czechoslovakia, in conjunction with the Amiot 143M (see above). A few were also employed as transports by the Vichy Air Force.

Fokker C. X

Purpose: Reconnaissance bomber.
Engine: One 650 h.p. Rolls-Royce Kestrel V inline.

Max. Speed: 200 m.p.h.
Normal Range: 500 miles.

This single-engined biplane first appeared in 1935, and in 1938 twenty were delivered to the Dutch Air Force, ten of them being assigned subsequently to the Netherlands East Indies. The remaining ten were still in Dutch service when Holland was overrun in May 1940, and a further

Fokker C.X., Finnish Air Force/*Eino Ritaranta*

batch of 35, powered by Bristol Mercury engines, served with the Finnish Air Force, the latter sometimes employing a ski landing gear. The first five C.Xs to be built featured an open cockpit, but an enclosed position was standardised on subsequent machines. Bomb load of the C.X was 880 lb., and a defensive armament of two machine guns was normally carried.

Fokker C. XI-W

A float-fitted reconnaissance biplane with a crew of two, 18 of which were delivered in 1938 to the Dutch naval air arm for use as shipborne spotter aircraft. Hr.N.M.S. *Tromp* and *De Ruyter* were fitted with catapults for the launcn of these aircraft, but the practice aboard other ships was to lower the aircraft on to the sea for a normal powered take-off from the water.

Fokker C. XIV-W

Purpose: Reconnaissance.   *Engine:* One 425 h.p. Wright Whirlwind radial.

Twenty-one of these two-seater biplanes were delivered to the Dutch Navy by May 1940, eleven of which were assigned to the East Indies. Owing to the low power of the Whirlwind engine, which did not confer a very high performance, the C. XIV-W was employed chiefly as a trainer.

Fokker D.XXI, Finnish Air Force/*Eino Ritaranta*

Fokker D. XXI

Purpose: Fighter.
Engine: One 830 h.p. Bristol Mercury VIII radial.
Span: 36 ft. 1 in.
Length: 26 ft. 10¾ in.
Weight Empty: 3,197 lb.

Weight Loaded: 4,519 lb.
Max. Speed: 286 m.p.h.
Service Ceiling: 31,360 ft.
Normal Range: 590 miles.
Armament: Four 7.9 mm. machine guns.

The prototype D. XXI was first flown on 27th March, 1936, being powered by a 645 h.p. Mercury VI-S engine. In 1937 the Dutch government ordered 36 production aircraft, to be powered by the Mercury VII or VIII, and in the same year the Finnish government ordered seven and obtained a production licence. Only 29 of tne original 36 Dutch machines were still in service when Holland was invaded, and the bulk of the D. XXIs produced were built elsewhere. The Finnish State Aircraft Factory built a total of 93, including 55 utilising the American Twin Wasp engine in place of the British Mercury. The Danish government bought three and built a further ten, these being powered by the Mercury VI-S engine of the first Dutch prototype. The Spanish government also acquired a licence, although none of the aircraft whicn they began to build was actually completed.

Fokker G.Ia

Fokker G. I

Purpose: Heavy fighter and ground attack.
Engines: Two 830 h.p. Bristol Mercury VIII radials.
Span: 56 ft. 3¼ in.
Length: 37 ft. 8¾ in.
Weight Empty: 7,326 lb.

Weight Loaded: 10,560 lb.
Max. Speed: 295 m.p.h. at 13,990 ft.
Service Ceiling: 30,500 ft
Normal Range: 945 miles.
Armament: Nine 7.9 mm. machine guns.

One of the small band of twin-boom aircraft designs to see service in World War 2, the Fokker G. I was evolved as a private venture and first flown on 16th March, 1937, at Eindhoven, powered by two 750 h.p. Hispano-Suiza 80-02 engines; this powerplant was later replaced by a pair of Twin Wasp Junior SB4Gs of similar power. A production order was placed for the G I in 1937, and deliveries of the first of this batch of 36 began in 1938. Of these, 23 were still serviceable when Holland was invaded, but many were destroyed on the ground and the remainder were taken over by the Luftwaffe as fighter-trainers—though not before they had made their presence felt. Twelve G.Ib, ordered by Spain, were still in Holland at the time of the invasion, and neither of the other two foreign orders—26 for Denmark and 18 for Sweden—was able to be delivered. The G. Is in service with the Luchtvaartafdeling (Army Air Service), or LVA, carried a crew of three and were capable of mounting an 880 lb. bomb load for strafing missions.

Fokker T.V

Fokker S. IX

Purpose: Trainer.

Engine: One 165 h.p. Menasco Buccaneer or Armstrong Siddeley Genet Major radial.

This biplane two-seat trainer was first flown in 1937; 24 were delivered to the Army and 27 to the Navy during 1938.

Fokker T. V

Purpose: Medium bomber.
Engines: Two 925 h.p. Bristol Pegasus radials.

Max. Speed: 280 m.p.h.
Max. Range: 1,000 miles.

Sixteen of these medium bombers were delivered in 1938 to the LVA, nine still being serviceable at the time of the invasion. Bomb load was 2,200 lb., and defensive armament one cannon and four machine guns.

Fokker T. VIII-W

Purpose: Torpedo bomber and reconnaissance.
Engines: Two 830 h.p. Bristol Mercury XI radials.
Span: 65 ft. 7 in.
Length: 49 ft. 10 in.
Weight Empty: 9,955 lb.

Weight Loaded: 14,520 lb.
Max. Speed: 222 m.p.h.
Service Ceiling: 22,300 ft.
Normal Range: 1,056 miles.
Armament: Two 7.9 mm. machine guns.

First flown in 1938, the Fokker T. VIII-W had a general appearance not unlike a Bristol Beaufort mounted on a pair of floats. Up to the time of the German invasion of Holland, 11 of these aircraft had been delivered to the Dutch Navy, and nine succeeded in escaping to the United Kingdom where they were formed into No. 320 Squadron of R.A.F. Coastal Command. A further five machines still on the assembly lines were completed under German supervision and used by the Luftwaffe on anti-shipping and coastal reconnaissance missions. A landplane version, the T. VIII-L, was under construction at this time for Finland, but the sole example of this version was taken over and completed for the Luftwaffe.

Hanriot 232

Purpose: Advanced trainer.
Engines: Two 220 h.p. Renault 6Q inlines.
Span: 41 ft. 10¼ in.

Length: 28 ft. 0½ in.
Weight Loaded: 4,938 lb.
Max. Speed: 214 m.p.h.

The prototype of this two-seat French trainer, the H-230, appeared in 1937 powered by two 170 h.p. Salmson inline engines. With tandem seating and a fixed undercarriage, it was generally similar to the H-220, the predecessor of the Hanriot NC-600 fighter. The H-231, which flew on 29th July, 1937, had two 250 h.p. Salmsons and a twin fin and rudder assembly, but the third machine, the H-232, which appeared in 1938, reverted to the single fin arrangement, and was powered by 220 h.p. Renault 6Qs. The production H-232 retained this powerplant, but settled after all for the twin-fin arrangement. Just over 50 H-232s were built altogether.

I.A.R. 37, 38 and 39

The construction of this series of 3-seat biplanes was begun in 1938 by the Industria Aeronautica Romana to replace the obsolescent French types previously in service with the Rumanian Air Force. Their function was primarily light bombing and reconnaissance.

I.A.R. 80˙

Purpose: Fighter.
Engine: One 940 h.p. licence-built Gnome-Rhone 14K radial.
Span: 32 ft. 10 in.
Length: 26 ft. 9½ in.
Weight Empty: 3,930 lb.

Weight Loaded: 5,040 lb.
Max. Speed: 317 m.p.h. at 13,000 ft.
Service Ceiling: 34,500 ft.
Max. Range: 590 miles.
Armament: Two 20 mm. cannon and four 7.7 mm. machine guns.

The only quantity-produced fighter of Rumanian design to appear during World War 2, the I.A.R. 80 embodied many facets of the Polish PZL P-24E fighter which the Industria Aeronautica Romana had built under licence in the late 1930s. The prototype I.A.R. 80 flew at the end of 1938, and the type entered production in 1941. It went into squadron service at the beginning of 1942, and about 125 were produced altogether. The I.A.R. 81 was a developed version for fighter-bomber duties, carrying two 220 lb. bombs, but only a few of these were produced.

251

Ikarus IK-2

Purpose: Fighter.
Engine: One 860 h.p. Hispano-Suiza 12 inline.
Span: 37 ft. 4¾ in.
Length: 25 ft. 10¼ in.
Weight Empty: 3,175 lb.
Weight Loaded: 4,255 lb.

Max. Speed: 266 m.p.h. at 16,400 ft.
Max. Ceiling: 34,450 ft.
Normal Range: 248 miles.
Armament: One 20 mm. cannon and two 7.92 mm. machine guns.

The IK-2 was the second prototype of the IK-1 high-wing fighter monoplane which first appeared in 1935. Despite an accident to the first machine, the IK-2 design went ahead, making its first flight in 1936. Series production of the IK-2 amounted only to 12 aircraft, delivered in 1937, and by the outbreak of World War 2 only eight of these remained, being used mainly for ground attack missions.

Royal Netherlands Air Force

Koolhoven F.K. 51

The LVA and the Dutch Navy respectively received 44 and 24 of these 2-seat biplane trainers prior to the war, the former assigning 24 of its quota to the Netherlands East Indies. Those that remained serviceable when Holland was invaded were pressed into service for observation duties.

Koolhoven F.K. 58

Purpose: Fighter.
Engine: One 1,080 h.p. Hispano-Suiza 14 radial.
Span: 36 ft. 1 in.
Length: 28 ft. 6½ in.
Weight Empty: 3,960 lb.

Weight Loaded: 5,610 lb.
Max. Speed: 313 m.p.h. at 14,760 ft.
Service Ceiling: 34,110 ft.
Normal Range: 466 miles.
Armament: Four 7.5 mm. machine guns.

The prototype of the F.K. 58, bearing the Dutch civil registration PH-ATO, made its first flight on 22nd September, 1938, and the design was rewarded two months later by an order from the French government for 50 aircraft of the type. These were to be of two models: the F.K. 58 with the Hispano-Suiza motor and the F.K. 58A powered by the Gnome-Rhone 14N/16. Of this order, 18 (seven F.K. 58 and eleven F.K. 58A) had been delivered by September 1939. Meanwhile, 40 F.K. 58s with a Bristol Taurus powerplant had been ordered for the LVA by the Dutch government, but these were never delivered; only the French machines were ever operational—and these were flown by Polish pilots!

Lioré et Olivier LeO 45

The LeO 45 medium bomber began to enter service with the Armée de l'Air in the autumn of 1939, and was the only really modern bomber in French service when war broke out. The few that had been delivered continued to serve with the Vichy Air Force, and some were also seen in the North African theatre.

Loire-Nieuport LN-40

This French attack bomber went into production in the late 1930s and equipped two shore-based squadrons of Aéronavale at the beginning of World War 2. At the outset they were engaged on coastal anti-submarine patrol, but after France was invaded they were used also in the support of ground forces.

J. B. Cynk

L.W.S. RWD-14 Czapla (*Heron*)

Purpose: Army co-operation.
Engine: One 420 h.p. PZL G.1620B Mors II
  radial.
Span: 39 ft. 0¾ in.
Length: 29 ft. 6¾ in.
Weight Empty: 2,542 lb.

Weight Loaded: 3,747 lb.
Max. Speed: 154 m.p.h. at sea level.
Service Ceiling: 16,400 ft.
Normal Range: 361 miles.
Armament: Two 7.7 mm. machine guns.

The Czapla, first flown in 1935, was put into production in Poland by the Lubelska Wytwornia Samolotow in 1938, and by early the following year a total of 65 of these aircraft had been built. Despite early teething troubles and the loss of two prototypes, the RWD-14 was a good quality army co-operation machine with an excellent short-field performance, and all but five of those built were still operational at September 1939.

I.W.M.

Morane-Saulnier 406

Purpose: Fighter.
Engine: One 860 h.p. Hispano-Suiza 12Y-31
  inline.
Span: 34 ft. 9¾ in.
Length: 26 ft. 9¼ in.
Weight Empty: 4,189 lb.

Weight Loaded: 5,364 lb.
Max. Speed: 301 m.p.h. at 16,400 ft.
Service Ceiling: 30,840 ft.
Normal Range: 497 miles.
Armament: One 20 mm. cannon and two
  7.5 mm. machine guns.

Numerically, the M.S. 406 was by far the most important fighter in French service when the war broke out. It was developed from the M.S. 405 of 1934, the prototype of which was flown on 8th August, 1935. A year later, a pre-production batch of 15 was ordered, differing from the first machine in various constructional details. One such model was later built under licence in Switzerland as the D-3801. The final definitive version of the M.S. 405 was given the new designation of M.S. 406, and 1,000 of these fighters were ordered in March 1938; up to the fall of France in the summer of 1940, 1,037 had actually been completed, and French pilots scored well over 250 "kills" against enemy aircraft, including the Bf 109. Among foreign orders for the M.S. 406 extant at the outbreak of war were 12 for Lithuania and 160 for Poland (which were not delivered), 45 for Turkey, 30 for Finland and 13 for China.

Plage and Laskiewicz Lublin R. XIII

Purpose: Reconnaissance and Army co-opera-
tion.
Engine: One 220 h.p. licence-built Wright
Whirlwind radial.
Span: 43 ft. 4 in.
Length: 27 ft. 9¾ in

Weight Empty: 1,956 lb.
Weight Loaded: 2,933 lb.
Max. Speed: 121 m.p.h.
Service Ceiling: 14,600 ft.
Normal Range: 323 miles.
Armament: One 7.7 mm. machine gun.

Between 1932 and 1936 a total of 300 R. XIIIs of all versions was built, the principal model
being the R. XIIID to which the above data apply. About 150 R. XIIIs remained in service
at the time of the invasion, these mostly being either the D version or the R. XIIIG which had a
380 h.p. Mors engine; about 30 more " hydro " versions, fitted with twin floats, were in service
with the Polish Navy.

Potez 54

Purpose: Bomber and reconnaissance.
Engines: Two 690 h.p. Hispano-Suiza 12X
radials or 780 h.p. Lorraine 12H inlines.

Cruising Speed: 150 m.p.h.
Normal Range: over 800 miles.
Bomb Load: 2,200 lb.

Over 220 examples of this twin-engined reconnaissance bomber were built, the principal versions
being the Potez 540 with Hispano-Suiza motors and the Potez 542 with Lorraine engines; 147
and 59 of these versions were built respectively. The prototype aircraft first flew on 14th November
1933 with a twin-fin tail assembly, but a single fin was standardised on production aircraft. The
Potez 54 was a monoplane with a high braced wing, the engines being mounted on short stub-
wings sprouting from the base of the fuselage. A civil variant, the Potez 62, entered service in
1935 with Air France; 35 of these were built, one being converted as a V.I.P. transport for the
French Air Minister. A further 50 aircraft, based on the Potez 62 but designated P.650, were
built for the Air Force as 14-passenger troop transports.

Potez 63

Data apply to P.631-C.3.
Purpose: Fighter.
Engines: Two 670 h.p. Gnome-Rhone 14M3/4
radials.
Span: 52 ft. 6 in.
Length: 36 ft. 3¾ in.
Weight Empty: 6,526 lb.

Weight Loaded: 9.921 lb.
Max. Speed: 277 m.p.h. at 13,120 ft.
Service Ceiling: 29,530 ft.
Normal Range: 745 miles.
Armament: Two 20 mm. cannon and eight
7.5 mm. machine guns.

The Potez 63 was a multi-purpose aircraft, produced as a fighter, attack aircraft, light bomber,
dive bomber and reconnaissance type. The prototype flew on 25th April, 1936, and in May of

the following year the first production series, the Potez 630 three-seat fighter, was begun: 80 of these were completed with 640 h.p. Hispano-Suiza engines, followed by 214 Potez 631s with Gnome-Rhone motors. The other chief production versions were the Potez 633 two-seat attack variant (115 built), the Potez 637 three-seat observation (61 built) and the Potez 63-11 reconnaissance three-seater, of which 717 were completed. Up to May 1940, Avions Henry Potez had completed about 1,250 of the different versions, though probably no more than 500 actually reached operational service. Varying numbers of the different models were exported to Greece, Rumania and Switzerland, and orders which remained unfulfilled were received from Finland and China. A number of ex-Vichy Air Force machines were used by the Luftwaffe for communications duties.

J. B. Cynk

P.W.S. 26

Purpose: Training and liaison.
Engine: One 220 h.p. licence-built Wright Whirlwind radial.
Span: 29 ft. 6¾ in.
Length: 23 ft. 0¾ in.
Weight Empty: 1,874 lb.

Weight Loaded: 2,469 lb.
Max. Speed: 135 m.p.h.
Service Ceiling: 15,157 ft.
Normal Range: 286 miles.
Armament: One 7.7 mm. machine gun.

Two hundred and forty of these two-seat aircraft were used by the Polish Air Force for training and liaison missions, and a few were also employed operationally on reconnaissance and light bombing. A development of the P.W.S. 26 was the P.W.S. 35 Ogar fighter-trainer, a few captured examples of which were employed by the Luftwaffe.

P.W.S. RWD-8

Purpose: Primary trainer.
Engine: One 110 h.p. Walter Junior inline.
Span: 36 ft. 1 in.
Length: 26 ft. 3 in.
Weight Empty: 1,102 lb.

Weight Loaded: 1,649 lb.
Max. Speed: 106 m.p.h.
Service Ceiling: 16,404 ft.
Normal Range: 270 miles.

Out of a total of 650 of these 2-seat Polish Air Force primary trainers, 400 were completed by the Podlaska Wytwornia Samolotow for the training role, and a further 40 for liaison duties. In the latter role, the RWD-8 sometimes carried a single light machine gun for defence.

PZL P-7

Purpose: Fighter.
Engine: One 485 h.p. licence-built Bristol Jupiter VIIF radial.
Span: 33 ft. 9½ in.
Length: 23 ft. 6 in.
Weight Empty: 2,062 lb.

Weight Loaded: 3,047 lb.
Max. Speed: 203 m.p.h. at 16,400 ft.
Service Ceiling: 32,808 ft.
Normal Range: 435 miles.
Armament: Two 7.7 mm. machine guns.

A development of the 1929 P-1 fighter, the P-7 prototype first flew in 1930. A total of 150 was built by the Panstwove Zaklady Lotnicze (Polish State Aircraft Factory), but by the outbreak of World War 2 most of these were useful only for training purposes, and the 27 that were still with fighter squadrons were too obsolete to be of any effective value.

255

P.7a/J. B. Cynk

P.11c/J. B. Cynk

PZL P-11 and P-24

Data apply to P-11C.
Purpose: Fighter and fighter-bomber.
Engine: One 645 h.p. licence-built Bristol
  Mercury VI-S2 radial.
Span: 35 ft. 2 in.
Length: 24 ft. 9½ in.

Weight Empty: 2,524 lb.
Weight Loaded: 3,960 lb. (max.).
Max. Speed: 242 m.p.h. at 18,000 ft.
Service Ceiling: 36,080 ft.
Max. Range: 503 miles.
Armament: Two or four 7.7 mm. machine guns.

A single-seat monoplane with a high, braced gull wing, the P-11 was developed from the P-7 and made its maiden flight in September 1931. The P-11A, of which 25 were built, was powered by a 500 h.p. Mercury VI-S2, entering production in 1933 and service in 1934. Major production model for the Polish Air Force was the P-11C, 175 of which were completed up to 1937. The P-11A and C formed the greater part of PAF fighter strength in September 1939. The P-11B was an export model for Rumania: fifty, with 595 h.p. Gnome-Rhone K.9 engines, were supplied from Poland, and the P-11B was subsequently built by licence in Rumania in limited numbers. A P-11 airframe, re-engined with a 770 h.p. Gnome-Rhone 14K, became in 1933 the prototype for the P-24. This was broadly similar to the P-11, the chief external difference being a " spatted " undercarriage. The P-24 was never employed by the PAF, but was supplied to or built under licence in various Balkan countries. These included Turkey (40 P-24C and licence), Rumania (6 P-24E and licence), Greece (36 P-24F and G) and Bulgaria (24 P-24G).

PZL P-23 Karas (*Carp*)

Data apply to P-23B.
Purpose: Bomber and reconnaissance.
Engine: One 680 h.p. licence-built Bristol
  Pegasus VIII radial.
Span: 45 ft. 9½ in.
Length: 31 ft. 9½ in.

Weight Empty: 3,912 lb.
Weight Loaded: 6,918 lb.
Max. Speed: 198 m.p.h. at 11,975 ft.
Service Ceiling: 23,950 ft.
Max. Range: 932 miles.
Armament: Three 7.7 mm. machine guns.

Following its first appearance in prototype form in 1934, the P-23 entered production (Karas A) the following year, powered by a Bristol Pegasus II, as an operations trainer. In 1936 the major

production version, the P-23B Karas B reconnaissance-bomber, went into production, 210 of this version being completed. A further 54 P-23Bs were built 1937-39 for Bulgaria, under the designation P-43, and another Karas B became a test-bed for components of the P-46 Sum, large numbers of which were on order when Poland was invaded: just over 200 P-23s were then operational with the PAF.

PZL P-37 Los (Elk)

Data apply to P-37B.
Purpose: Bomber.
Engines: Two 925 h.p. licence-built Bristol
  Pegasus XX radials.
Span: 58 ft. 10¼ in.
Length: 42 ft. 4½ in.

Weight Empty: 9,314 lb.
Weight Loaded: 18,739 lb.
Max. Speed: 273 m.p.h. at 12,140 ft.
Service Ceiling: 19,685 ft.
Max. Range: 1,615 miles.
Armament: Three 7.7 mm. machine guns.

The prototype Los (two 873 h.p. Pegasus XII) was flown in 1936, and featured a twin-fin tail assembly. Thirty Los A were ordered for the PAF, these having a single fin and the Pegasus XX powerplant; they were followed by about 70 Los B with similar engines and twin fins and rudders. Export models under evaluation in September 1939 were the Los C (900 h.p. Gnome-Rhone 14N-01) and Los D (1,050 h.p. Gnome-Rhone 14N-20), and an enlarged development of the original design with two 1,300 h.p. Bristol Hercules III, a four-man crew, very heavy armament and a 4,900 lb. bomb load. Sixty-one Los Bs were in service with the PAF at the invasion, but nearly fifty of them succeeded in escaping to Rumania, and some while later were employed operationally against the Russian forces.

Rogozarski IK-3

Purpose: Fighter.
Engine: One 920 h.p. licence-built Hispano-
  Suiza 12 inline.
Span: 33 ft. 9½ in.
Length: 27 ft. 4¾ in.
Weight Empty: 4,123 lb.

Weight Loaded: 5,291 lb.
Max. Speed: 327 m.p.h. at 17,715 ft.
Service Ceiling: 26,250 ft.
Normal Range: 310 miles.
Armament: One 20 mm. cannon and two
  7.92 mm. machine guns.

Powered by an 890 h.p. Hispano-Suiza 12Y engine, the prototype IK-3 was first flown in the spring of 1938, and a production order for 12 aircraft was placed. The first of these was delivered in the summer of 1940, and an order for a further 25 had just begun when Yugoslavia was invaded by the Nazis in April 1941.

257

V.L. Myrsky II (*Storm*)

Purpose: Fighter.
Engine: One 1,065 h.p. Swedish-built Pratt & Whitney SC3G Twin Wasp radial.
Span: 36 ft. 1 in.
Length: 27 ft. 4¾ in.
Weight Empty: 5,141 lb.

Weight Loaded: 6,497 lb.
Max. Speed: 329 m.p.h.
Service Ceiling: 29,500 ft.
Normal Range: 310 miles.
Armament: Four 12.7 mm. machine guns.

Designed by the Valtion Lentokonetehdas (State Aircraft Factory) around the SFA-built Twin Wasp engine obtained from Sweden, the prototype Myrsky I flew for the first time during 1942. This and the next three machines were all lost during testing, but from the fifth machine onwards (Myrsky II) various improvements were incorporated, and altogether 47 Mysrky IIs were built up to 1944. They were very little used during the German withdrawal from Finland, being a somewhat unsatisfactory design and rather unpopular with their pilots. Ten examples of an improved Myrsky III were under construction when VE-day terminated further development.

Eino Ritaranta

V.L. Pyry II

Another design of the Finnish State Aircraft Factory, the Pyry II appeared in prototype form some 2-3 years before the outbreak of World War II, and was intended as a fighter-trainer. Production was suspended during 1940, but during 1941 forty of these aircraft were completed.

Other Types

(Experimental and less important operational aircraft)

GERMANY

Arado Ar 199. Two/three-seat naval floatplane trainer; similar to, but slightly larger than, the Ar 96B.

Arado Ar 233. Project under development in Occupied France for an amphibious twin-engined medium transport. Not produced.

Bachem Ba 349 Natter (Viper). Rocket-propelled interceptor fighter with a fantastic climb rate of 37,000 ft. per minute. Nearly 40 had been completed when the war ended.

Blohm und Voss Ha 139. Four-engined, twin-float seaplane for long range maritime reconnaissance and minelaying. Pre-war design, not used widely.

Blohm und Voss Bv 141. One of the war's oddest-looking aircraft; consisted of a " fuse-lage " bearing only the single engine, the tail fin and a half-tailplane on the port side. A separate pilot's nacelle was mounted on the staiboard wing. Only a small test batch was produced and employed in Russia and over the U.K. as observation aircraft.

Blohm and Voss Bv 141 prototype

Blohm und Voss Bv 142. Land-based modification of Ha 139 (see above); also used for troop-carrying and general transport duties.

Blohm, und Voss Bv 144. Twin-engined, twin-finned medium transport design featuring a variable-incidence wing. Two prototypes completed in France by Breguet.

Blohm und Voss Bv 155. Originally designated Me 155, was a radical development of the Bf 109 intended as a high altitude shipboard interceptor. Taken over and further modified by Blohm und Voss in 1943, only two prototypes were completed.

D.F.S. 228. Short-range reconnaissance aircraft powered by a rocket motor. Still under development at VE-day, though ten pre-production machines had been ordered for 1945.

Dornier Do 26. Pre-war transatlantic mail carrier for D.L.H., used in small numbers for reconnaissance. Four engines, mounted in pairs back to back.

Dornier Do. 214. Design for an outsize transport flying boat with a 197-foot span; abandoned in 1942.

Dornier Do 335 Pfeil (Arrow). Unconventional twin-DB 603 fighter, one engine forward and one aft with cockpit in between. Single-seat (Do 335A) and two-seat (Do 335B) versions almost ready for service at VE-day. Armament of 30 mm. cannon and 450 m.p.h. top speed. Do 435 project similar with higher-powered engines.

Dornier Do 635. A union of two Do 335 fuselages and outer wing sections, joined together by a new centre section. Not operational.

Dornier Do 335 VI   **259**

Flettner Fl 282 Kolibri (Humming Bird) and Fl 285. Small observation helicopters, developed during the war but not put into production.
Flettner Fl 339. Large transport helicopter, still in design stage at the end of hostilities.
Focke-Wulf Fw 44 Stieglitz (Goldfinch). Single-engined biplane, used in small numbers as primary trainer.
Focke-Wulf Fw 58 Weihe (Kite). Twin-engined monoplane for training and light communications. Also produced in floatplane version.
Focke-Wulf Ta 154. Twin-engined two-seat night fighter. Sometimes known unofficially as Moskito, only a couple of dozen built. Although put into service, they were not a success. Long-span development was designated Ta 254.
Focke-Wulf Ta 183. Single-jet fighter design with sharply-swept wings and vertical tail surfaces. Development well advanced, and type would have been in service later in 1945.
Focke-Wulf Fw 187 Falke (Falcon). Twin-engined fighter, first flew 1937. Only three prototypes completed, which saw action 1939-43 later becoming test-beds for the Ta 154.
Focke-Wulf Fw 191. Twin-engined medium bomber, first flew 1942. Six completed, but unsatisfactory powerplant and other troubles led to abandonment the following year.
Focke-Wulf Fw 300 and Ta 400. Designs only, for successor to the Fw 200.
Gotha Go 345. Design of 1944 for medium transport glider, not unlike the U.S. Hadrian in appearance.
Heinkel He 59. Obsolescent in 1939: large float biplane used for a while on air/sea rescue duties in small numbers.
Heinkel He 60. Another biplane floatplane, obsolescent when the war started, being replaced for shipboard reconnaissance by the Ar 196.
Heinkel He 100D. Single-engined fighter designed to same specification as Bf 109. Only small batch completed.

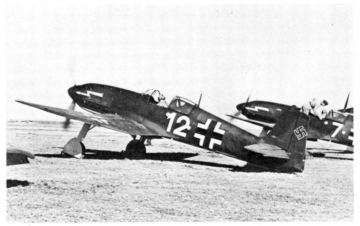

Heinkel He 100D-1

Heinkel He 114. Single-engined twin-float biplane used for coastal patrol and reconnaissance in early war years.
Heinkel He 119. Single-engined, two-seat bomber/reconnaissance aircraft, development of which was abandoned early during the war.
Heinkel He 274. Four-engined long range development of He 177, to same specification as the Me 264. Two prototypes begun in late 1943.
Heinkel He 280. Twin-jet fighter (the world's first) which first flew 1941. Eight prototypes completed before development abandoned in 1942.
Heinkel He 343. Four-jet day and night fighter, bomber and reconnaissance project. One prototype (a night fighter) completed but never flew.
Henschel Hs 130. Twin-engined high altitude reconnaissance monoplane developed from experimental Hs 128.
Henschel Hs 132. Single-jet prone-pilot dive bomber project resembling He 162. Three prototypes completed, but none flown.
Henschel Hs 293. Radio-controlled glider bomb with aeroplane configuration and small rocket to provide initial acceleration after launching from " mother " aircraft. Spanning about 10 feet, it was released at around 5,000 feet and 5 miles from its target, to which it was guided by a controller in the launching aircraft. Explosive warhead 1,100 lb. of H.E.
Horten Ho 9. Intriguing design for twin-jet, tail-less fighter-bomber, ordered into production at Gothaer factory in March 1945 as Go 229, but only three prototypes completed.
Junkers Ju 89. Originally intended as four-engined heavy bomber; only two machines completed (pre-war), these employed as transports.
Junkers Ju 248. Development of Me 163, later designated Ju 8-263; not operational. (*See also Me* 263.)
Junkers Ju 287. Six-jet bomber design with *forward*-swept wings. Only one or two completed.

Junkers Ju 288. Despite numerical similarity, was no connection with Ju 88 "family". It was a bomber project (two Jumo 222 engines), but did not go into quantity production.
Junkers Ju 390. Six-engined bomber/transport generally similar to Ju 290; not operational.
Junkers Ju 488. Proposed four-engined bomber utilising outer wing panels of Ju 188. One prototype completed, but did not fly.
Kalkart Ka 430. Utility transport glider. Not operational.
Messerschmitt Me 209. Correct designation of so-called "109R" World Speed Record holder of 1939. Was in fact a completely new fighter design, but only four prototypes completed before project was abandoned in 1944.
Messerschmitt Me 261. Twin-engined, ultra-long range aircraft, known as "Adolphine" and bearing resemblance to Bf 110. Built in 1939 and flown in 1940, only three machines completed, these used as mailplanes. Also formed the basis for the Me 264 design.
Messerschmitt Me 263. Development of Me 163 interceptor; not operational.
Messerschmitt Me 264. Four-engined long range "New York bomber", first flew late 1942. Only one fully completed, two others began construction.
Messerschmitt Me 309. Experimental fighter (one DB 603); development abandoned.
Messerschmitt Me 328. Fighter/ground attack design for cheap and speedy production. A few prototypes (Me 328B), powered by two pulse-jets of the kind fitted to the FZG-76, completed but unsuccessful. Projected Me 328C (one Jumo 004) did not materialise.

GREAT BRITAIN

Airspeed A.S.39 Fleet Shadower. To same specification (S. 23/37) as the G.A.L.38 (see below), which it closely resembled. One completed and another started before project was abandoned.
Airspeed A.S.45. Advanced trainer design to T.4/39. Two prototypes built, but aircraft not produced.
Airspeed Envoy. Similar appearance to Oxford (page 23), was development of civil Courier. Several used during war for communications.
Avro Lincoln. "Stretched" development of Lancaster to B.14/43, originally designated Lancaster IV and V. First flown 1944 and in service early 1945, but too late for operational use.
Avro Rota. Licence-built version of Cierva C.30A Autogiro, equipping one wartime R.A.F. squadron.
Blackburn B.20. Twin-engined flying boat project in which the whole hull bottom acted as a retractable landing gear. Only one built.
Blackburn B.44. Small single-engined seaplane, designed to have same retractable hull principle as B.20 but not built.
Blackburn Firebrand. Strike aircraft to N.11/40, first flown 1942 and in production by middle war years, but not in service until September 1945.
Blackburn Shark. Blackburn's last biplane, used in limited numbers for communications and torpedo training.
Boulton Paul Overstrand. Twin-engined biplane bomber of the middle 'thirties, of which a small number were used up to 1941 for gunnery training.
Boulton Paul P.92. Twin-Vulture turreted fighter project, to F.11/37. Half-scale prototype only (P.92/2) with Gipsy Majors.
de Havilland Albatross. Two prototypes of civil airliner impressed for R.A.F. service; destroyed in August 1941 and April 1942.
de Havilland Hornet. Development of the Mosquito as a long range fighter, was in production late 1944 but not in service until 1946. Was fastest R.A.F. piston-engined fighter.
de Havilland Vampire. Second British production jet fighter, designed to E.6/41. First flown 1943 but not in service until 1946.
Fairey Spearfish. Barracuda replacement to Spec. O.5/43, first flown July 1945 and too late for war service. Only four built.

Fane F.O.P. Ultra-light Flying Observation Post aircraft, prototype only with civil registration G-AGDJ.

General Aircraft Cygnet. Single-engined, twin-finned lightplane used in small numbers for communications.

General Aircraft G.A.L.38 Fleet Shadower. Special purpose aircraft, one only built to Spec. S.23/37. Four engines, low speed and STOL capability.

General Aircraft G.A.L.47. Ultra-light private venture design for A.O.P. duties. Not produced.

General Aircraft G.A.L.55. Small, two-seat training glider to TX.3/43. Two prototypes only.

General Aircraft G.A.L.56. Small research glider for " flying-wing " flight. Only three or four built, beginning trials late 1944.

Gloster E.28/39. Britain's first reaction-propelled aircraft, first flown 15th May, 1941. Powered by a single Whittle W.2/7000 jet engine.

Gloster E.28/39, first prototype/*I.W.M.*

Gloster F.9/39. Resembling a twin-finned Beaufighter, was a project for a fast twin-engined fighter. Two built, one with Taurus and one with Peregrine powerplant. No production.

Hawker Fury. Development of Tempest II to F.2/43, was first flown 1944 but eventually produced for export only.

Hawker Sea Fury. Naval counterpart of Fury, to N.7/43, was last F.A.A. piston-engined fighter, entering service after end of war.

Martin-Baker M.B.5. Single-seat fighter to F.18/39, resembling the P-51 Mustang. First flown late 1944, maximum speed of 465 m.p.h., but only one completed.

Miles Falcon. Elementary trainer, not unlike the Mentor (page 218). One R.A.F. squadron on communications until 1940.

Miles M.20. Utility fighter of 1940, designed, built and flown in just over nine weeks. Fixed undercarriage, Merlin XX engine and many Master components; was nearly as fast as the Spitfire but only two were completed.

Miles M.35. Research aircraft for a revolutionary fleet fighter, with canard layout and single " pusher " engine. Designed, built and flown in six weeks.

Miles M.39B Libellula. Flying scale model for a multi-engined bomber or transport. Canard layout, twin engines and triple tail assembly.

Miles Monitor. Twin-engined specialised target tug to Q.9/42. Prototype flown 1944, originally intended for R.A.F. but only 20 built, which served with the Royal Navy.

Short Seaford. Development of the Sunderland (page 151) to R.8/42 and originally designated Sunderland IV. In production (31 built) but not in service during war. Subsequently converted to civil Solents.

Slingsby Hengist. Fifteen-passenger glider to Spec. X.25/40. Four prototypes and 18 production aircraft only, and role changed to equipment transport.

Supermarine Seafang. Naval counterpart of Spiteful (see below) to N.5/45; 150 ordered May 1945 but only eight delivered.

Supermarine Spiteful. Straight-winged Spitfire development to F.1/43. First flown 1944 but too late for war service and production cancelled after only a few had been completed.

Supermarine Type 322. Nicknamed " Dumbo ", was designed to same Specification (S.24/37) as the Barracuda and featured a variable-incidence wing. Two prototypes only.

Vickers-Armstrongs Type 432. Design to F.7/41 for a pressurised twin-Merlin high altitude fighter and unofficially christened " Mayfly ". Did not progress beyond prototype stage.

Vickers-Armstrongs Windsor. Four-motor heavy bomber with elliptical wing form. Abandoned after only one or two prototypes were completed.

Vickers-Armstrongs Windsor, first prototype

Vickers Vildebeest. Biplane torpedo-bomber of 1930.—A few, mostly Mk. IV, served briefly during the early war years.
Vickers Vincent. Single-engined general purpose biplane, entered service 1934; a few remained active until 1941.

Westland Wallace equipped for target towing

Westland Wallace. Single-engined general purpose biplane of 1934, small numbers remaining in service converted to target towing until 1943.
Westland Welkin. Single-seat twin-Merlin high altitude fighter. Only a few built, which were too late for war service.

ITALY

Breda Ba 25 and Ba 28. Biplane trainers of mid-1930s vintage, used in limited numbers during the war.
Breda Ba 88 Lince (Lynx). Twin-engined fighter/bomber/reconnaissance type; a small number were employed by the Regia Aeronautica, but they were not a great success.

Breda Ba 88 Lince/*Italian Air Ministry*

263

Caproni-Vizzola F.5. Single-seat fighter. Only a small batch built, equipping one Regia Aeronautica squadron.

Caproni-Vizzola F.5 prototype/*Italian Air Ministry*

Meridionali Ro 43 and Ro 44. Shipboard biplanes of largely similar appearance, designed as fighter/reconaissance aircraft. Very few in service when Italy entered the war and not widely used.
Savoia-Marchetti S.M.75 Marsupiale. Trimotor military transport derived from pre-war airliner and similar to the S.M. 79 Sparviero in general layout.

JAPAN

Aichi D1A2-K. Trainer (one Hikari 1 radial) used in limited numbers by J.N.A.F. Code name *Susie*.
Aichi M6A1 Seiran (*Moubtain Haze.*) Atsuta-powered floatplane bomber to be carried in pairs by ocean-going submarines. Only 28 completed, none operational.
Aichi S1A1 Denko (*Lightning*). Homare 22-powered night interceptor. Two prototypes begun, both destroyed by bombing.
Kawanishi E7K2. Land- and cruiser-based reconnaissance floatplane; in production until 1941 and service until 1942. Code name *Alf*.
Kawanishi E15K1 Shiun (*Violet Cloud*). Reconnaissance floatplane which could jettison its entire float unit to increase getaway speed. Fifteen built, of which six only were operational. Code name *Norm*.
Kawasaki Ki. 32. Single-engined bomber, widely used in China but withdrawn from service shortly after outbreak of World War 2; about 800 built. Code name *Mary*.
Kawasaki Ki. 55. Advanced trainer, modification of the Tachikawa Ki. 36, with single 450 h.p. Hitachi Ha. 13A radial.
Kawasaki Ki. 64. Experimental "heavy" fighter with tandem Ha. 40 engines fore and aft of the cockpit. One only, first flown December 1943; development later suspended. Code name *Rob*.
Kawasaki Ki. 108. Pressurised, twin-engined high altitude fighter project of 1943. Only four completed, two modified from Ki. 102b.
Kawasaki Ki. 119. Single-engined project to replace Ki. 67 *Peggy* bomber. Completion of prototype prevented by Allied bombing.
Kyushu E9W1. Submarine-borne reconnaissance type (one Amakaze 12), similar in appearance to the *Glen*. Also built by Nakajima as the E9N1, but not widely used. Code name *Slim*.
Kyushu J7W1 Shinden (*Magnificent Lightning*). Promising "canard" type pusher-engined interceptor. First of two prototypes flown 3rd August 1945, scheduled for intensive production later that year.
Kyushu K11W1 Shiragiku (*White Chrysanthemum*). Single-engined bombing and gunnery trainer, 798 built. Also used for reconnaissance and anti-submarine duties.
Mitsubishi A7M2 Reppu (*Hurricane*). Zero development, first flown 6th May 1944. Only eight production aircraft completed before VJ day, and none was operational. Code name *Sam*.
Mitsubishi B5M1. Torpedo-bomber conceived as a rival to the Nakajima *Kate*; only 125 built.
Mitsubishi C5M2. Later version of the 1939 C5M1; only 30 built, appeared 1941 on long range reconnaissance. Code name *Babs*.
Mitsubishi J8M1 Shusui (*Rigorous Sword*). Rocket-powered interceptor designed broadly on the basis of the Me 163, following the loss en route to Japan of an actual specimen intended to inaugurate licence production. First flown 7th July 1945, crashing due to engine failure; few only completed by VJ day.
Mitsubishi Ki. 30. Single-engined bomber; some 700 built by Mitsubishi and Tachikawa used extensively for short time in China and the Philippines. Code name *Ann*.
Mitsubishi Ki. 109. Development of the Ki.67 *Peggy* as a high altutide B-29 interceptor abandoned as a failure after 22 completed.

264

Kyushu J7W1 Shinden, first prototype/*H. J. Nowarra*

Nakajima G5N1 Shinzan (*Deep Mountain*). Four-motor bomber (Mamoru 11 radials), based on Douglas DC-4 prototype. First flown 10th April 1941, abandoned after only **four completed. Code name** *Liz*.
Nakajima G8N1 Renzan (*Mountain Range*). Four-motor bomber (Homare 21 radials), first flown October 1944; four prototypes only completed. Code name *Rita*.

Nakajima G8N1 Renzan prototype/*H. J. Nowarra*

Nakajima G10N1 Fugaka (*Mount Fuji*). Formidable bomber project with 12 engines (six coupled pairs), 485 m.p.h. speed and 49,000 ft. ceiling. In advanced stage of completion at VJ day.
Nakajima J5N1 Tenrai (*Heavenly Thunder*). Twin-engined high altitude interceptor, first flown July 1944. Of six completed, four were lost in crashes or on the ground and none was operational.
Nakajima Ki. 34. Twin-engined, eight-passenger transport, 299 built. Code name *Thora*.
Nakajima Ki. 115 Tsurugi (*Sword*). Designed from outset purely for suicide attack, powered by single 1,170 h.p. Ha. 115 radial. About 105 completed by VJ day but none was ever used.
Nippon Ki. 59 Twin-engined transport; 59 built, later replaced by K1. 54. Code name *Theresa*.
Nippon Ki. 76. Liaison type resembling the Fi 156; one 280 h.p. Hitachi Ha. 22 radial. Code name *Stella*.
Nippon Ki. 86. Bucker 131 Jungmann trainer licence-built by Nippon (1,037 for Army) and Kyushu (217 for Navy as K9W1 Momiji (*Maple*)). Later models had 110 h.p. Hitachi Ha. 47 engine. Code name *Cypress*.
Nippon Ku. 7 Manazuru (*Crane*). Twin-boom glider first flown 15th August 1944, later modified with two 950 h.p. Ha. 26B radials as the Ki. 105 Ohtori (*Big Bird*) powered transport. Only nine completed, which were still under test at VJ day. Code name *Buzzard*.
Rikugun Ki. 79. Advanced trainer (one 450 h.p. Hitachi Ha. 13A), modified from the Ki. 27 *Nate*.
Showa L2D2. Modified version of the Douglas DC-3 built by Showa (380) and Nakajima (70). Code name *Tabby*.
Tachikawa Ki. 9. Single radial-engined biplane primary trainer; used in moderate numbers during early war years. Code name *Spruce*.

Tachikawa Ki. 36. Reconnaissance and army-co-operation type used in China 1938 and during early war years. Code name *Ida*.
Tachikawa Ki. 70. Reconnaissance project with twin 1,730 h.p. Mitsubishi Ha. 104ru radials; two only completed. Code name *Clara*.
Tachikawa Ki. 74. High altitude long range bomber, first flown May 1944. Sixteen prototypes completed, later ones with two 1,900 h.p. Ha. 104ru radials, but none operational. Code name *Patsy*.
Tachikawa Ki. 77. High aspect-ratio research aircraft (two 1,170 h.p. Ha. 115), first flown 18th November 1942; set two endurance records during war. Two prototypes completed, second lost two months after completion.
Yokosuka H5Y1. Twin-motor flying boat torpedo bomber and maritime reconnaissance aircraft; six only completed, none operational. Code name *Cherry*.
Yokosuka K5Y. Intermediate trainer (one Amakaze 11 radial), built as K5Y1 landplane and K5Y2 seaplane. Code name *Willow*.
Yokosuka R2Y1 Keiun (*Lucky Cloud*). Fast reconnaissance project based on the He 119. Two coupled engines gave 447 m.p.h. top speed, but this version cancelled in favour of turbojet R2Y2. Flight tests unsatisfactory, further work curtailed by end of war.

RUSSIA

Berezniak-Isaev BI-1. Rocket-powered interceptor project studied by Red Air Force in 1941/42. Abandoned after completion of prototype.
Chetverikov ARK-3. Flying boat reconnaissance bomber with two 650 h.p. M-25 radials mounted in tandem. Not believed to have been used in great numbers.
Mikoyan/Gurevich MiG-5. Radial-engined development of the MiG-3, in service in small numbers during 1943 but ousted by the La-5.
Nikitin-Sevchenko IS-1. Novel single-seat Russian biplane fighter with retractable lower wings and undercarriage; proved practicable but project abandoned.
Shcherbakov Shche-2. Built as a Po-2 replacement, but not put into production. Used during war for evacuation of partisans and casualties. Two M-11 radials.
Sukhoi Su-2. Two-seat Red Air Force bomber, also known as BB-1. One 1,100 h.p. M-88 radial. Not extensively used.
Tupolev ANT-20*bis*. Giant Russian six-motor transport; about sixteen built for trooping and freight transport during World War 2.
Tupolev ANT-44. Flying boat with four radial motors, not produced in great numbers.
Yakovlev Yak-4. Fighter-bomber similar in appearance to the Pe-2; not entirely successful and only comparatively few built. Two 1,100 h.p. M-105 inlines.
Yermolaev ER-2 and ER-4. Twin-engined medium bombers used in moderate numbers by the Red Air Force.

U.S.A.

Aeronca TG-5. Three-seat training glider evolved from the YO-58 Defender lightplane.
Allied Aviation LRA-1 and -2. Twelve-seat amphibious gliders produced in 1943 for U.S. Navy.
Beechcraft XA-38. Twin-engined, twin-finned attack aircraft with 75 mm. cannon. Experimental only.
Bell FM-1 Airacuda. Twin pusher-engined long range escort fighter. Thirteen only for U.S.A.A.F.
Bell XP-77. Small all-wood fighter design, not produced for service; two prototypes only.
Boeing 314A. Four-motor transatlantic flying boat impressed for military service.
Boeing XPBB-1 Sea Ranger. Long range patrol flying boat, first flown July 1942. Ordered 1942, cancelled, re-ordered 1944 and cancelled again. Only one built.

Boeing XPBB-1 Sea Ranger

Brewster XA-32. Torpedo and dive bomber project: two prototypes only.
Budd RB-1 Conestoga. Twin-engined all stainless steel transport, first flown October 1943. Army contract cancelled for six hundred C-93, Navy's two hundred RB-1 cut to twenty-five. Latter completed as JRB-3 but sold out to civil operators and never served with U.S.N.
Consolidated B-32 Dominator. Conceived as a B-29 " insurance "; entered production January 1944, first fifteen to Pacific April 1945. Only about twenty sorties flown before VJ day, when production cancelled.
Consolidated-Vultee R2Y-1. Long range transport with new and enlarged fuselage mated to B-32 wings, motors and undercarriage, and tail similar to PB4Y-2. One only, converted to civil use but later abandoned.
Curtiss AT-9 Jeep. Twin-engined advanced trainer, similar in appearance to the Bobcat.
Curtiss C-76 Caravan. Twin-engined all-wood assault transport. Only twenty-five built, did not enter service.
Curtiss SNC-1 Falcon. Two-seat advanced trainer resembling the Texan, equipped for naval gunnery, bombing and instrument training.
Curtiss XP-55 Ascender. Experimental tail-first pusher-engined fighter, first flown 13th July 1943. Did not go into production.
Douglas XSB2D-1 (later XBTD-1). Carrier-based attack project: three prototypes and four pre-production only. Development cancelled.
Douglas XTB2-D1. Carrier-based torpedo bomber project: two prototypes flew, production order for twenty-three cancelled at VJ day.
Fisher P-75A Eagle. Fighter originally designed (XP-75) in 1942 to utilise components of other production aircraft. First prototype had F4U undercarriage, P-40 wings and A-24 tail unit, total resemblance to P-39, including rear-engine layout. Development led to completely new design in 1944, but a production order for the P-75A was subsequently cancelled.
Fletcher FBT-2. Two-seat cheap utility " unit construction " basic trainer, built during early war years.
Frankfort TG-1A. Two-seat training glider, military version of pre-war Cinema.
General Airborne Transport XCG-16A. Experimental twin-boom " flying wing " glider for forty troops or four-ton payload.
Grumman F7F Tigercat. Twin-engined day/night fighter, two prototypes appeared 1944, but few only in service before VJ day.
Grumman F8F Bearcat. Hellcat successor, first flown 21st August, 1944, but none operational before VJ day.
Grumman XP-50. Land version of XF5F-1 Skyrocket. Sole prototype crashed on first flight May 1941, and development was abandoned.
Howard Nightingale. Four-seat, single-engined personnel transport (UC-70/GH-1), ambulance (GH-2 and -3) and instrument trainer (NH-1), adapted from commercial DGA-15 high wing cabin monoplane.
Interstate L-6 Grasshopper. Two-seat light observation and liaison aircraft developed from the 1940 Cadet lightplane. Some acquired civil Cadets were designated L-8.
Kellett YO-60. Observation autogyro, seven of which were completed for evaluation in 1943. Development abandoned.
Laister-Kauffmann TG-4A. Two-seat dual control training glider.
Laister-Kauffmann XCG-10A. Thirty-seat military transport glider, two completed in 1944. The XCG-7 was of similar layout but smaller.
Lockheed Model 12. Twin-engined six-passenger aircraft appearing in 1936; did war duty in many countries as a command transport.
Lockheed P-80 Shooting Star. America's first large-scale production jet fighter, first flew late in 1943 but not in service before VJ day.

Lockheed P-80A Shooting Star

267

McDonnell XP-67. Twin-engined high altitude fighter with pressure cabin and armament of six 37 mm. cannon, semi-flying wing configuration. Only two built.

Martin XA-22. One only with U.S. designation. Export version for France diverted to Britain, who eventually received two hundred and twenty-five as the Maryland Mks. I and II. Used mainly as reconnaissance bombers by the R.A.F. in the Mediterranean and North Africa; one mission was the reconnaissance leading to the attack on the Italian Fleet at Taranto in November 1940. Also served with S.A.A.F.

Martin XPB2M-1R Mars. Giant flying boat patrol bomber (span 200 ft.), virtually a scaled up Mariner. Converted to transport with single fin, but original order for twenty cut to only five aircraft.

North American XB-28. Design for a twin-engined pressurised medium bomber, flew in 1942 and later played an important part in development of the B-29.

Northrop N-3PB. Single-engined twin-float fighter bomber of 1940. None in U.S. service, but twenty-four used from 1941 onwards by Royal Norwegian Air Force from bases in Iceland.

Northrop XP-56. Small cruciform wing/tail pattern fighter design with single pusher engine, flown in 1943. Did not enter production.

Ryan PT-16, -20, -21, -22 and -25. Series of primary trainers produced for U.S.A.A.F. Large numbers of PT-16 and -20 included exports to Netherlands East Indies, Guatemala, China, Honduras, Mexico and others. PT-22 replaced in production 1942 by PT-25 which utilised non-strategic materials.

Sikorsky JRS-1/OA-8. Designations of the VS-43B commercial two-motor amphibian impressed for military service.

Sikorsky JR2S-1. Designation of VS-44A Excalibur four-motor flying boat impressed for military service.

Vought XTBU Seawolf. Torpedo bomber whose production was to have been undertaken by Vultee as the TBV-1, but contract cancelled before any were delivered.

Vultee XP-54. Design for single-seat pressurised high-altitude fighter, with pusher engine and twin-boom layout. Only two built, in 1943.

Waco CG-3A. Nine-man trooper, eventually used as a training glider. One hundred built.

Waco UC-72. Designation of pre-war cabin biplane used by U.S.A.A.F. as light personnel transport.

Index

270

271